THE ALCOHOLIC REPUBLIC

THE
ALCOHOLIC
REPUBLIC

AN AMERICAN TRADITION

W. J. RORABAUGH

OXFORD UNIVERSITY PRESS
Oxford   New York   Toronto   Melbourne

Oxford University Press

Oxford London Glasgow
New York Toronto Melbourne
Nairobi Dar es Salaam Cape Town
Kuala Lumpur Singapore Hong Kong Tokyo
Delhi Bombay Calcutta Madras Karachi

and associate companies in
Beirut Berlin Ibadan Mexico City

First published by Oxford University Press, New York, 1979
First issued as an Oxford University Press paperback, 1981

Library of Congress Cataloging in Publication Data
Rorabaugh, W J
The alcoholic republic, an American tradition.

Bibliography: p.
Includes index.
1. Alcoholism—United States—History. 2. United
States—Social conditions—To 1865. I. Title.
HV 5291.R67   362.2'92   79-650
ISBN 0-19-502584-9
ISBN 0-19-502990-9 (pbk.)

printing, last digit: 20 19 18 17 16 15 14 13 12 11

Printed in the United States of America

For
AGNES and IRVIN RORABAUGH
and
ELIZABETH ROSENFIELD

THE GROG-SHOP

O come let us all to the grog-shop:
The tempest is gathering fast—
There surely is nought like the grog-shop
To shield from the turbulent blast.

For there will be wrangling Willy
Disputing about a lame ox;
And there will be bullying Billy
Challenging negroes to box:

Toby Fillpot with carbuncle nose
Mixing politics up with his liquor;
Tim Tuneful that sings even prose,
And hiccups and coughs in his beaker.

Dick Drowsy with emerald eyes,
Kit Crusty with hair like a comet,
Sam Smootly that whilom grew wise
But returned like a dog to his vomit

And there will be tippling and talk
And fuddling and fun to the life,
And swaggering, swearing, and smoke,
And shuffling and scuffling and strife.

And there will be swapping of horses,
And betting, and beating, and blows,
And laughter, and lewdness, and losses,
And winning, and wounding and woes.

O then let us off to the grog-shop;
Come, father, come, Jonathan, come;
Far drearier far than a Sunday
Is a storm in the dullness of home.

GREEN'S
ANTI-INTEMPERANCE
ALMANACK (1831)

PREFACE

THIS PROJECT began when I discovered a sizeable collection of early nineteenth-century temperance pamphlets. As I read those tracts, I wondered what had prompted so many authors to expend so much effort and expense to attack alcohol. I began to suspect that the temperance movement had been launched in the 1820s as a response to a period of exceptionally hearty drinking. The truth was startling: Americans between 1790 and 1830 drank more alcoholic beverages per capita than ever before or since. Little has been written about this veritable national binge, and some reflection concerning the development of American historiography explains the neglect.

In the first place, throughout most of American history alcohol has been a taboo subject. While nineteenth-century librarians filed references to it under a pejorative, the 'liquor problem,' proper people did not even mention strong beverages. Neither did historians, who long neglected the fact that the United States had been one of the world's great drinking countries. A recent biographer of Patrick Henry, George Willison, tells us that one of Henry's early biographers transformed that patriot's tavern-keeping for his father-in-law into occasional visits to that drinking house. And a few years later Henry's grandson wrote a biography that did not even mention the tavern. Sometimes, late nineteenth-century authors became politely vague. When Richard H. Collins in his *History of Kentucky* (Louisville, 1877), 767, described Thomas F. Marshall, a drunkard nephew of Chief Justice John Marshall, he wrote, "In spite of his great weakness—a weakness which often made him disagreeable and unwelcome to his best friends, the weakness most common among men of brilliant promise—he was in truth a remarkable man. . . ." Thus was the innuendo closed with a dash, as the author retreated behind a facade of respectability.

In the second place, American historians traditionally have focused upon political events, especially upon such obvious turning points as the Revolution and the Civil War, with the consequence that life during the years between those wars has often been ignored. Even scholars who have written on the early nineteenth century have emphasized politics, including Arthur M. Schlesinger, Jr., in his path-breaking *The Age of Jackson*. That work, published in 1945, led a generation of historians to see Jacksonian America primarily as the era that gave birth to modern liberal values. This view gave the period a favorable reputation until it was discovered that Andrew Jackson, that primordial liberal, had been a holder of slaves and a slayer of Indians.

During the 1960s, while scholars were recoiling from Jackson and losing interest in his times, Americans were living through unprecedented turmoil. We discovered that social change had the potential to be as tumultuous and alarming as political change. Historians began to examine more closely the social changes that had occurred in the United States in past times, and they began to question the utility of such turning points as the Revolution or the Civil War. A number of studies of New England towns during the colonial period pointed to the importance of evolutionary change as the basis for long-term rearrangements of the social order. The impact of industrialization during the mid-nineteenth century began to attract more attention, and that interest stimulated a number of works focusing on such developments as the American railroad. A rising consciousness about ethnicity led to studies of immigrant groups. The changing roles of women were investigated. Most of these inquiries, either explicitly or implicitly, eroded the importance of such customary dividing points as the Revolution or the Civil War, and, indeed, the proliferation of social history threatened to leave much of the American past without significant turning points.

The present study suggests a new turning point. The changes in drinking patterns that occurred between 1790 and 1840 were more dramatic than any that occurred at any other time in American history. Furthermore, the association of particular patterns in the consumption of alcohol with certain social and psychological traits has led me to conclude that the United States in those years underwent such profound social and psychological change that a new national character emerged. Indeed, the American of 1840 was in assumptions, attitudes, beliefs, behavior, and mind closer to the American of 1960 than to his own grandfather. In other words, the early nineteenth century was a key formative period in American social history.

This project began with more modest aims. As I began to investigate the period of high consumption during the early nineteenth century, I considered who drank, what they imbibed, when and where they consumed. Had this work never advanced beyond those questions, it would have been a suggestive though inchoate essay in manners. What has enabled me to consider broader questions has been the use of the theoretical literature on the consumption of alcohol. From the work of social scientists who examined the drinking mores in particular cultures and made cross-cultural comparisons of drinking in primitive societies, I learned that drinking customs and habits were not random but reflective of a society's fabric, tensions, and inner dynamics, and of the psychological sets of its people. Because the wealth of this material enabled me to apply social science theory to many of my observations of drinking patterns in nineteenth-century America, I was able, consequently, to draw conclusions concerning the psychology and social behavior of Americans in that period. At the same time, this inquiry became a kind of laboratory in which to test hypotheses from the literature on alcohol. In that sense, theorists of drinking motivation can view the work as a historical case study.

And here I will add a warning. Because this book mixes history and the social sciences, it employs methods that are not traditional to any single discipline, and its conclusions are sometimes more suggestive than rigorously proved. My justification for such speculation is that there is a need for books that provide questions rather than answers. It matters less that my speculations are correct, although I hope that some of them will be proved in time, than that I have provoked the reader to think and explore for himself. That is why I wrote the book.

Finally, by way of appreciation, I would like to offer several toasts. First, to the many cooperative librarians, particularly those at the Congregational Society Library and Harvard's Baker Business Library Manuscripts Department; to helping friends, Suzanne Aldridge, Steve Fish, Bill Gienapp, Keith Howard, Tony Martin, Steve Novak, Roy Weatherup, Hugh West, and Kent Wood; and to friendly critics, Joe Corn, Harry Levine, Charles Royster, Joseph Ryshpan, and Wells Wadleigh. I also raise my glass to David Fischer for suggesting a logical format for presenting consumption statistics; to Bruce Boling and Kerby Miller for access to many Irish immigrant letters; to Edward Pessen for comments on my dissertation; and to Michael McGiffert and Gary Walton for critiquing early drafts of chapters two and three, respectively. An earlier version of my consumption estimates appeared in "Estimated U.S. Alcoholic Beverage Consumption, 1790–1860," *Journal of Studies on Alcohol*, 37 (1976), 357–364. The next round honors Alfred Knopf, Inc.; the Maryland Historical Society, Baltimore; and the Rhode-Island Historical Society, respectively, for permission to reproduce three illustrations. Photographs were made at the University of California, Berkeley, and the University of Washington. Permission was given to quote from several manuscript collections: Benjamin Rush Papers, Historical Society of Pennsylvania; Michael Collins Papers, Duke University; Robison Family Papers, Maine Historical Society; J. H. Cocke Papers, Mrs. Forney Johnston and the University of Virginia; and Bacon Family Papers, Yale University.

I also salute the members of my thesis committee at Berkeley, Troy Duster, Winthrop Jordan, and especially chairman Charles Sellers. He shepherded this work from its inception to its completion as a thesis, warned me of numerous pitfalls, and made many helpful suggestions, including the title. The University of California, Berkeley, gave financial support as a Teaching Assistant and as a Dean's Fellow with a travel allowance. I owe a special toast to Elizabeth Rosenfield. Her generosity in providing a place to write and inimitable dinner conversation sped my thesis to its conclusion. Mine was the sixth dissertation written in her home. More recently, she has exercised her editorial skill upon the manuscript. We did not always agree: her whiskey is Scotch; mine, as a native of Kentucky, is not. My final salutes are to Richard R. Johnson, Otis Pease, and my other colleagues at the University of Washington; to Ann Pettingill, whose assistance was made possible by a grant from the University of Washington Alcoholism and Drug Abuse Institute; to Sheldon Meyer, who gave early encouragement; to Susan Rabiner, Phyllis Deutsch, and everyone at Oxford; and to my sister, Mary Rorabaugh, who helped solve a last minute crisis.

W. J. R.

Seattle
June 13, 1979

CONTENTS

Chapter

1   A NATION OF DRUNKARDS   3

2   A GOOD CREATURE   23

3   THE SPIRITS OF INDEPENDENCE   59

4   WHISKEY FEED   93

5   THE ANXIETIES OF THEIR CONDITION   123

6   THE PURSUIT OF HAPPINESS   147

7   DEMON RUM   185

Appendix

1   ESTIMATING CONSUMPTION OF ALCOHOL   223

2   CROSS-NATIONAL COMPARISONS OF
    CONSUMPTION   237

3   COOK BOOKS   240

4   REVIEW OF DRINKING MOTIVATION
    LITERATURE   241

Contents

5   QUANTITATIVE MEASUREMENTS 247

6   A RECIPE 250

Bibliographical Note 251

Key to Abbreviations 254

Notes 256

Index 295

THE ALCOHOLIC REPUBLIC

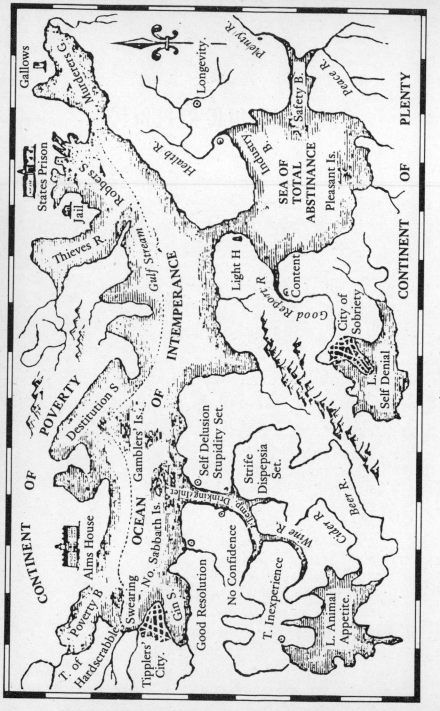

A geography lesson.

CHAPTER

A NATION OF DRUNKARDS

The thing has arrived to such a height, that we are actually threatened with, becoming a nation of drunkards.

GREENE and DELAWARE MORAL SOCIETY
1815

W<small>AS</small> <small>EARLY</small> nineteenth-century America really a nation
of drunkards? Certainly the clergymen who were crusad-
ing for temperance thought so, as excerpts from their sermons and addresses attest. These self-appointed moral
guardians, convinced that a hearty indulgence in alcohol
was commonplace, increasing, and unprecedented, were
filled with apprehension, their sermons filled with despair. Intemperance, they warned, was widespread, "too
obvious not to be noticed;" "so common, as scarcely to be
thought criminal;" "the fashionable vice of the day."
They noted, too, that the United States was among the
most addicted of nations, that in this respect it had outstripped all Europe, and that "no other people ever indulged, so universally." Even more alarming in their eyes
was the fact that this intemperance was spreading "wider
and wider;" "like the plague;" "throughout our country;"
"with the rapidity and power of a tempest." Not only did
they see excessive use as the crying sin of the nation, but
they believed it to be "a *growing* evil;" "*still increasing*;"
until America "was fast becoming a nation of drunkards."[1]

A similar alarm was voiced by the nation's most prominent statesmen. It was not so much the use of alcohol
that worried them—they all drank to some extent—as its
excessive use. George Washington, a whiskey distiller

5

himself, thought that distilled spirits were "the ruin of half the workmen in this Country. . . ." John Adams, whose daily breakfast included a tankard of hard cider, asked, ". . . is it not mortifying . . . that we, Americans, should exceed all other . . . people in the world in this degrading, beastly vice of intemperance?" And Thomas Jefferson, inventor of the presidential cocktail party, feared that the use of cheap, raw whiskey was "spreading through the mass of our citizens." In 1821 George Ticknor, a wealthy Boston scholar, warned Jefferson, "If the consumption of spirituous liquors should increase for thirty years to come at the rate it has for thirty years back we should be hardly better than a nation of sots." The Founding Fathers, fearful that the American republic would be destroyed in a flood of alcohol, were anguished and perplexed.[2]

Other observers, more dispassionate but no less articulate, found American drinking habits deplorable. Foreign travellers, for instance, were surprised and shocked at the amount of alcohol they saw consumed. A Swedish visitor, Carl D. Arfwedson, reported a "general addiction to hard drinking," while a visitor from England, Isaac Holmes, noted that intoxication pervaded all social classes. It was not surprising that Basil Hall, a retired Royal Navy Captain hostile to the new nation's democratic ideals, should be "perfectly astonished at the extent of intemperance." But even the sympathetic English reformer, William Cobbett, deplored American tippling. "I almost wished," he wrote, "that there were Boroughmongers here to *tax* these drinkers."[3]

The more discerning visitors observed that while heavy drinking was widespread, public drunkenness was not common. This fact led William Dalton to suggest that Americans better deserved the appellation of tipplers than of drunkards. Infrequency of conspicuous drunkenness, however, was not inconsistent with an extensive overuse of alcohol. As a shrewd Scot by the name of Peter Neilson pointed out, the nation's citizens were "in a certain degree *seasoned*, and consequently it [was] by no means common to see an American *very* much intoxicated." In other words, as a result of habitual heavy drinking Americans had developed a high degree of tolerance for alcohol. Even so, in the opinion of Isaac Candler, Americans were "certainly not so sober as the French or Germans, but perhaps," he guessed, "about on a level with the Irish."[4]

American travellers expressed similar views. They found "a great want of economy in the use of spirituous liquors," noted that drunkenness was "everywhere prevalent," and pronounced the quantity of alcohol consumed to be "scandalous." The well-travelled Anne Royall, who spent much of her life crisscrossing the country in stage coaches, wrote, "When I was in Virginia, it was too much whiskey—in Ohio, too much whiskey—in Tennessee, it is too, too much whiskey!"[5]

It was the consensus, then, among a wide variety of observers that Americans drank great quantities of alcohol. The beverages they drank were for the most part distilled liquors, commonly known as spirits—whiskey, rum, gin, and brandy. On the average those liquors were 45 percent alcohol, or, in the language of distillers, 90 proof. It was the unrestrained consumption of liquors of such potency that amazed travellers and alarmed so many Americans. And there was cause for alarm. During the first third of the nineteenth century the typical American annually drank more distilled liquor than at any other time in our history.

A brief survey of American alcohol consumption from the colonial period to the present will help us put the early nineteenth century in proper perspective. As Chart 1.1 shows, during the colonial period the annual per capita consumption of hard liquor, mostly rum, reached 3.7

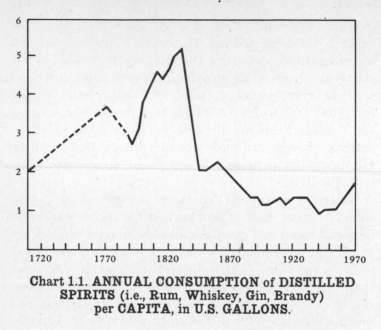

Chart 1.1. **ANNUAL CONSUMPTION of DISTILLED
SPIRITS (i.e., Rum, Whiskey, Gin, Brandy)
per CAPITA, in U.S. GALLONS.**

gallons. After the Revolution, because of decreased trade
with the West Indies, high import duties on West Indian
rum and on the West Indian molasses from which New
England rum was made, and a new tax on domestic whiskey, the consumption of distilled liquors declined by
one-quarter. But by 1800, prosperity, improved distilling
technology, the growing popularity of whiskey together
with illicit and therefore untaxed distilled spirits had
combined to raise per capita consumption to the 1770
level. Then, between 1800 and 1830, annual per capita
consumption increased until it exceeded 5 gallons—a rate
nearly triple that of today's consumption. After 1830 the
temperance movement, and later on high federal taxation
discouraged the drinking of distilled beverages. Annual
per capita consumption fell to less than 2 gallons, a level
from which there has been little deviation in more than a
century.

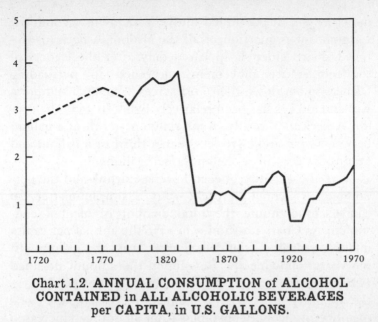

Chart 1.2. **ANNUAL CONSUMPTION of ALCOHOL CONTAINED in ALL ALCOHOLIC BEVERAGES per CAPITA, in U.S. GALLONS.**

In addition to distilled spirits, Americans drank weaker fermented beverages: beer (5% alcohol), hard cider (10%), and wine (18%). Colonial beer consumption was negligible, except for home brewed 'small beer,' which was only one percent alcohol. Until 1850 annual per capita consumption of commercial beer at no time reached 2 gallons, and it was not until after the Civil War that it rose dramatically toward today's rate of more than 18 gallons. But hard cider was a different matter. Pre-Revolutionary cider consumption, heaviest in the apple country from Virginia northward, was probably as high if not higher than in the early nineteenth century. In fact, so much cider was drunk that colonial Americans probably ingested more alcohol from that beverage than from their much more potent rum. And even with the increased popularity of distilled spirits after 1800, the annual per capita consumption of hard cider was 15 or

9

more gallons. It continued until the 1830s to account for a significant proportion of all the alcohol Americans imbibed. Hard cider disappeared only after the leaders of the temperance movement succeeded in persuading farmers to cut down their apple trees. Wine consumption was and always has been relatively light. In 1770 the typical American annually drank only one-tenth of a gallon; between 1770 and 1870 less than a third of a gallon; and even today less than one and a half gallons.

From the quantity of each beverage drunk and the percentage of alcohol in each, it is a simple matter, of course, to compute the total amount of alcohol consumed. As Chart 1.2 shows, in 1770 the annual per capita intake of alcohol from all sources was 3.5 gallons. In the years following the Revolution the amount declined as the consumption of spirits declined. But after 1800, as the quantity of spirits consumed increased, the total quantity of alcohol consumed from all sources increased until it reached a peak of nearly 4 gallons per capita in 1830. This rate of consumption was the highest in the annals of the United States. After reaching this peak, consumption fell sharply under the influence of the temperance movement, and since 1840 its highest levels have been under 2 gallons—less than half the rate of consumption in the 1820s.[6]

Drinking in the young nation was obviously hearty, not to say excessive. However, the charge made by alarmed clergymen and statesmen that in this respect America had outstripped every other nation was exaggerated. A comparison of the annual per capita intake of alcohol in the United States with that in other countries during the early nineteenth century shows that Americans drank more than the English, Irish, or Prussians, but about the same as the Scots or French, and less than the Swedes. The nations with high consumption rates tended to share certain characteristics. Except for France, where wine predominated, the remaining heavy drinking countries, Scotland, Sweden, and the United States, were distilled spirits strongholds. These nations were agricultural, rural, lightly populated, and geographically isolated from foreign markets; they had undercapitalized, agrarian, barter economies; they were Protestant. In all three cheap, abundant grain fed the distilleries. By contrast, consumption was low in Ireland and Prussia because their economies lacked surplus grain and, hence, could not support a high level of distilled spirits production. In England high spirits taxes had encouraged the populace to switch from whiskey and gin to beer. Although early nineteenth-century Americans did not drink more than relatively affluent Europeans of that era, by modern standards they drank a lot. A recent survey of alcohol consumption in ten European countries shows only France with a higher per capita consumption than the American rate during the early nineteenth century and shows five countries drinking at less than half that rate.[7]

So the typical American was drinking heartily, but not all Americans drank their share. It is impossible to obtain an exact accounting, but the American Temperance Society estimated that during each year of the late 1820s nine million women and children drank 12 million gallons of distilled spirits; three million men, 60 million gallons. At this high point the average adult male was imbibing nearly a half pint a day. Few, however, were average. It was calculated that half the men drank 2 ounces a day; one-quarter ("habitual temperate drinkers"), 6 ounces; one-eighth ("regular topers, and occasional drunkards"), 12 ounces; and another eighth ("confirmed drunkards"), 24 ounces. Thus, half the adult males—one-eighth of the total population—were drinking two-thirds of all the distilled spirits consumed.[8]

While men were the heartiest topers, women were not

Men were the heartiest topers.

faint-hearted abstainers. Little, however, can be learned
about either the reputed 100,000 female drunkards or the
more numerous women who consumed from one-eighth
to one-quarter of the nation's spirituous liquor. The subject received scant attention because it was "too delicate"
to be discussed. The ideal of femininity did discourage
tippling, for a woman was supposed to show restraint
consistent with virtue, prudence consonant with delicacy, and a preference for beverages agreeable to a fragile
constitution. The public was not tolerant of women
drinking at taverns or groceries, unless they were travellers recovering from a day's arduous journey. Then the
ladies might be permitted watered and highly sugared
spirituous cordials.[9]

The concept of feminine delicacy led women to drink
alcohol-based medicines for their health; many who
regarded spirits as "vulgar" happily downed a highly al-

12

coholic "cordial or stomachic elixir." Furthermore, there were some social occasions when it was proper for women to imbibe freely and openly. For example, eastern ladies drank in mixed company at society dinners, suppers, and evening parties; and at pioneer dances the "whiskey bottle was . . . passed pretty briskly from mouth to mouth, exempting neither age nor sex." A surprised Frances Kemble learned that New York ladies who visited the public baths were "pretty often" supplied with mint juleps. Still, because a woman had to conform, at least outwardly, to the social precepts of the day, she was most likely to drink in the privacy of her own home. There she could suit herself. The usual roles of male and female were reversed when temperance reformer Edward Delavan called upon Dolly Madison. After the teetotaling Delavan declined a drink, the flustered hostess declared that "such an example was worthy of imitation" and proceeded to mix herself a toddy.[10]

Southern slaves, like women, drank less than their share of liquor. Masters usually provided watered spirits as a work incentive during harvest time, and many allowed their bondsmen a three-day spree at Christmas. The law, however, generally prohibited blacks from drinking at other times. This prohibition was only partially effective. Blacks in some districts were reputed to be a majority of tavern customers, and slaves often found that they could acquire liquor by bartering their own garden vegetables or hams purloined from the master. One Warrenton, North Carolina man complained that on Sunday afternoon the streets were "infested with drunken negroes stagering from side to side." This observer concluded that custom was "stronger than law." Defiance of the liquor laws led to tougher statutes. North Carolina, for example, in 1798 prohibited retailers from selling alcohol to slaves if their owners objected; in 1818 forbade slaves from vending liquor; and in 1833 forbade them from buying spirits under any condition. But these legal restraints against slaves drinking were less effective in discouraging consumption than was the plantation system under which there was neither the opportunity to obtain liquor nor the money to buy it. As Eugene Genovese has pointed out, the slaves' principal drinking problem was the drinking of their masters.[11]

White males were taught to drink as children, even as babies. "I have frequently seen Fathers," wrote one traveller, "wake their Child of a year old from a sound sleap to make it drink Rum, or Brandy." As soon as a toddler was old enough to drink from a cup, he was coaxed to consume the sugary residue at the bottom of an adult's nearly empty glass of spirits. Many parents intended this early exposure to alcohol to accustom their offspring to the taste of liquor, to encourage them to accept the idea of drinking small amounts, and thus to protect them from becoming drunkards. Children grew up imitating their elders' drinking customs. Boys who played 'militia' expected the game to end, like their fathers' musters, with a round of drinks. Adolescents perceived drinking at a public house to be a mark of manhood. Sometimes the swaggering young male made a ridiculous picture. "It is no uncommon thing," wrote one man, "to see a boy of twelve or fourteen years old . . . walk into a tavern in the forenoon to take a glass of brandy and bitters. . . ." Men encouraged this youthful drinking. Many a proud father glowed when his son became old enough to accompany him to the tavern where they could drink as equals from the same glass.[12]

The male drinking cult pervaded all social and occupational groups. A western husbandman tarried at the tavern until drunk; an eastern harvest laborer received daily a half pint or pint of rum; a southern planter was considered temperate enough to belong to the Methodist Church if he restricted his daily intake of alcohol to a

quart of peach brandy. A city mechanic went directly from work to the public house where he stayed late and spent his day's wages. Alcohol was such an accepted part of American life that in 1829 the secretary of war estimated that three-quarters of the nation's laborers drank daily at least 4 ounces of distilled spirits. Liquor was so popular that the army dared not bar the recruitment or reenlistment of habitual drunkards. If such a policy were adopted, warned the surgeon general, the army might have to be disbanded. The middle classes were scarcely more sober. Attorneys disputed with physicians as to which profession was the more besotted. Even more shocking was the indulgence of clergymen. One minister who considered himself temperate systematically downed 4 glasses of spirits to help him endure the fatigues of Sunday. At Andover Seminary, one of the most important centers of temperance activity, students regularly drank brandy toddies at the local tavern. Perhaps this practice was necessary to prepare would-be ministers for keeping up with their future congregations.[13]

Drinking by these enthusiastic topers was done in a variety of places, including, of course, taverns. Although the original purpose of public houses had been to provide travellers a place to obtain refreshment, most localities had so few travellers that tavern owners found it necessary for their economic survival to attract local customers to the bar. Even so, the typical early nineteenth-century tavern recorded fewer than fifty visits a week. Half of these trips were made by the same four or eight men, the regulars who gathered every day or two around the pot-bellied stove to talk about the crops and weather, to argue politics, to quarrel and fight over insults, and, of course, to drink. They usually treated, that is, each man bought a half pint of whiskey, which was passed around the room. Since every man was expected to treat in turn, by evening's end each had drunk half a pint. With so few regulars, the solvency of most public houses depended upon the Saturday trade, when as many as twenty men might gather to drink a half pint apiece. It appears that the typical man patronized a public house once a week, that these visits provided him with 13 quarts of distilled spirits a year, and that this amount represented about one-fifth of his annual consumption.[14]

Most liquor was drunk in the home, where whiskey and rum provided mealtime drinks, customary refresheners, and hospitable treats for guests. Fashionable people owned ornate liquor cases or elaborate sideboards that contained numerous bottles of various cordials, including mild, sweet, fruit-flavored elixirs for the ladies. Even the poorest host proffered his whiskey jug. While some of this liquor was made on the premises, bartered from neighbors, or bought at a distillery, much came from the

general store, where its sale was often the most important item of business. Although some merchants curried favor with their customers by plying them with free samples of their spirits, less liquor was given away than was sold for home use. A study of one New Hampshire store's records from 1810 to 1833 showed that farmers who purchased supplies usually bought liquor along with their other purchases. During the early 1820s one-quarter of the value of this store's total sales was alcohol; typically, at that time, in a transaction that was for more than $1 and that included the sale of alcohol, distilled beverages accounted for more than half the value of the sale. A decade later less than one-tenth of the value of total sales was liquor; in a transaction over $1 that included alcohol, spirits were but one-third the value of the sale.[15]

Leaving home, however, did not require that an American forego his favorite beverage. When journeying by stage coach, travellers could obtain liquor at the inns where the horses were changed. During one arduous seventeen-hour, sixty-six mile trip across Virginia, the stage stopped ten times, and two of the passengers had drinks at each way station: ten drinks apiece. Such habits led one foreign observer to conclude that "the American stage coach stops every five miles to water the horses, and *brandy the gentlemen!*"[16] With the invention of steamboats, Americans were provided with yet another place to drink. Whereas stage travellers had been able to imbibe only when their vehicle rested at a wayside inn, boat passengers usually found a bar conveniently situated in the gentlemen's compartment, on the middle deck above the engine room. This arrangement is telling. The location of the bar not only discouraged female travellers from drinking; it also indicates that the bar was the boat's central feature. Of all forms of public transportation, only the steamboat focused so much attention on the bar. In part, this design reflected the owners' hopes for high profits from liquor sales; some boats were little more than floating saloons. More important is the fact that the steamboat was conceived at a time when drinking was central to American society. Boat designs that stressed bars conformed to a cultural imperative.[17]

Americans drank not only any place but also any time. Some began to imbibe even before breakfast with an eye opener concocted of rum, whiskey, or gin mixed with bitters. In one Rhode Island factory town, laborers going to work made their way through the dawn's early light to

the tavern "to take a little drop." Gentlemen adjourned
from business at 11:00 A.M. for the old-fashioned equiva-
lent of the coffee break, the 'elevens,' an occasion for par-
taking of spirituous liquor. When the weather was cold,
they might have hot toddies made of whiskey or rum,
sugar, and hot water, or hot slings made of gin, sugar,
and hot water. At times a little lemon juice, cherry
brandy, or bitters was added. The Virginia gentry gathered at 1:00 P.M., an hour before dinner, for the purpose
of taking juleps compounded of peach brandy or whiskey, sugar, and ice. Sometimes crushed mint was added
to make a mint julep. Throughout America early afternoon dinner was accompanied by hard cider or distilled
spirits mixed with water; in late afternoon came another
break; then supper with more refreshment. Finally, in
the evening it was time to pause and reflect upon the
day's events while sitting by the home or tavern fireside
sipping spirits.[18]

Americans drank on all occasions. Every social event
demanded a drink. When southerners served barbecue,
they roasted hogs and provided "plenty of whiskey."
Guests at urban dances and balls were often intoxicated;
so were spectators at frontier horse races. Western new-
lyweds were customarily presented with a bottle of whiskey to be drunk before bedding down for the night.
Liquor also entered into money-making and business affairs. When a bargain was negotiated or a contract
signed, it was sealed with a drink; auctioneers passed a
whiskey bottle to those who made bids. After the harvest, farmers held agricultural fairs that ended with dinners laced with dozens of toasts. Whiskey accompanied
traditional communal activities such as house-raisings,
huskings, land clearings, and reaping. It was even
served when women gathered to sew, quilt, or pick the
seeds out of cotton.[19]

Liquor also flowed at such public events as militia

musters, elections, and the quarterly sessions of the
courts. Militiamen elected their officers with the expectation that the elected officers would treat. One newly
elevated colonel pledged, "I can't make a speech, but
what I lack in brains I will try and make up in rum."
Voters demanded and received spirits in exchange for
their ballots. Electoral success, explained one Kentucky
politico, depended upon understanding that "the way to
men's hearts, is, *down their throats.*" At trials the bottle
was passed among spectators, attorneys, clients—and to
the judge. If the foreman of a jury became mellow in his
cups, the defendant stood an excellent chance for acquit-
tal.[20]

Alcohol was pervasive in American society; it crossed
regional, sexual, racial, and class lines. Americans drank
at home and abroad, alone and together, at work and at

play, in fun and in earnest. They drank from the crack of dawn to the crack of dawn. At nights taverns were filled with boisterous, mirth-making tipplers. Americans drank before meals, with meals, and after meals. They drank while working in the fields and while travelling across half a continent. They drank in their youth, and, if they lived long enough, in their old age. They drank at formal events, such as weddings, ministerial ordinations, and wakes, and on no occasion—by the fireside of an evening, on a hot afternoon, when the mood called. From sophisticated Andover to frontier Illinois, from Ohio to Georgia, in lumbercamps and on satin settees, in log taverns and at fashionable New York hotels, the American greeting was, "Come, Sir, take a dram first." Seldom was it refused.[21]

Early nineteenth-century America may not have been 'a nation of drunkards,' but Americans were certainly enjoying a spectacular binge.

CHAPTER

A GOOD CREATURE

Drink is in itself a creature of God,
and to be received with thankfulness.

INCREASE MATHER
1673

To UNDERSTAND the great alcoholic binge of the early nineteenth century, we have to go well back into the eighteenth century to examine changes that were then taking place: changes in the social structure, in philosophical ideas, in business and industry, and, most particularly, in beliefs and habits related to the consumption of alcohol.

At the beginning of the eighteenth century, tradition taught, and Americans, like Englishmen and Europeans, universally believed, that rum, gin, and brandy were nutritious and healthful. Distilled spirits were viewed as foods that supplemented limited and monotonous diets, as medications that could cure colds, fevers, snakebites, frosted toes, and broken legs, and as relaxants that would relieve depression, reduce tension, and enable hard-working laborers to enjoy a moment of happy, frivolous camaraderie. Such favorable views led to a widespread use of strong drink. Before 1750 nearly all Americans of all social classes drank alcoholic beverages in quantity, sometimes to the point of intoxication.[1]

Virginia slaves, at the bottom of the social scale, indulged in such frequent intoxication that one governor of the colony was persuaded to offer his servants a bargain. If they agreed to stay sober on the Queen's birthday, he promised that they would be allowed to get drunk an-

other day. His offer was accepted, and the bargain was
fulfilled. White laborers were also great imbibers, and,
according to diarist William Byrd, the Virginia populace
got drunk regularly at militia musters, on election days,
and during quarterly court sessions. The North was as
given to drink as the South. One New Englander wrote:

> *There's scarce a Tradesman in the Land,*
> *That when from Work is come,*
> *But takes a touch, (sometimes too much)*
> *Of* Brandy *or of* Rum.

Even on the western frontier, rum was a dietary staple.
When William Byrd's party surveyed the Virginia-North
Carolina boundary, one backwoods host served them a
dinner of fat bacon soaked in rum.[2]

Nor was hearty drinking confined to the lower classes.
At auctions in Philadelphia it was the custom to serve
liquor to any merchant who made a bid. On one occasion, the bidders drank 20 gallons of rum while the
total sales came to less than £200. Diarist Byrd recorded
many instances of intoxication among the Virginia elite
and particularly noted a doctor friend who frequently
"came drunk to dinner." Another physician who drank
freely was Dr. John Potts. While governor of Virginia he
continued a medical practice that consisted principally of
prescribing distilled spirits for his patients and himself.[3]

There was little opposition to such robust drinking.
While William Byrd did not condone public drunkenness
that led to disorder, he expressed equal indifference toward intoxication among members of the Governor's
Council and among his own servants. He considered occasional drunkenness a natural, harmless consequence of
imbibing. At that time inebriation was not associated
with violence or crime; only rowdy, belligerent inebriation in public places was frowned upon. Such excesses
were discouraged in part by the high price of distilled

spirits and in larger part by the fact that the upper classes
monitored public drinking. Since all classes of colonial
society had the same attitude toward drinking and the
same easygoing drinking style, upper class efforts to restrain public drunkenness were, on the one hand, made
in a tolerant spirit and, on the other, accepted as necessary for the preservation of order.[4]

That the upper classes were able to monitor drinking
and to impose restraints was due to the hierarchical nature of colonial society. Although men were deemed
equal before the law and before God, their social and political inequalities were recognized and respected. New
Englanders followed the advice of their educated, socially
prominent Congregational clergy, and in free and open
elections they chose men from the upper classes as tith-
ingmen, school overseers, town selectmen, and legislative
representatives. New York's Hudson River valley pa-
troons not only demanded but received their tenant
farmers' support, and further south, Virginia planters,
whose prestige was based on owning vast acreage and
numerous slaves, vied only with each other for election
to the House of Burgesses.[5]

One way in which the upper classes monitored drinking was by controlling the taverns. During the first half
of the eighteenth century the public house was a focus of
community life. Americans met there not only to enjoy
themselves but also to transact business and debate politics. In Virginia, for example, where the law allowed
only one tavern per county, this drinking place most
often adjoined the courthouse. Before trials it was common for defendants, attorneys, judges, and jurymen to
gather there to drink, and sometimes matters were settled
'out of court.' At other times, when a controversial case
attracted a crowd, it was necessary to hold the trial in the
tavern, which was the only public building roomy
enough to accommodate the spectators. New England

public houses were often built next door to meeting houses so that Sunday worshippers could congregate there before and after service. During the winter, churchgoers warmed their posteriors in front of the tavern fire and their interiors with rum before yielding to the necessity of entering the unheated meeting house. After worship, they thawed out at the tavern.[6]

Because taverns played such an important role in local affairs, the upper classes believed that they should be well regulated, orderly, and respectable, that only men and women of good moral character should operate them, and that this requirement could best be met through the device of licensing. In late seventeenth-century Massachusetts, for example, the law provided that only voters and church members, the colony's elite, were eligible to hold licenses. Such regulations led to the kind of situation that existed in the town of Danvers, where the licensed taverners included two deacons and an ordained Congregational minister. Even when members of the upper classes did not themselves manage the public houses, the licensing system kept publicans subservient to the town or county authorities who held the power to grant or deny permits.[7]

Yet licensing itself was only one mechanism by which the upper classes asserted their authority. Control was also exercised through informal channels. One Massachusetts minister insisted that a public house be located next to his own dwelling so he could monitor tavern traffic through his study window. If he observed a man frequenting the place too often, the clergyman could go next door and escort the drinker home. Ministers, however, were not the only men of authority who enforced liquor regulations. In 1714, for example, some holiday drinkers refused to leave a Boston public house at closing time, and their defiance was brought to the attention of Judge Samuel Sewall. The judge immediately left home

and proceeded to the tavern. There he "Found much
Company. They refus'd to go away. Said were there to
drink the Queen's Health, and they had many other
Healths to drink. Call'd for more Drink: drank to me, I
took notice of the Affront to them. Said must and would
stay upon that Solemn occasion. Mr. John Netmaker
drank the Queen's Health to me. I told him I drank
none; upon that he ceas'd. Mr. Brinley put on his Hat to
affront me. I made him take it off. I threaten'd to send
some of them to prison; that did not move them. . . . I
told them if they had not a care, they would be guilty of
a Riot." With that warning the drunken mob departed.
Although Sewall had not found it easy to disperse the
men, their capitulation underscores the reality of upper
class control of the taverns.[8]

This hearty, carefree, freewheeling, benign drinking,
monitored and to some extent controlled by the upper
classes, would probably have prevailed indefinitely if the
per capita consumption of distilled spirits had remained
stable. All signs, however, indicate that rum drinking
increased after 1720. Nor was this increase surprising,
for the price of distilled spirits fell. At Boston the price
of a gallon of rum plummeted from 3 shillings 6 pence in
1722 to 2 shillings in 1738. At that low price a common
laborer could afford to get drunk every day. Georgians
were no more sober than Bostonians. In 1735, when
James Oglethorpe investigated delays in the construction
of a lighthouse, he learned that workmen labored only
one day in seven, for a day's wages would buy a week's
inebriation. Lower prices had naturally stimulated demand. Boston rum production rose substantially during
the 1730s, and in the following decade New England imports of both rum and molasses for distillation increased.
By the middle of the century, Boston, Providence, New
Haven, and Philadelphia had emerged as centers of a
burgeoning distilling industry.[9]

This high tide of rum brought with it a new style of drinking. Public drunkenness became a vehicle for the expression of anger and hostility. It also became evident to some people that drunkenness led to thievery, lechery, and brutality. The association of rum with crime and disorder caused these Americans to perceive inebriation itself as a major social problem. In 1736, when Benjamin Franklin reprinted an English article against liquor, he added a preface in which he said, "Perhaps it may have as good an Effect in these Countries as it had in England. And there is as much Necessity for such a Publication here as there; for our RUM does the same Mischief in proportion, as their GENEVA."[10]

Among the first to be alarmed by the increase of drunkenness and alcohol-induced disorder were, as we might expect, American clergymen. Evangelist George Whitefield condemned inebriation, and troubled New England ministers bewailed the iniquities befalling God's Saints. This apprehension about alcohol, provoked by extensive public drunkenness, contrasted with a more restrained traditional Puritan view. In the late seventeenth century the Rev. Increase Mather had taught that drink was "a good creature of God" and that a man should partake of God's gift without wasting or abusing it. His only admonition was that a man must not "drink a Cup of Wine more then is good for him." Only a few years later, however, and even before cheap rum had had its full effect, his son was expressing a less serene view.[11]

In 1708 Cotton Mather affirmed his father's teaching that rum was "a *Creature of God*," that spirits had nutritional and medical value, and that people could drink moderately to gain strength. Drunkenness, however, he condemned. Mather saw inebriation as a source of social unrest, as a sign of divine affliction, and as a warning of eternal damnation. He had cause for alarm, for intoxication among God's Saints was not uncommon. What the

Puritan Mather feared especially was that the "Flood of RUM" would "Overwhelm all good Order among us." By this he did not mean simply that intoxication would lead to increased crime, pauperism, gaming, and whoring. The "Order" he feared for was the class structure of New England society. Rum, he believed, was a threat to the existing social hierarchy. The menace that Mather feared was a consequence of the intertwining of popular beliefs about the virtue of the good creature rum with the rising availability of that cheap, plentiful beverage. In a culture in which liquor was respected, its use was limited only by how much people could afford. The source of Mather's alarm was that the wealthy elite, whom he addressed, could best afford to buy rum and were, therefore, the most likely to overindulge.

To Mather, upper class inebriation had frightening consequences. "The *Votaries* of *Strong Drink*," he warned, "will grow numerous; . . . they will make a *Party*, against every thing that is *Holy, and Just, and Good*." Society was threatened by a tide of upper class inebriates who would sweep away the authority of the righteous; the church would yield to the tavern, the minister to the barkeeper. This upheaval would lead to new values throughout the hierarchy until the day came when children called for their drams and a wife became *"Mistress of a Bottle."* This unnatural and unrighteous society would then be punished by God. There was, however, one way to prevent this catastrophe. The higher ranks of society must renounce drunkenness in order to be a model for the rest. "Let persons of the *Best Sort*, be Exemplary for this piece of *Abstinence;* and then," he predicted, "Let the *Lowest of the People*, be in that point, we'll consent unto it, *As Good as the Best*." Thus would the 'good order' be preserved.[12]

Whatever effect Mather's warnings may have had in New England, it is clear that elsewhere the upper classes continued to drink heartily. For example, in 1744, nearly two decades after Mather's death, when Dr. Alexander Hamilton of Annapolis recorded his travels through several colonies, he rated cities and regions by their flow of spirits. He was disappointed in Philadelphia's low rate of consumption, but he disliked even more the poor quality of New England's beverages. That region, he wrote, provided better for horses than for men. When visiting New York, he found that a reputation for hearty drinking was essential for admission to the best society. On one occasion he matched bumpers with Governor George Clinton, whom he fondly labelled a "jolly toaper." He enjoyed the high quality of the drinks served him in New York but deplored the efforts of New Yorkers to make him intoxicated by proposing too many toasts. Dr. Hamilton preferred moderation to excess—not more than one bottle of wine each evening.[13]

Gentlemen who by reason of their wealth, prestige, and popularity set the tone for society belonged to drinking clubs that met privately in the back rooms of taverns. These retreats, modelled after the London clubs immortalized by Samuel Johnson, flourished in cities such as Charles Town, New York, and Annapolis. Dr. Hamilton's club in Annapolis had fifteen witty, raucous, fun-loving members who put away at each weekly meeting not less than a quart of Madeira wine apiece. While Hamilton and his friends downed expensive, imported Madeira, poorer Americans were drinking more and more cheap, domestic rum.[14]

One of the early consequences of cheaper, more plentiful rum was that the upper classes began to lose control of the taverns. As the price fell, people were able to buy more spirits, and this increased demand attracted a plethora of new purveyors. In the cities there began to appear many small private dealers who sold spirits to friends and neighbors without licenses; in Boston it was reported

The Grand Clubical Battle of the Great-Seal, and the decathedration of the Lord President

Dr. Hamilton's Sketch of the Tuesday Club. By permission of the Maryland Historical Society, Baltimore.

that liquor could be bought at one of every eight houses. In the hope of retaining some measure of control and authority, public officials were driven to increasing the number of permits for public houses. In Boston the number of licensed premises rose from 72 in 1702 to 155 in 1732. Although this rate of increase only slightly exceeded the rate by which the city's population had grown, the larger number of public houses proved to be more than the upper classes could watch effectively.

"Taverns are multiply'd among us," complained Thomas Foxcroft, "beyond the bounds of real Necessity, and even to a Fault, if not a Scandal."[15]

The proliferation of weakly controlled licensed public houses led eventually to efforts to have the number of permits reduced. In 1760, at Braintree, Massachusetts, John Adams launched one such crusade. He argued that taverns and inns, which were necessary for travellers and town people on public occasions, were otherwise nuisances; that too many permits had been granted, so that publicans, in order to reap a profit, were forced to sell to immoral people; and that the licensing of tavern keepers selected from among the most worthy had given way to licenses for the multitude. The public, however, favored a liberal licensing policy, and when Adams asked the Braintree town meeting to consider reducing the number of public houses, he was ridiculed.[16]

Members of society's upper classes, having failed in their efforts to reduce the number of licensed taverns, then sought to impose stricter laws for their regulation. Measures were enacted to discourage Sunday sales; to require all taverns to provide lodging for travellers; to revoke licenses if gaming were permitted on the premises; to prohibit sales to seamen; and to stop a slave from buying liquor without his master's consent. These provisions, judging from their frequent modifications and reenactments, failed to stop the erosion of upper class authority. By the middle of the century, when the upper classes found that they were no longer able to control public houses, many agreed with Franklin's *Pennsylvania Gazette*, March 29, 1764, that taverns were "a Pest to Society."[17]

To those who presumed that they had the right to mold society's institutions, the unregulated tavern's independence, like the growing independence of the lower classes, was a sign of chaos and disorder. Men such as

John Adams came to blame public houses for the weakening of religious influence and the creation of political factions. Adams complained that a clever politician who cultivated publicans would win the support of the masses, that taverngoers in many towns were a majority of the populace, and that drinking houses were "the nurseries of our legislators." Among the articulate, taverns had few defenders, although Hunter's *Virginia Gazette*, July 24, 1752, did print an article warning that license regulations that frustrated the common people in their "Pursuit of Independence" from upper class control would lead them to feel "crushed by Authority."[18]

Whether or not taverns were "nurseries" of the legislatures, they were certainly seed beds of the Revolution, the places where British tyranny was condemned, militiamen organized, and independence plotted. Patriots viewed public houses as the nurseries of freedom, in front of which liberty poles were invariably erected. The British called them public nuisances and the hot beds of sedition. There is no doubt that the success of the Revolution increased the prestige of drinking houses. A second effect of independence was that Americans perceived liberty from the Crown as somehow related to the freedom to down a few glasses of rum. Did not both freedoms give a man the right to choose for himself? Upper class patriots found it difficult after the Revolution to attack the popular sentiment that elite control of taverns was analogous to English control of America. As a consequence, drinking houses emerged from the war with increased vitality and independence, and the legal regulation of licensed premises waned.[19]

While opposition to the taverns developed and then collapsed in the throes of the Revolution, upper class attitudes toward liquor were undergoing change. By the middle of the eighteenth century many educated people had begun to doubt that spirituous liquor was ever a good creature, and some began to condemn it altogether. This change of mind was stimulated by a number of impulses, among which were the spread of rationalist philosophy, the rise of mercantile capitalism, advances in science, especially the science of medicine, and an all pervasive rejection of custom and tradition. It was a time when men had begun to think of the world in new ways. They expressed the hope that rather than depending upon faith and custom mankind would progress through the capacity of the human mind for reasoning and the acquisition of knowledge. Many of those imbued with a rationalist philosophy were opposed to drinking because they considered that the gratification to be had from taking spirituous liquor was more than offset by its detrimental effect on the reasoning process.[20]

Mercantile capitalists opposed the use of spirits for practical reasons. They had developed far-flung business empires by employing new, improved business methods: they evolved better bookkeeping practices, took only limited risks, calculated their risks more accurately, shared their risks through mutual insurance, and settled for smaller but surer profits. Businessmen whose fortunes were based on these more precise methods commonly traded in rum, but they came to view the extensive use of rum or any other distilled spirits by their employees, agents, or business associates as a threat to their commercial success.[21]

We should not be surprised to find that among the first Americans to condemn the use of distilled beverages were the Quakers, a sect whose members were not only educated and reform minded but also mercantile oriented. Anthony Benezet, the best known early opponent of spirituous liquors, was a wealthy Philadelphia Quaker. He had extensive commercial connections and was well aware of the conditions necessary for the successful operation of a modern business. Imbued with the spirit of reform, he was drawn to advanced positions on a variety of social questions. Today he is best remembered for his hostility to slavery and for starting a movement that led to the emancipation of northern bondsmen. However, he was no less hostile to distilled liquor and during the Revolution attacked both rum and slavery, which he jointly characterized in one pamphlet as *The Potent Enemies of America*. He argued that the Revolution's success in ending British rule would be a hollow victory if Americans failed to rid themselves of these twin evils. A republic of free men, he contended, had no place for the bondage of men either to other men or to distilled spirits; Americans must liberate themselves from customs that impeded the nation's development as a haven for free, rational men. Here for the first time we see liberty viewed in a new light, not as a man's freedom to drink unlimited quantities of alcohol but as a man's freedom to be his own master, with the attendant responsibility to exercise self-control, moderation, and reason.[22]

Starting early in the eighteenth century, long before the advent of Benezet, Quakers had begun to practice restraint in the use of distilled spirits, and this restraint increased through the years. In 1706 the Pennsylvania Yearly Meeting advised Friends not to drink even small quantities of distilled liquors at public houses. In 1726 Quakers were forbidden to imbibe spirits at auctions. Quaffing the auctioneer's liquor, it was reasoned, raised the cost of the goods being offered for sale; in other words, such self-indulgence fostered bad business practices. At mid-century, when other Americans drank heartily at funerals, Quaker custom called for passing the spirits bottle only twice. Even restrained use came under attack, first by Benezet and later by the Pennsylvania Yearly Meeting, which, during a wartime bread shortage in 1777, ordered Friends neither to distill grain nor to sell grain to be distilled. After the war, there were new restrictions: in 1784 Friends were neither to import nor to retail distilled spirits; in 1788 not to use liquor as a medicine without caution; in 1789 not to use distilled beverages at births, marriages, or burials. By the 1780s Quaker opposition to all drinking of spirituous liquors was widespread and vigorous.[23]

During the eighteenth century Methodists were the only other principal religious denomination that shared the Quakers' opposition to distilled spirits. Many of the Methodists, unlike the Quakers, were uneducated and lower class people who were little influenced by the rise of rationalist philosophy, science, or business efficiency. Their hostility to liquor arose from two other sources. First, all innovative, new movements have a need to assert themselves by rejecting tradition. Thus the Methodist refusal of the customary dram was in itself a radical act symbolizing the new sect's determination to root out old customs and habits. Second, founder John Wesley represented a peculiar rationalism, expressed in his goal to restructure religion through 'method.' Methodists saw the drinking of spirits as a hindrance to the process of reordering and purifying both the church and society. American Methodists joined the Quakers in condemning distilled spirits in the 1780s, long before tradition-bound Baptists and Presbyterians.[24]

While rationalist philosophy, commercialism, and the rejection of tradition were influential in changing attitudes toward distilled spirits, it was the new, scientific approach to medicine that had the greatest effect. As early as the 1720s some scientists had concluded that alcohol was poisonous, and by the 1730s this view was gaining support. James Oglethorpe, for example, attempted to ban rum from his Georgia colony at the urging of the Rev. Stephen Hales, one of the colony's trustees, a physiologist, and the author of two antispirits treatises. Then, during the 1740s, American doctors began to investigate the quaintly named West Indies Dry Gripes. This was a painful, debilitating malady that we now recognize as lead poisoning caused by drinking rum made in lead stills. Contemporaries were puzzled until Philadelphia's Dr. Thomas Cadwalader identified rum as the cause of the disease and recommended abstinence, a novel proposal that was contrary to traditional opinion concerning rum's healthful qualities.[25]

People opposed to liquor for any reason soon recognized that the health argument was the most potent weapon in their arsenal. That was why Anthony Benezet cloaked his moral and philosophical opposition to spirits by devoting most of his antiliquor tracts to a recitation of diseases purportedly caused by strong drink. This line of attack was encouraged by the medical theories being taught at the Edinburgh College of Medicine, where Benjamin Rush, who was to lead the post-Revolutionary campaign against distilled spirits, studied in the 1760s. To men captivated by the Enlightenment spirit, the discovery that a too extensive consumption of alcohol produced illness and disease had two important implications. First, the information itself was a sign of progress, a sign of the triumph of rational, experimental inquiry over irrational tradition and custom. Second, the realization that alcohol was detrimental to health would be certain, it seemed, to lead men to abstinence and, as a consequence, to rationality.[26]

As early as 1772, Rush, by then a physician living in Philadelphia, condemned distilled spirits in a pamphlet in which he urged moderate drinking, eating, and exercise. In this work, addressed to the upper classes, he argued for the right of physicians to propose new theories. He hoped that the "same freedom of enquiry" could be extended "to medicine, which has long prevailed in religion." This attack on orthodoxy resulted from Rush's scientific training. His Edinburgh education had led him to question the dogma that alcohol was healthful. In fact, he had concluded from observing his patients that spirituous liquor was a powerful stimulant that destroyed the body's natural balance. Although he noted in his pamphlet the potential dangers to health caused by immoderate drinking, his conclusions were tentative, and he did not at that time recommend abstinence. Despite the inconclusive nature of his findings, he published the work and sent two copies to London, one to a bookseller for republishing and the other to Benjamin Franklin, who was then a colonial agent in England.[27]

The doctor's conviction was strengthened during the Revolutionary War when he served for a time as the Continental Army's surgeon general. The army's traditional rum ration, Rush asserted, caused numerous diseases, particularly fevers and fluxes. The poor health of American soldiers contrasted with the vigor and vitality of the warriors of the Roman Republic. Their canteens, he incorrectly and perhaps naively stated, had contained "nothing but vinegar." Rush's wartime experience and medical ideals drove him in 1782 to write "Against Spirituous Liquors." This newspaper article urged farmers not to supply their harvest laborers with distilled spirits, which, he claimed, failed to aid physical labor, injured health, crippled morals, and wasted money. As substitutes he proposed various mixtures compounded of milk, buttermilk, cider, small beer, vinegar, molasses, and water.[28]

These early works showed a growing hostility to distilled spirits that culminated in Rush's 1784 essay, *An Inquiry into the Effects of Spirituous Liquors*. This piece, first published as a newspaper article and then as a pamphlet, combined in compact form the arguments that the doctor had encountered and those he had employed in his long antiliquor crusade. He catalogued liquor's defects: it protected against neither hot nor cold weather, for on hot days it overstimulated and on cold ones it produced temporary warmth that led to chills; it caused numerous illnesses—stomach sickness, vomiting, hand tremors, dropsy, liver disorders, madness, palsy, apoplexy, and epilepsy. Spirituous liquor, he believed, should be replaced with beer, light wine, *weak* rum punch, sour milk, or switchel, a drink composed of vinegar, sugar, and water. The pamphlet was a masterpiece. Its rational arguments, logic, and incisive examples made it both the century's most effective short piece and also a model for later temperance publications; by 1850 more than 170,000 copies had been circulated. Even in 1784 its impact was such that enthusiastic readers wrote Rush admiring letters. From frontier Pittsburgh Hugh Henry Brackenridge reported that he had quit drinking spirits, and from Charleston Dr. David Ramsay announced that he had arranged for Rush's "unpopular" views to be reprinted in the local press.[29]

Why, we might ask, was this particular article such a success? For one thing, Rush showed an extraordinary capacity for marshalling the evidence to support his convictions. His skillful presentation of the subject, however, does not fully explain why the *Inquiry* produced such a sympathetic and vigorous response. The doctor seems to have struck a public nerve, and his success depended far less upon his literary talent and skill as a propagandist than upon his scientific ideals. By the 1780s, Rush's medical and social theories had passed into the mainstream of educated American opinion. Whereas his training at Edinburgh had once made his medical views the object of suspicion, by the eighties his beliefs were respectable, even fashionable. Intelligent, articulate people agreed with Rush that bodily imbalances caused disease, that the duty of the physician was to restore balance, and that the most effective remedies were purgatives and bleeding. Then, too, as a highly regarded medical pioneer, Rush was able, unlike other doctors, to argue new propositions convincingly. No man understood his opportunities better than Rush, who assailed liquor in the belief at this point that physicians could serve the cause better than ministers or legislators.[30]

We should not, however, attribute the *Inquiry*'s success solely to Rush's preeminent position in medicine, his skillful presentation, and the receptive mind of the public, for much of its appeal to readers was derived from the author's sociology. To understand how the doctor's antiliquor pamphlet had employed a new methodology, it is necessary to consider two of his other essays, "An Account of the Manners of the German Inhabitants of Pennsylvania" and "An Account of the Progress of Population, Agriculture, Manners, and Government in Pennsylvania." The former was a pioneering work in cultural anthropology, the first analysis of American ethnic assimilation. The latter was an equally original contribution to sociology, a brilliant account of how distinct social classes succeeded one another on the American frontier. Both pieces employed a new analytical method. Whereas the usual technique in an eighteenth century pamphlet had been to proceed from lists of observations to an analytical conclusion, Rush employed a two-step approach. First, he arranged data in categories, each of which he analyzed; then, in a second step, he compared the results of these analyses and arrived at a conclusion. In "German Inhabitants," he first analyzed the mores of German Pennsylvanians and the mores of English Pennsylvanians and then compared the results of these analyses and concluded that intermingling would eventually diminish ethnic differences. In "Progress," an analysis of each of three types of frontier social classes led to an examination of how one class would displace another. The *Inquiry* followed the same method in proceeding from preliminary analyses of the several categories in which distilled spirits were shown to be undesirable to a masterly summary in which Rush concluded that abstinence was imperative.[31]

The *Inquiry*'s popularity led Rush to embark on a campaign to spread its message. Following its first printing in 1784, the article was reproduced in the Philadelphia papers each autumn as a warning to farmers who supplied their harvest laborers with spirituous liquor. In 1788, Rush issued the work as a pamphlet, an event that led to correspondence with Jeremy Belknap, a Boston minister who later became president of Harvard College. Belknap gave Rush even more encouragement than had Charleston's Dr. Ramsay. He arranged for the work to be reprinted in Boston and, shortly afterward, reported, "I assure you your piece on spirituous liquors is read & admired & has produced a good effect. I have had the pleasure of hearing Dr. Rush quoted more than once against grog-drinking & I know some families where it was freely used who have left it off since that publication." Pleased with his success, Rush urged Belknap to be "a pioneer in this business in Massachusetts." With the help of Ramsay and Belknap, he hoped to start a movement that would grow and prosper, so that by "1915 a drunkard . . . will be as infamous in society as a liar or a thief, and the use of spirits as uncommon in families as a drink made of a solution of arsenic or a decoction of hemlock."[32]

The minister and physician became collaborators. Rush published a "Moral and Physical Thermometer" that correlated beverages with various conditions. Water, milk, and small beer brought health, wealth, and happiness; mixed drinks made with spirits—sickness, idleness, and debt; straight rum and whiskey—crime, chronic disease, and severe punishment; incessant drinking—death. When Belknap saw this 'thermometer,' he recommended

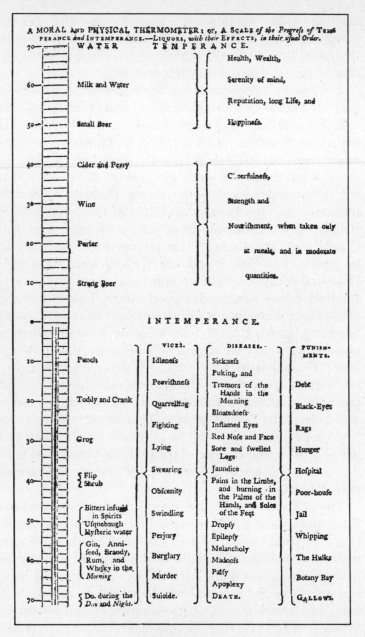

A MORAL AND PHYSICAL THERMOMETER; or, A SCALE of the Progress of Temperance and Intemperance.—LIQUORS, with their Effects, in their usual Order.

WATER   TEMPERANCE.

70	WATER		Health, Wealth,	
60	Milk and Water		Serenity of mind,	
			Reputation, long Life, and	
50	Small Beer		Happiness.	
40	Cider and Perry			
			Cheerfulness,	
30	Wine		Strength and	
			Nourishment, when taken only	
20	Porter		at meals, and in moderate	
			quantities.	
10	Strong Beer			

0

INTEMPERANCE.

		VICES.	DISEASES.	PUNISHMENTS.
10	Punch	Idleness	Sickness	
		Peevishness	Puking, and Tremors of the Hands in the Morning	Debt
20	Toddy and Crank	Quarrelling	Bloatedness	Black-Eyes
		Fighting	Inflamed Eyes	Rags
30	Grog	Lying	Red Nose and Face Sore and swelled Legs	Hunger
40	Flip Shrub	Swearing	Jaundice	Hospital
		Obscenity	Pains in the Limbs, and burning in the Palms of the Hands, and Soles of the Feet	Poor-house
	Bitters infused in Spirits Usquebaugh Hysteric water	Swindling	Dropsy	Jail
50		Perjury	Epilepsy	Whipping
	Gin, Anniseed, Brandy, Rum, and Whisky in the Morning	Burglary	Melancholy Madness	The Hulks
60		Murder	Palsy	Botany Bay
			Apoplexy	
70	Do. during the Day and Night.	Suicide.	DEATH.	GALLOWS.

Rush's Thermometer.

that it be added to the next edition of the *Inquiry*, and this suggestion was adopted. Later, Rush asked Belknap to estimate the per capita consumption of distilled spirits in New Hampshire, a subject on which the minister was writing a history. Belknap tried to obtain this information for Rush from his friends in New Hampshire, but it appears that he was unable to persuade any of them to furnish estimates. After a year of enthusiasm and optimism, Rush's hopes began to wane. In 1789 he reported that while the drinking of spirits had declined in Pennsylvania, complete success appeared impossible, and he reluctantly concluded, contrary to his earlier view, that only religion could secure victory for his cause. Shortly after this prediction, Belknap bought half of a new edition of the *Inquiry* and distributed more than one-third of his 456 copies to New Hampshire clergymen.[33]

Rush continued his campaign against spirits with a newspaper article entitled "To the Ministers of the Gospel of All Denominations," in which he advised clergymen to preach not only against intoxication but against any use of distilled spirits. He also wrote an antiliquor commencement address for Princeton, which, although never delivered, was printed in Carey's *American Museum*, and another article published in the same magazine advising western immigrants to forego taking with them "a brandy or whiskey case." His greatest triumph was the July 4, 1788, Phildelphia Independence celebration, when 17,000 people walked to a suburban estate to drink "nothing but Beer and Cider." These beverages Rush termed "those invaluable FEDERAL liquors" in contrast with distilled spirits, which were "*Antifederal*," the "companions of all those vices that are calculated to dishonor and enslave our country."[34]

Although Rush himself was discouraged, the campaign he had initiated did lead more and more Americans to give up distilled spirits. Foreign travellers observed that the Revolutionary War years had produced a marked change in upper class drinking practices. One Italian recalled that in 1774 his request for water at a Virginia dinner had caused such confusion that the host had asked if he could not choose another beverage. A decade later the scene would have been impossible, for some Americans drank water. Another visitor who returned to America after the war noted that gentlemen's drinking clubs had disappeared, that Americans appeared to drink less, and that the Virginia gentry no longer felt an obligation to send guests home drunk.[35]

Naturally, literate, educated people were most influenced by Rush's writings. Martha Laurens Ramsay, wife of Rush's South Carolina correspondent, rejected the easygoing manners of the past in a determined effort to prevent intoxication among her slaves. This was remarkable behavior for the daughter of the state's leading rum importer. In New York, a Columbia College student, Daniel D. Tompkins, later governor of New York and vice-president of the United States, joined what was becoming a fashionable chorus by writing an essay on the mass desertion of Bacchus. In New England, Jedidiah Morse spread Rush's message to children by inserting antiliquor lines in his widely used geography textbooks. But perhaps the most effective opposition to distilled spirits came from the graduates of Rush's Philadelphia College of Medicine. They spread themselves and Rush's views across the entire country—e.g., George C. Shattuck, Massachusetts; Richard Hopkins, Maryland; John Vaughan, Delaware; and Joseph Speed, Virginia. Speed wrote to Rush, "I conceived it a debt of gratitude I owed you to thank you for the impressive manner in which you advised your class in the winter of '94, '95 to lay an early restraint on themselves against the prevailing practise of dram & grog drinking."[36]

By 1790, while an appreciable number of people had

concluded that spirituous liquor sapped health, morals, and social order, they were still a minority. And they were well aware that most Americans had not digested the lessons of the eighteenth-century revolutions in business, medicine, and philosophy, that the masses continued to drink distilled spirits, and that drinking itself remained a traditional rite, rooted in custom and sanctioned by practice. Proposals that the upper class try to transform these habits met with little enthusiasm. The pledge by the leading agriculturalists of Litchfield, Connecticut, including Judge Tapping Reeve, that they would deny spirits to hired laborers was not copied elsewhere. Employers believed that hands would not work without distilled spirits, that, as the *New Haven Gazette* put it, "a laboring man must have his half pint or pint every day, and at night half his wages in rum." The common man was unenlightened. "The thirst for spirits in the back country is so ardent," Jeremy Belknap wrote of rural New Hampshire, "that in the fall & winter they will sell their wheat for this sort of pay, & then in the spring & summer following go 40 or 50 miles after bread."[37]

Those opposed to spirituous liquor had reasons for believing that persuasion would not move the masses to adopt new values and give up drinking. For one thing, the Enlightenment ideal contained a paradox destructive to the hope for spreading rationality: to be rational it was necessary to be receptive to reason; to be receptive to reason was itself an indication of rationality. The unenlightened man, therefore, was a poor prospect for enlightenment. Furthermore, the opponents of drinking believed that use of spirituous liquor itself blocked the attainment of rationality. To be rational was to control emotion with reason, but liquor unleashed emotion and destroyed reason. There was a need, as Dr. David Ramsay put it, for men to exercise "self-command, prudence and fortitude, and a strict discipline of the passions and appetites . . . to maintain the empire of reason over sense." Intoxication, wrote one author in the *Massachusetts Magazine*, served "no other purpose than to increase . . . passions." Viewed from the minority vantage point, the majority's thirst for strong drink had created a chronic dependency and, at the same time, crippled the rational faculty required to break the bonds of that dependency. Benjamin Rush, for example, had been warned by one correspondent that religious attacks against spirits would fail. Since drinking was an essential part of the mores of most men, it was foolish to believe that the exhortations of ministers could penetrate those well-soused minds and persuade them to espouse abstinence.[38]

Two circumstances influenced the direction that the crusade against distilled spirits would take. In the first place, despite the increased concern about alcohol on the part of Rush and other members of the upper classes, there were many from those very classes who continued to drink heartily. It was reported that most of the Virginia gentry were dissipated and that many South Carolina planters were sots who died young and left behind youthful, rich widows. Whenever the wealthy congregated, they imbibed great amounts. New York Governor George Clinton honored the French ambassador with a dinner at which 120 guests downed 135 bottles of Madeira, 36 bottles of port, 60 bottles of English beer, and 30 large cups of rum punch. Even in staid New England the upper classes continued to imbibe; at one Congregational minister's ordination in 1793 the celebrants consumed dozens of bottles of hard cider, wine, sherry, cherry brandy, and Jamaica rum.[39]

Second, the upper class continued to engage in the highly profitable business of supplying and distributing distilled spirits. The nation's leading rum importers and wholesalers were wealthy members of society such as

Robert Morris of Philadelphia, Peter Livingston of New York, and the Brown family of Providence. Distilling was a genteel occupation engaged in by such prominent figures as Silas Deane's two brothers and George Washington. When Maine landholder Thomas Robison proposed to build a distillery, Robert Jenkins counselled delay. "The gentleman, whome I purpose to get to draw you a plan of a *Distillhouse*," wrote Jenkins, "is a member of our General Assembly, which is now setting and when his hurry is a little over, he will do it." The power and prestige of the distillers was nearly matched by that of the retailers, who included such worthies as Thomas Chittenden, first governor of Vermont; James Garrard, second governor of Kentucky; and Samuel Fraunces of New York, George Washington's personal steward.[40]

The reform-minded minority, hostile to spirits, recognized that extensive imbibing by the upper classes together with their control of the liquor industry ruled out any chance of imposing a legal prohibition of distilled spirits. Since they also believed that moral suasion through ministerial exhortation would fail, they had to turn to some other plan, and they took as their model England's mid-eighteenth-century imposition of an excise tax, which had proved successful in cutting the consumption of gin. The cheapness of American distilled spirits had long been noted. If an excise tax were imposed, the price would rise, and, they hoped, spirits would become "too dear for people to purchase." However, proponents of an excise found that the outlook for such a measure under the Articles of Confederation was not bright. As early as 1782, financier Robert Morris had proposed an excise to refinance the nation's war debts, but Congress had been unable to obtain the unanimous consent of the states, which was necessary for its enactment.[41]

By the late eighties, opponents of liquor had begun to act at the state level. They persuaded the Massachusetts legislature to encourage the use of beer in place of distilled spirits by exempting brewery equipment from property taxes. This measure, however, failed to reduce the consumption of spirits. The Virginia legislature forbade the importation of distilled spirits into that state. The provision was supported by both antispirits men and western whiskey distillers, but it so outraged the planters of the Tidewater region that it was soon repealed. In Pennsylvania, Quaker George Logan proposed a state tax on distilled spirits. When the measure was debated in the legislature, one member suggested, with reference to lobbying by Benjamin Rush, that the proposal be referred to the College of Physicians. Rep. Richard Peters then rose to observe that this action might lead the doctors to bring in a bill—and he had seen enough medical bills already. Logan's proposal died amid laughter.[42]

The failure of state action was painfully clear to the reformers. The antispirits *New Haven Gazette* diagnosed the problem as "a want of *federal power*." Only after a "continental power to impose uniform duties on importations" had been established would distilled spirits be taxed sufficiently to reduce their consumption. The timing of the demand for a spirits tax meshed with many other commercial and political motives favorable to a new constitution to replace the Articles of Confederation. After the Constitutional Convention had met at Philadelphia and drafted a new constitution during the summer of 1787, federalists openly campaigned for its adoption on the ground that it would help reduce the consumption of distilled spirits. Alexander Hamilton, for example, argued in *Federalist #12* that a high spirits excise would reduce consumption and, thereby, improve agriculture, business, morals, and health. After the new constitution had been ratified, advocates of a spirits tax began to lobby for their proposal. The Philadelphia College of Physicians, ever under Rush's wing, petitioned the new Congress "to impose such heavy duties upon all distilled spirits, as shall be effectual to restrain their intemperate use in our country."[43]

When the new government was installed in 1789, Alexander Hamilton was appointed secretary of the treasury. In that office, he was responsible for proposing taxes to finance the new government. The administration's decision to underwrite the state war debts necessitated raising a large revenue. Although most of the money was expected to come from import duties, experience during the 1780s suggested that imports alone would not provide sufficient funds. The shortfall would have to be covered by other taxes, such as real estate taxes or domestic excises. Hamilton himself favored a duty on domestic spirituous liquors. It was fair, he later declared, because distilled beverages were consumed "throughout the United States." No tax could "operate with greater equality. . . ." Any variations in consumption reflected "relative habits of sobriety or intemperance. . . ." Hamilton's sweeping endorsement of a spirits excise was politically sound. First, he knew that it would be easy to persuade Congress to enact a tax on domestic distilled spirits because politicians would find it difficult to oppose a measure designed both to reduce drunkenness and to raise money. Second, a domestic excise, when combined with Hamilton's tariff program, would preserve price ratios between whiskey and rum. The latter faced an import duty because it was either imported or distilled from imported molasses. This balance was essential if Hamilton was to gain sufficient political support from New England to get his economic program enacted.[44]

Hamilton's proposed domestic spirits excise was not adopted immediately. Congress, in its first session, was preoccupied with government organization, and it imposed only import duties in the hope that they alone would yield a sufficient revenue. The secretary of the treasury's attempt to tie a distilled spirits excise to the tariff bill was defeated in the House of Representatives. Opposition came from a combination of New Englanders hostile to levies on imported molasses and rum and southerners hostile to a whiskey tax. On that occasion, however, one North Carolinian claimed that he followed his conscience. Dr. Hugh Williamson, who professed to be a lifelong opponent of distilled spirits, voted for the measure in order, he said, to reduce the consumption of spirituous liquor and, thereby, improve people's health. It is possible, however, that he may have had another reason for favoring a tax on whiskey, since he had at one time owned a rum distillery. In any event, the good doctor predicted correctly that his vote insured that whiskey-drinking Carolinians would not return him to Congress.[45]

Six months later, when it had become clear that additional funds were needed, the proposal for a levy on domestic distilled spirits was resurrected. House floor debates revealed a mixture of sectional politics and moral arguments. North Carolina Congressman John Steele complained that his state would pay ten times the amount Connecticut did, a sentiment echoed by Georgia Rep. James Jackson, who noted that the South had neither cider nor beer—beverages that would escape taxation. The excise, he warned, would "deprive the mass of the people of almost the only luxury they enjoy, that of distilled spirits." The bill trapped James Madison between his role as Hamilton's floor leader and his role as representative of his Virginia district. Although "principled against excises," he voted for this particular measure, a decision that nearly cost him his seat at the next election. Most northern representatives favored the proposal. Massachusetts Congressman Theodore Sedgwick believed the bill necessary to raise revenue and attacked members who backed it for any "consideration of morality." New Hampshire's Samuel Livermore thought it a good idea to be "drinking down the national debt." At the roll call, the measure was approved, with a unanimous New England casting half the ayes (17-0), the middle states splitting (13-8), and the South standing in opposition (5-13).[46]

Hamilton's whiskey tax was not a success. Protests arose in the South and West almost immediately, and petitions from Georgia demanded the exemption of peach brandy, a "necessary of life . . . in this warm climate." Throughout the South, the secretary of the treasury found it difficult to hire tax collectors; in Kentucky, it was impossible to organize the state as an excise jurisdiction. Such difficulties led President Washington, in his annual address to Congress in October, 1791, to admit that in much of the country the new law had led "to some degree of discontent." He expected these sentiments to disappear with the rise of "a just sense of duty." This change, however, did not occur, and in 1792 public outrage at the levy forced Congress to modify the law. Congress exempted 'personal stills' from taxation, a change that Hamilton accepted reluctantly, because he knew that it would lead to widespread tax fraud. Already an embarrassed secretary of the treasury was compelled to acknowledge that the excise on domestic distilled spirits was the most expensive tax to collect and that it had yielded less than two-thirds of its anticipated revenue. When President Washington addressed Congress in November, 1792, he conceded that collection of the duty was difficult but then added that the impediments were lessening. Washington's belief, bordering on fantasy, was a reflection of Hamilton's. To his agent in Salisbury, North Carolina, the secretary wrote, "If the people will but make trial of the thing, their good-will towards it will increase." He was gratified by "the late symptoms of acquiescence . . . which you announce in your quarter. . . ."[47]

Hamilton received something other than reports of acquiescence from other quarters. In 1792, western Pennsylvanians led by Albert Gallatin drafted a petition to Congress urging repeal of the duty. "Distant from a permanent market, and separate from the eastern coast by mountains," stated the memorial, ". . . we have no means of bringing the produce of our lands to sale either in grain or in meal. We are therefore distillers through necessity, not choice. . . ." This petition annoyed Hamilton, who felt that frontiersmen were parasitic. They contributed little to the treasury because they bought few imports, yet they demanded and received expensive military protection from Indian raids. The whiskey tax he thought a light contribution. Furthermore, the secretary observed, the western objection to the tax was rooted in economic error. The effect of the tax was not to bar the sale of western whiskey in the East but to raise its price, for "the duty on all they send to those markets will be paid by the purchasers." Westerners could object only if they were "greater consumers of spirits than those of other parts of the country." In that case, it was to "their interest to become less so."[48]

While this acerbic advice may have been congruent with sound economic theory, it failed to take into account the West's principal difficulty, which was a lack of money. Frontiersmen were unable to pay the excise because the government demanded payment in specie or currency. Although Hamilton did not mention the West's shortage of cash, he was aware of it, as evidenced by his having authorized the army to purchase much of its ration of distilled spirits in the West in order to pump money into that region's barter economy. This policy, however, failed to stem western discontent. In 1794 an exasperated assistant informed Hamilton, "The state of things in the western country raises some doubts whether it will be practicable to procure in that quarter Spirits *lawfully distilled* for the military supply of 1795."[49]

When the government, in 1794, attempted to enforce the excise in western Pennsylvania, that region revolted in what came to be called the Whiskey Rebellion. After an infuriated Hamilton persuaded a reluctant Washington to call up thousands of troops, Hamilton himself directed the military action that crushed the revolt. But the secretary's triumph was far from complete. Hamilton's suppression of the insurrection led his enemies to intensify their opposition against the administration, and the rebellion itself, as an expression of deep-seated hostility to the spirits tax, assured its eventual demise. As a revenue measure the excise had already failed, for it had proved impossible to collect the tax in the West, expensive to employ a body of excisemen for a single duty, and difficult, if not impossible, to monitor distilling. Even in Philadelphia, the federal capital, illicit distilling was common. When the government hired James Newport to investigate Philadelphia tax evasion, he reported that in six weeks four major distilleries had paid taxes on only 3,277 of the 5,277 gallons they had produced. Fortunately, such chronic problems were offset by rising revenues from import duties, and in 1802 a southern and western majority in Congress followed President Jefferson's recommendation and repealed the excise tax.[50]

What had killed the spirits excise? It had not died because western distillers had no cash, for the government could have arranged to accept barter payments. Nor had it died because of illicit and underreported distilling, for adequate inspection could have overcome that difficulty. And its end had not come because of the providential rise in imports, although the government was lucky enough to have that source of income to replace the whiskey tax. The excise failed, in part, because it was not in line with economic reality. America was a rural nation in which farmers produced a grain surplus that could be marketed only as distilled spirits. These small farmers hated the whiskey tax because it adversely affected the market for their surplus grain.[51]

More important, however, is the fact that Americans in general hated the excise on domestic distilled spirits because it clashed with post-Revolutionary principles. Consider, for example, Gallatin's 1792 petition opposing the excise as an "unequal" measure that taxed "the common drink of a nation" and that fell "as heavy on the poorest class as on the rich." At first glance we might conclude, as Hamilton erroneously did, that this complaint was primarily economic. While couched in economic terms, however, I would contend that the argument itself was rooted in American concepts of equality and liberty. The majority of Americans resented a measure that appeared to favor the rich who drank Madeira over the poor who drank whiskey. They condemned what they considered to be both an infringement of their freedom to drink and an effort on the part of the government to control their customs and habits. Furthermore, in the 1790s a fierce republican pride caused most Americans to resist any attempt by the wealthy and powerful to set standards of morality and coerce the ordinary man to adopt them. The excise tax, aimed at curbing the use of distilled spirits, was seen as just such an attempt. And so the measure failed. As for the antiliquor reformers, they emerged from the wreckage of the whiskey tax controversy with neither a policy nor a program. They watched with bewilderment and apprehension as the postwar tide of liquor rolled onward, engulfing America.[52]

By 1800 traditional colonial society had all but disappeared. The time when Harvard students were listed in the college roster by their parents' social rank had passed; the wearing of powdered wigs and knee breeches was nearing an end. The assumptions that had maintained the power of the old elite were everywhere giving way, and the style of the upper classes had changed. Once to be of high station had implied an obligation to demonstrate power through display; it was necessary to be 'drunk as a lord.' When cheap spirits enabled every man to be as drunk as a lord, the prestige of drunkenness declined. Yet the adoption of a new, sober style by many of the upper class did not result solely from the fact that their heavy drinking had been imitated by the lower classes and was no longer a sign of wealth and status; the new habit of sobriety resulted from a number of much more significant social changes. The elite class was itself being transformed by economic change that had raised up a new group of broad-minded, international merchants in place of country gentry, by an ideology of liberty and equality that vigorously challenged tradition, and by the upheavals of the Revolution that had enabled the masses to take political control of the taverns. Amid these shifting social processes was the gradual decay of the old belief that spirituous liquor was God's good creature, the rise of a contrary belief, and the beginnings of a quarrel about alcohol that would become a curious theme threading its course throughout American history.

CHAPTER

THE SPIRITS
OF INDEPENDENCE

Come on, then, if you love toping;
for here you may drink yourselves blind
at the price of sixpence.

WILLIAM COBBETT
1818

By 1800 the influence of the upper class minority hostile to distilled spirits had declined, while a majority of Americans continued to uphold a hearty drinking tradition. That tradition survived and flourished with a readily available and plentiful supply of strong drink. Indeed, as the availability of inexpensive distilled spirits, particularly whiskey, increased, drinking increased. It was during the early nineteenth century that domestic whiskey supplanted rum as the favorite spirituous beverage, that technological improvements in distillation increased the output of distilled spirits, and that western settlers began to turn large quantities of surplus corn into cheap, abundant whiskey.

Distilled spirits had long played a significant role in the American economy. Before the Revolution, molasses and rum accounted for one-fifth of the value of all goods imported from British possessions, and from Philadelphia northward the distillation of rum from imported molasses was the leading manufacturing process. After the Revolution, the production of spirituous liquor continued to be important to the nation's economy. During the 1790s molasses and rum still acounted for one-fifth of the value of American imports, and by 1810 whiskey, rum, and other distilled spirits ranked behind cloth and tanned hides as the third most important industrial product, worth 10 percent of the nation's manufactured output. When we consider that distilling was less likely to be a cottage industry than were spinning, weaving, and tanning, we can view distilling as the era's principal industry. Tracing the economic role of rum and whiskey during the colonial and early national years will show why these beverages were inexpensive and available and how they affected the economy and society.[1]

In the eighteenth century, when Americans occupied only a fringe of the continent along the Atlantic shore, they struggled to keep their foothold, worked hard to make the wilderness yield a living, and looked to England for the means to maintain and improve their new-won land. They expected to receive their necessaries from the trading vessels that docked at American seaports. From across the ocean came the seeds for their crops, the implements to work their fields, the cattle for their pastures, and even the indentured servants and slaves to work for them. On the return voyage these same ships carried back to the mother country tobacco, indigo, rice, timber, and foodstuffs. Unfortunately, however, England needed colonial produce less than the colonies needed English goods. This constant imbalance in trade created a chronic deficit in the colonial balance of payments. Gold and silver flowed away from America, leaving the colonies short of hard currency.[2]

As a consequence, American merchants needed a substitute for money as a medium of exchange. One possible substitute was credit, but eighteenth-century banking was ill equipped to meet colonial demands. The nearest financiers were in London, separated from the colonies by geography and time, by tradition and psychology. Few English bankers wished to invest money in remote ventures or to risk their capital with strangers at such a distance. Although established traders could obtain credit, it was inconvenient and had other disadvantages.

If a London financier went bankrupt, for example, an American merchant might be caught months later holding a worthless bill of exchange. Then, too, the value of commerical paper fluctuated so much that a trader was often unable to ascertain the worth of his credits or debits.[3] Because profits in the shipping industry depended upon the stability of prices, the trader preferred to have his assets in a form that was less subject to change than commerical paper. Lacking hard money and fearful of credit, American merchants turned to barter.

One important item for barter was rum. Its usefulness for this purpose resulted from the nature of colonial trade and from the commodity's own unique qualities. Much American trade was carried on along the seaboard: South Carolina rice exchanged for Massachusetts salted fish, North Carolina tar and pitch for Connecticut rum, Virginia tobacco for Pennsylvania white pine spars. This coastal trade not only encouraged ship building and helped to integrate the colonies' economies, it also stimulated an interest in commercial opportunities in more remote markets. A merchant might buy molasses in the French West Indies, ship it home, distill it, trade the rum in Africa for slaves, transport the slaves to the Caribbean cane plantations, and trade them for more molasses. This triangular shipping pattern was then repeated. However, the more common pattern was one in which shippers exported American foodstuffs to the West Indies and traded them there for either molasses or rum. The British West Indies distilled their own rum, and Americans who traded there were forced to accept payment in rum rather than in molasses. American merchants preferred to trade in the French, Spanish, or Danish West Indies, where they could get molasses, take it home, and distill it at a profit, either selling the rum in America or exporting it to Africa, Canada, or back to the non-British West Indies. The patterns of these commodity exchanges made molasses and rum the predominant items for barter, and in some respects rum was the more attractive. Unlike other goods, including molasses, rum shipped easily, could be warehoused cheaply, withstood any climate and improper handling, and increased in value as it aged. Rum was the currency of the age.[4]

The rise of American shipping flooded the colonies with British West Indian rum. First, as American commerce expanded, merchants who sold agricultural produce in the British islands were obliged to accept ever larger volumes of rum as payment. Traders preferred to fill their holds with rum rather than to ship more speculative commodities, accept bills of exchange, or travel with worthless ballast. High quality rum was often dumped on the American continent at a loss in order to load vessels with more profitable cargoes. Second, the growth of American trade in molasses, which was distilled at home into cheap, low quality rum and then shipped to Africa and the Caribbean, had caused the British West Indies to lose those markets. The result was that the principal sales of Caribbean rum were in North America, and as both West Indian and American rum glutted the colonial market, the price inevitably fell. At Philadelphia in the 1740s New England rum sold for 2 shillings, 2 pence to 4 shillings, 4 pence per gallon; from 1763 to 1775 it varied from 1 shilling, 7 pence to 2 shillings, 5 pence per gallon. As noted earlier, rum became so cheap that a casual laborer could earn in one day money enough for a week's drunk. This sharp drop in the price of rum was in contrast to the more stable price of a basic commodity like flour.[5]

In 1770, on the eve of the Revolution, the colonies imported 4 million gallons of rum and distilled another 5 million gallons. Of this prodigious amount, Americans themselves drank seven-eighths. Although rum was important as an item of trade that enabled American merchants to participate, through barter, in the international market, it had greater significance as a catalyst in the home economy. The large-scale and highly profitable distilling industry in the principal colonial seaports employed many laborers, stimulated capital formation and investment, and encouraged the development of managerial talent. As economic historian John J. McCusker, Jr., has pointed out, distilling was essential to the infrastructure of the shipping complex that then dominated the American economy.[6]

During the Revolutionary War, the British blockaded molasses and rum imports. Although distillers temporarily switched from making rum to making whiskey, they were unable to manufacture enough spirits to meet wartime demand. Distilled liquor was often unavailable, and when it could be procured, the price was high. Diarist William Pynchon of Salem, Massachusetts, for example, recorded in 1777 that a friend had bought a house for only 4 shillings more than the price of a hogshead of rum. That beverage was so scarce that Patrick Henry, as wartime governor of Virginia, embarrassed his friends by serving home-brewed beer to important guests. In 1778, when the British Army evacuated New Haven, the local council was delighted, until they learned that the departing troops had carted away the town's rum supply. Then they were furious. American farmers were not able to provide their laborers with traditional allowances of rum, and hands were obliged to take such substitutes as spruce, pumpkin, or persimmon beer. Often even Continental Army soldiers did without, when supply contractors failed to deliver the troops their daily 4-ounce rum ration. Spirituous liquor was so precious, recalled one man, that "in a severe battle, General Putnam, who was almost perforated with bullets, complained most of all, that a shot had passed through his canteen and spilt all his rum. . . ."[7]

After the war, rum distillers resumed capital-intensive and large-scale operations. Shipping merchants dominated the industry because, as a practical matter, a successful distiller needed a constant flow of molasses. In Providence, Rhode Island, for example, the Browns, a family with a far-flung business empire, established a distillery to generate cash to pay for other ventures. Between 1789 and 1794 they produced more than 500,000 gallons of rum. Throughout the New England seaboard, there were large rum works. New Haven's two rum factories, operated by Abner Kirby and Elias Shipman & Co., together distilled as much as 10,000 gallons a year. In contrast, the interior county of Hartford had dozens of small fruit and grain stills that altogether yielded only a fraction of this gallonage. Even on the lightly populated Maine coast rum production was great, with Thomas Robison's Falmouth rum works making more than 5,000 gallons during the first four months of 1785.[8]

However, despite extensive capital outlay, the postwar rum distillers lost their economic preeminence when their molasses sources began to disappear and their markets began to collapse. It became increasingly difficult to import molasses, because the European West Indies followed the British West Indies in distilling their own rum, and the French joined the British in closing their colonies to American trade. The American rum industry also faced the loss of its markets in Africa, Canada, and other British colonies, where a significant portion of the American product had been sold. At the same time, consumption fell within the United States. Americans in 1770 drank 8 million gallons of rum; by 1789, with a population that had nearly doubled, only 7 million gallons.[9]

Erratic supplies and higher prices for rum had encouraged a shift to beer, cider, and whiskey, but rum also suffered from rising nationalism. Imported molasses and rum were symbols of colonialism and reminders that America was not economically self-sufficient. Whereas the colonists once had been proud of obtaining such commodities from the British Empire, independent Americans now believed that having to import those items signified an economic weakness that could lead to political subjugation. To sell foodstuffs or other articles to the West Indies was desirable because it was profitable; to buy rum from those same islands was foolish and unpatriotic because it was harmful to American distillers and their workmen. "I reckon every horse exported and returned in rum," wrote one American, "as so much property lost to the general interest."[10]

Furthermore, the destruction of colonial trade patterns, wartime experimentation with beverages other than rum, and the thrust for economic independence left the American rum industry vulnerable to political attack. In 1783, Congress had proposed financing the central government by levying import duties. This plan necessitated an amendment to the Articles of Confederation. The Articles, however, could only be amended by unanimous consent, and Rhode Island, whose rum distillers feared a molasses tariff, voted against the proposal. It was the industry's last victory. After the federal government was established under the new constitution in 1789, Congress imposed rum and molasses duties. The only concession to the rum industry was the enactment of a whiskey tax, which was supposed to maintain the ratio that then existed between the prices of rum and whiskey. Even this levy could not stop the drift of Americans from expensive rum distilled from imported molasses to cheap whiskey made from domestic grain. Rum distillers faced an unpleasant situation; before the Revolution rum had been the universal beverage, and whiskey had been rare, so rare in 1774 that one author who used the word felt obliged to define it for his readers; but by 1790 rum accounted for only two-thirds of all the hard liquor consumed, and whiskey had become so popular that, along with domestic fruit brandy, it accounted for the remaining one-third.[11]

The rum industry was ruined when the attempt to use taxes to equalize the price of rum and whiskey failed. The impost and excise did lead to higher prices for both beverages. In Boston, local rum more than doubled from 1 shilling, 8 pence per gallon in the late 1780s to 3 shillings, 6 pence in the early 1790s. In New York, similar increases occurred, with the price of Jamaica rum doubling and that of whiskey rising by as much as 50 percent. It does not appear, however, that these higher prices significantly reduced consumption. Perhaps during the 1790s Americans could afford to pay more for alcoholic beverages because they were prospering from the sale of agricultural produce to war-ravaged Europe. Then, too, while the domestic excise raised the price of whiskey, it did not curb the growth of the supply. If there had been no whiskey tax, the price of that beverage would have fallen, and its use increased even more. In any event, whiskey gained at rum's expense, for the duties on molasses and rum were both higher than the whiskey tax and more difficult to evade.[12]

Repeal of the whiskey tax in 1802 doomed the rum industry. Since rum importers and distillers continued to pay rum and molasses duties, their product became too high priced to be competitive, except along the seaboard. Annual molasses imports remained steady at about 1 gallon per capita, at a time when spirits consumption was rising. While the domestic rum industry stagnated, imports of rum fell sharply. From 1790 until the United States embargo of 1808, annual rum imports were above

1 gallon per capita, from 1808 to 1827 less than a half gallon, and from 1828 to 1850 below one-fifth of a gallon.[13]

The decline of the rum industry was accompanied and hastened by the rise of cheap, plentiful whiskey. The success of the whiskey industry was due, in part, to the fact that many Scottish, Irish, and Scotch-Irish grain distillers had immigrated to America during the last quarter of the eighteenth century. These whiskey-drinking peoples had experimented with distillation for two centuries and had developed efficient stills that produced large amounts of fairly high quality liquor. When these Irish and Scots settled on the American frontier, they found conditions favorable for the exercise of their talents: plentiful water, abundant grain, and ample wood to fuel their stills. Travellers to western Pennsylvania observed that in that region one of every thirty families or an even greater proportion owned stills. In parts of Kentucky these instruments were the only manufactured items that had been brought from the East.[14]

In addition to the arrival of these highly skilled craftsmen, the American whiskey industry benefited during the early nineteenth century from radical technological improvements in stills. To understand these improvements, it is necessary to know how a still works. (See Chart 3.1.) The process begins when prepared fermented matter (the mash) is placed in a closed container (the still bowl) and heated until an alcoholic steam is produced. This steam then escapes through an outlet at the top of the bowl, passing through a pipe (the worm) which is cooled either by contact with the air or by passing through a series of tubs of cold water. The steam is recaptured as a liquid in a second closed container (the condenser). Each time a distiller follows this procedure of adding mash to the still bowl he has run off a batch, and each batch is one of a series that forms a run. It is generally

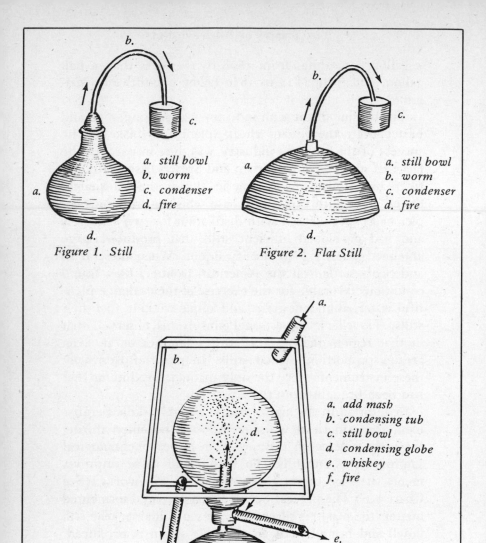

a. still bowl
b. worm
c. condenser
d. fire

Figure 1. Still

a. still bowl
b. worm
c. condenser
d. fire

Figure 2. Flat Still

a. add mash
b. condensing tub
c. still bowl
d. condensing globe
e. whiskey
f. fire

Figure 3. Perpetual Still

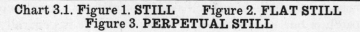

**Chart 3.1. Figure 1. STILL   Figure 2. FLAT STILL
Figure 3. PERPETUAL STILL**

agreed that the middle portion of batches from the middle of a run yields the highest quality distilled spirits. Stills operate on two physical principles: first, that fermented mash contains alcohol; second, that alcohol boils at a lower temperature than water. The device operates to pass a largely alcoholic steam into the condenser while leaving a watery, nonalcoholic waste in the still bowl. Condensers, worms, and still bowls can vary in size and shape. The selection of a particular design for a still depends upon local conditions. If wood or other fuel is scarce, a design that minimizes heat loss is preferable; if copper, the material most commonly used to make a still, is expensive, the still will be small; if water for cooling is difficult to obtain, slow condensation is carried out by exposing a long, coiled copper worm to the air.

One of the early advances in still design came about 1800, after the British government placed a steep excise on stills according to their capacity. Canny Scots, seeking to minimize the tax, devised a flat, shallow still of small capacity that could produce quickly large quantities of liquor. The flat still heated so rapidly that a distiller could run off a batch in as little as three minutes. However, while this design increased the rate of output and saved fuel, it required more labor. In America, where fuel was cheap, labor dear, and the equipment was taxed lightly or not at all, the stills were not so flat as those used in Scotland. Even so, American whiskey distillers discovered that the shallow bowl cut the size and, hence, the expense of the still, reduced wastage at the beginning and end of runs, and produced a higher quality liquor. This shallow, flat still was of no use to rum distillers, for while grain mash could be heated rapidly and intensely, molasses would scorch.[15]

A second improvement in still design raised yields and reduced both labor and fuel requirements. With a traditional apparatus, or even a flat still, the most efficient results could be attained only with a large unit run at full capacity. A high-capacity still had lower costs per gallon of output than a smaller unit, because labor costs depended upon the number of batches run rather than their size. A large still also used heat more efficiently and thereby cut fuel costs. These facts had favored rum distillers who operated large units over whiskey distillers who had to use small units because they lacked significant capital, plentiful grain supplies, and large markets. This competitive edge vanished with the invention and perfection of the 'perpetual' still.[16]

The principle of this apparatus was a heat exchange that saved both fuel and cooling water. As Chart 3.1 shows, the exchange of heat was effected by the addition of a third chamber called a condensing tub, which was built around the condenser, now called the condensing globe. The mash was fed into the condensing tub and descended to the still bowl where it was heated; the steam rose into the condensing globe and emerged as whiskey. The advantage of this design was that the heat given off by the condensing globe as the steam cooled inside it warmed the mash in the surrounding tub before it reached the still bowl. In addition, as the mash in the tub absorbed heat from the globe, it acted to cool the alcoholic vapors in the globe. In the earlier designs the heat given off by the condenser had been wasted; in the perpetual still some of the heat generated in the still bowl and passed on to the condensing globe was returned to the still bowl by way of the warmed mash. Similarly, earlier designs had often used coiled worms that were passed through tubs of water in order to cool and condense the alcoholic vapors. Now the cooling of the vapors in the globe of the perpetual still was accomplished by the globe being surrounded by the condensing tub filled with mash. Thus, the perpetual still eliminated coiled worms and water tubs used for cooling and significantly reduced the need for fuel. The perpetual still had an added advantage: it could be fed continuously. It was no longer necessary to make liquor in batches. As a consequence, labor costs were cut and the poor quality spirits produced at the beginning and end of runs was reduced. Because this invention made small stills nearly as efficient as large ones, it enabled small-scale whiskey producers to compete with large-scale rum manufacturers.

The perpetual still was just one of many improvements in distillation patented during the early nineteenth century. From 1802 through 1815 the federal government issued more than 100 patents for distilling devices. These patents were more than 5 percent of all patents granted, and they were issued both in a higher proportion and in greater numbers than in later years. The great number of early patents is evidence of a widespread interest in still technology. Scientists concerned themselves with distilling problems; the nation's leading magazines published articles on the subject; and self-taught experts published distilling manuals. Among prominent Americans who were interested in methods of distillation were Tench Coxe, Hamilton's aide and one-time excise collector, who followed international technical developments with the hope of applying some innovations to domestic manufacturing; Dr. Samuel L. Mitchill, a leading New York physician active in the temperance cause; and Thomas Cooper, Dickinson College chemistry professor, who claimed that he had perfected the perpetual still in the Philadelphia laboratory of English exile Joseph Priestly. Perhaps more representative of the general interest in distillation was George Washington. On retiring from the presidency and moving to Mount Vernon in 1797 he built a distillery where he processed his neighbors' surplus grain and in 1798, his best year, earned £344.[17]

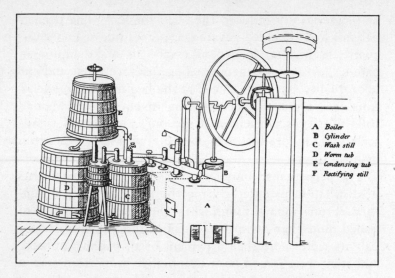

Anderson and Hall's Patented Steam Distillery.

The process of distillation interested Americans because it performed a vital economic function by transforming fragile, perishable, bulky, surplus fruit and grain into nonperishable spirits that could be easily stored, shipped, or sold. Unlike other commodities, spirituous liquor could be shipped at a profit, even when shipping required the payment of high overland transportation costs. A farmer could realize handsome profits from processing his grain into spirits, since a bushel of corn worth 25¢ yielded 2½ gallons of spirits worth $1.25 or more. Even if the farmer did not do his own distilling and had to give a commercial distiller half the output in payment for his service, he could increase the value of his corn by 150 percent.[18]

Although many farmers wanted a part of their grain to be distilled, not all could afford to buy stills. Boilers, worms, and still bowls were expensive because they had to be made by highly skilled craftsmen from copper, which was scarce. When a western husbandman found that $200 would buy either a 100-gallon still or 200 acres of uncleared land, he was inclined, if he had the money, to purchase the land. Indeed, he could justify the capital outlay for a still only if he could keep it occupied by processing not only his own grain but also his neighbors'. The result was that only wealthy agriculturalists had stills and that farmers who needed a distiller's services paid heavily for their dependency. Before 1820, the capitalist-distiller could make large profits from this captive market.[19]

Distilling manuals forecasted high earnings. For example, Harrison Hall, author of one distilling manual, calculated that a distillery that processed twelve bushels of grain a day and shipped 3,000 gallons of spirits to a nearby market would produce, in three months, $700 profit, an amount more than one-third of its gross sales. Here are his estimates:[20]

CAPITAL REQUIRED

125 gal. patent still	$ 240
100 gal. doubling still and worm	100
125 gal. boiler	100
50 hogsheads	75
misc. equipment	169
110 hogs	440
TOTAL	1124

EXPENSES

600 bu. corn at 50¢ per	300
300 bu. rye at 60¢ per	180
100 bu. malt at 60¢ per	60
500 lb. juniper berries	100
hops	2
100 barrels	100
transportation at 6¢ per gal.	180
33 cords wood	66

EXPENSES (CONT.)

grinding grain	50
wages	125
leakage, commissions, repairs	139
TOTAL	1302

RECEIPTS

3000 *gal. spirits at* 55¢ *per*	1650
gain on hogs	328
TOTAL	1978

PROFIT 676

Hall's figures indicate that within six months a small distillery would not only pay its expenses but also recover the value of invested capital. A close inspection of his estimates, however, shows that these rosy projections allowed no margin for error or mishap. For one thing, as Rep. James Buchanan once observed in Congress, many distillers' profits depended less upon whiskey than upon the hogs fattened on distillery slop. If the hogs died or the pork market became depressed, the distiller lost money. There could be other difficulties: a workman might spill the mash, the barrels might leak, the still might explode, or the spirits might not bring as high a price as expected. The prospect of profits that lured men to buy and operate stills created competition that inevitably drove down the price of whiskey. When the price dropped to 25¢ a gallon or less, as it did in the West during the 1820s, receipts would no longer meet expenses, much less recover capital invested in the still. By that time stills were no longer scarce and, being common, they lost their value as money mills.[21]

At the opening of the century, the West was the center of the burgeoning whiskey industry. By 1810, when distilling was concentrated in upstate New York, western

Pennsylvania, Ohio, and Kentucky, those four states produced more than half the nation's grain and fruit spirits. An important element in making the western frontier the center for whiskey distilling was the fact that it was separated from the East by the Appalachian Mountains. This physical barrier dictated a particular pattern of frontier settlement and economy. When the frontier had been on the eastern side of the mountains, settlers had moved along river valleys that kept them in touch with developed areas downstream. But settlers who crossed the Appalachians were out of touch with the seaboard. They were isolated and cut off from the East, and they were forced to develop their own resources, products, and markets. Land transportation across the mountain barrier was expensive and impractical. From Bedford, Pennsylvania, for example, it was said to be cheaper to haul goods 100 miles to Pittsburgh and then float them 2,100 miles down the Ohio and Mississippi rivers to New Orleans than to haul them 200 miles over the mountains of central Pennsylvania to Philadelphia. While water transport was nearly free, land carriage cost as much as 1¢ a pound per 100 miles. The West of necessity had to become self-sufficient.[22]

Although the region's commercial development was hindered by topography, the West did enjoy the advantage of soil superior to that of the East. "The valley of the Ohio," wrote one impressed foreign visitor, was "the richest and the most fertile . . . ever seen. The luxuriance and rapid growth of the vegetation were incredible." A settler needed to work "scarcely two hours a day to support himself and his family." Such reports led Americans to herald Kentucky as a paradise, a second Garden of Eden. This romantic vision was not entirely fanciful, as suggested by high agricultural yields. Whereas a typical Maryland farm yielded ten bushels of corn per acre, virgin Kentucky soil yielded forty. A diligent western farmer who planted and harvested ten acres got 400 bushels of corn, four times what his family and cattle could consume.[23]

Disposing of this surplus grain was difficult. Such lush production caused food prices in the Ohio valley to fall until they were the lowest in the world. Apples and peaches were free for the picking, and many were allowed to rot on the ground. Corn sold for as little as 25¢ a bushel, corn-fed pork 5¢ a pound. The western husbandman could make no money selling produce in this glutted local market, so he tried to sell his surplus elsewhere. During the Napoleonic Wars much of the grain was sent via New Orleans to Europe, but after 1815 a peaceful Europe no longer needed American produce. As for sending grain to the East, corn was so bulky that a horse could not carry enough across the Appalachian Mountains to provide his own feed. Indeed, it was calculated that grain could not be sent profitably by land more than twenty miles. The farmer was forced to ship his grain by water down the Mississippi to New Orleans, where he was at the mercy of a single market serving the entire western region. Sometimes the planter's corn rotted on the wharves, or he was paid so little that he lost money on the trip. Farmers found these grain shipments to be so unprofitable that many chose to feed their corn to hogs, thereby turning a corn glut into a hog glut. Although Cincinnatians boasted of their town as Porkopolis, most hogs were marketed through New Orleans, where a large supply and limited demand yielded a low price.[24]

To market their surplus grain more profitably, western farmers turned to distilling. Whiskey could be shipped to eastern markets either through New Orleans or overland. A man could make money sending his whiskey overland by pack animal because distillation so reduced the bulk of

Two views of a small distillery.

grain that a horse could carry six times as much corn in that form. Thus, a western planter could load his horse with liquor, head across the mountains, trade some of the alcohol for feed en route, and arrive in the East with a surplus to sell in a favorable eastern whiskey market. Whereas corn sold for 25¢ a bushel in Kentucky, whiskey brought, after trip expenses, four times that amount in Philadelphia. This price differential was due not so much to the conversion of corn into whiskey as to a significant difference between eastern and western grain markets. Grain in the West sold in a low-priced buyer's market created by the farmer's need to sell; he feared spoilage, lacked storage, and needed cash from his grain sales to pay taxes and buy manufactured goods. The mountain barrier dictated that corn and wheat grown in the West had to be sold locally or in a glutted New Orleans market. On the other hand, grain grown in the East sold in a high-priced seller's market at as much as three times the western rate. The East had barely enough grain for its own needs because of low acreage yields and a large nonfarming population.[25]

The existence of two distinct grain markets was a consequence of the geographical barrier. Since distilled spirits could be transported across the mountains, the two grain markets were united into a single, new, national whiskey market. However, little high-priced eastern grain was distilled, because the whiskey produced would have been more expensive than rum. Consequently, cheap western grain, in the form of whiskey, could be sold in the East at prices nearly as high as rum. Westerners rushed to enter this lucrative trade, inhibited only by a shortage of stills. Stills became more common, the rapid increase of western population increased the grain surplus, and the collapse of the European market for American grain in 1815 spurred more farmers to market whiskey in the East. The results were predictable. Cheap western spirits first stole the rum market by undercutting West Indian and New England rum, and then in the early 1820s whiskey itself became a surplus commodity. At Philadelphia, where rye whiskey before 1820 had sold at wholesale for more than 60¢ a gallon, its price was halved.[26]

This overproduction of whiskey contributed to the West's financial problems during the 1820s. For one thing, distilled spirits had been one of that region's important mediums of exchange. Whiskey had functioned as money on the frontier, much as rum had on the seaboard a half century earlier. The cash-short West needed some form of currency, and whiskey was a rational choice, for it was widely produced, universally used, and easily preserved, stored, shipped, and traded. It circulated like money, being readily interchangeable for all sorts of goods and services. One Ohio newspaper, for example, requested subscribers to pay cash or stipulated amounts of beef, pork, wheat, corn, or whiskey, and Cincinnati's First Presbyterian Church paid a portion of its minister's salary with 100 gallons of corn liquor. While whiskey, like rum, gained value when aged in storage, it was far from an ideal currency, for it had a limited home market in an area where every farmer was a potential distiller. When a western farmer bought a still, it appears that he often intended to make spirits not to sell but to pack his basement with liquid assets. As soon as he had filled the storeroom, he sold the still. There were few commercial distillers in the western country because there were few local buyers, a truth painfully learned by some New England investors whose Hope Distillery at Louisville failed when its product could not be marketed.[27]

Furthermore, the West was affected by whiskey's role in the national economy. After the first Bank of the United States had been allowed to die in 1811, the financing of American business depended heavily upon commodity exchanges. Naturally, one of the most important commodities for exchange on the part of the West was whiskey. The West needed its profits from the sale of whiskey in the East, especially after peace was established in Europe in 1815, in order to pay for the things that it needed to import. This funding system was inherently unstable, for it had developed when a shortage of stills and a small western population kept the whiskey supply low and its eastern price high. After increased westward migration and a greater number of stills raised production, the market became saturated, and, as noted above, prices broke. Following the Panic of 1819 the low price of spirituous liquors brought about by the whiskey surplus worsened the West's economic situation, since the surplus destroyed the trade that had been the financial mechanism linking East to West. Throughout the

1820s, the western economy stagnated, plagued by a chronic shortage of hard money and starved by a dearth of eastern capital. I believe that much of this economic hardship was a consequence of the whiskey glut.[28]

In the early 1820s, when a poorly paid agricultural laborer earned $1 a day, whiskey sold at retail for 25¢ to 50¢ a gallon.[29] From 1825 to the present most goods have declined in price, in terms of the labor required to purchase them; whiskey has increased. One reason for that increase is taxation. Whereas whiskey was not taxed in 1825, today it pays substantial state and local levies and a federal excise of $10.50 a gallon. The following comparisons illustrate that whiskey used to be a bargain:[30]

Table 3.1. RANKINGS of PURCHASING POWER
one day's wages

	1825	1975
	at $1 per Day	*at $25 per Day*
Loss		
whiskey	2 gallons	1 gallon
rent	10 days	6 days
beef	16 lbs.	14 lbs.
Even		
pork	16 lbs.	16 lbs.
Gain		
cheese	11 lbs.	17 lbs.
eggs	11 doz.	35 doz.
butter	6 lbs.	28 lbs.
milk	16 qts.	70 qts.
coffee	5 lbs.	21 lbs.
clothing	5% year's cost	25% year's cost
sugar	8 lbs.	42 lbs.
flour	20 lbs.	125 lbs.
tea	1⅓ lbs.	11 lbs.
wine	½ gallon	6¼ gallons
Madeira wine	¼ gallon	3 gallons

After 1815, just as whiskey was displacing rum as the dominant beverage in the East, other forces were at work stimulating the development of nationwide commerce and increasing the availability of cheap whiskey. In the West, farmers had used flatboats, keelboats, and rafts to float their produce down the Ohio and Mississippi rivers. Although these vessels were a cheap way to ship bulky agricultural products, they provided only a one-way trip. Ohio valley farmers found getting home from New Orleans inconvenient and even dangerous. Often they walked alone for four to six weeks, struggling to carry necessary purchases across desolate terrain and sparingly used highways that were infested by thieves and robbers. Then, too, floating produce down the river meant that western husbandmen had to sell their produce in a single competitive market at New Orleans, where they often had to sell at a loss.[31]

The invention of the steamboat and its rapid spread across western waters altered trade conditions. Now farmers who rafted produce to New Orleans could return home with their purchases rapidly, cheaply, and conveniently. More important, since steamboats could travel upstream, farm goods could be sold either at New Orleans or upriver, so that farmers in the Tennessee and Cumberland valleys, for example, turned to raising cotton after they began to receive foodstuffs from the Ohio valley. And this new transportation was cheap. One English visitor calculated that it cost 2¢ a mile to travel on a steamboat on the Mississippi River versus 23¢ a mile in a stage coach in Alabama or Georgia. Throughout the West, steamboats stimulated the movement of both passengers and freight. Trade boomed. In 1812, New Orleans received 11,000 gallons of whiskey; in 1816, 320,000 gallons; by 1824, 570,000 gallons. In 1810, Louisville tallied 250,000 gallons passing the falls; in 1822, 2,250,000 gallons.[32]

Canals were another stimulant to commerce, creating new markets and expanding old ones. When a canal was built, it substituted cheap water transportation for expensive overland transportation and thereby reduced shipping costs. These lower costs, in turn, radically altered markets. Some people found it cheaper to buy certain imported goods than to produce their own, and others discovered that they could now sell abroad products that had been unsalable. When the Erie Canal opened, a farmer was asked, "Where did you sell your staves and timber, before the canal was made?" And he replied, "No where." The New York, Pennsylvania, and Ohio canals facilitated the interchange of goods and helped the West to export its surplus corn by freeing that commodity from the monopoly of the New Orleans market. These new routes gave the western farmer a wider market, thereby increasing the demand for his produce and, consequently, increasing its price. At the same time, the eastern buyer could purchase low-priced western commodities with only small shipping charges added.[33]

Inexpensive transportation created a national grain market. Before the canal era, whiskey had been the only western commodity able to overcome the transportation barrier that divided the eastern and western grain markets, and, as we have seen, whiskey alone had enjoyed a national market. It was at that time the West's most profitable commodity. Before 1825, it was estimated that a farmer who sent 1,000 bushels of corn to New Orleans would be lucky to recover his shipping costs. If he could convert his corn into hogs, oxen, or horses, he might make $120. But if he shipped his corn as spirits, he could make $470. These differences in profits disappeared in the canal era, when national hog and corn markets began to compete with the national whiskey market.[34]

The market revolution altered not only prices but also trade patterns. Because of the new national grain market, westerners who observed that grain prices were rising relative to whiskey prices were less inclined to distill spirits. In one principal whiskey center, Dayton, Ohio, by 1832 nearly twice as much grain was milled as was distilled. Whiskey also began to decline as a proportion of western trade. From 1825 to 1834 the amount of Ohio valley spirits sent to New Orleans ceased to expand, while amounts of pork and corn increased. Central Ohio began to send its corn north over the Ohio Canal to the Erie line rather than south as spirits to New Orleans. Cheap western produce flooded the East, caused prices to fall, and produced even more radical changes. New York farmers who lived along the Erie Canal found that their worn-out lands could not compete with the West's virgin soil in producing grain for their local trading area. On the other hand, these same farmers discovered that the canal opened new markets for them further East. Until 1828 spirits shipments on the Erie Canal had increased because of the western distillers' increased penetration of the New York market as well as increased local distillation; then, in 1828 whiskey shipments peaked as westerners and New Yorkers began to shift from the production of whiskey to the production of grain for sale in New York City and New England. By 1835 the Erie Canal was such a grain conduit that Rochester, one of the cities along its route, could bill itself as the Flour City. In that year, flour accounted for half the value of the goods carried on the canal.[35]

The creation of a national grain market led to the rationalization of whiskey production, that is, whiskey production became concentrated in large-scale distilleries in those localities that could not compete in the raising and shipping of grain. By 1840 distilleries in southwest Ohio, upstate New York, and southeast and southwest Pennsylvania distilled more than half the nation's grain spirits. Each of these areas was in a disadvantageous location for

Advertizement for commercially distilled whiskey.

shipping corn. Neither Cincinnati nor Pittsburgh could
compete with the lower Ohio valley for the New Orleans
market or with northern Ohio and western New York for
the New England market. Although some upstate New
York farmers shipped grain, others turned to distilling
whiskey because they were better able than frontiersmen
to participate in an industry that required capital investment in stills. Southeastern Pennsylvania farmers
switched to distilling when their grain came into competition with cheaper grain brought down the Susquehanna
River and Pennsylvania canals.[36]

This geographic concentration coincided with a decrease in the number of distilleries. The decline after
1830 was in contrast with early nineteenth-century increases. One leading distilling center, for example, was

Lancaster County, Pennsylvania, which as late as 1786 had no distilleries; by 1814, there were 611; in 1830, only 203.[37] The number of distilleries in the entire country rose from 14,000 in 1810 to 20,000 in 1830 and then fell to half that number a decade later.[38] The decrease was the result of both a declining production of spirits and the fact that after 1830 small local units lost business to larger, more efficient competitors who produced for a national market. This change can be illustrated with data for the state of New York:[39]

Table 3.2. NEW YORK STATE DISTILLERIES, 1810–1860

Year	Number of Distilleries	Value of Product	Gallons
1810	591	1.7m$	2.1m
1821	1057	—	—
1825	1129	—	(18.0 ?)
1835	337	3.0	—
1840	212	—	12.0
1845	221	4.2	—
1850	93	4.7	11.7
1855	88	8.6	—
1860	77	7.7	26.2

The development of a large-scale, efficient, and concentrated distilling industry brought the spirits glut to an end. This was but the closing chapter in a story that began when economic conditions created an overabundance of cheap whiskey. In a sense, the period of plentiful spirits can be viewed as an episode in the maturation and development of the American economy. It occupied the years between 1790 and 1830 when a localized, rural, seaboard economy was beginning to be transformed into a modern, national, industrial economy. Whiskey's abundance also can be seen as part of an economic crisis that was brought on by the waning of traditional, agrarian society. Americans, like European peasants, had employed distillation to dispose of unmarketable agricultural surpluses. The early nineteenth-century enthusiasm for distilling had shown a lack of economic imagination, a kind of stale and mindless attachment to custom, and the inability of Americans to envision a better use for their agricultural surplus. This surplus grain had the potential to become either the food for industrial workers or, if sold in the market, the means of acquiring money that could be used as the capital to build factories. That Americans failed to use the surplus in either of those ways and preferred instead to drink indicated either that they were content with traditional society or, more likely, that they lacked the ingenuity or will to alter that society. In one sense, then, the whiskey glut exemplified the inability of Americans who clung to traditional agrarian values to promote change.

At the same time, I believe that the spirits surplus unleashed powerful influences for change. The plethora of whiskey resulted from overabundant agricultural production which, in turn, was caused by the fact that farmers were too great a proportion of the labor force. Laborers who worked on farms were available for new employment, if imaginative men would take the initiative to hire them for industrial jobs. When entrepreneurs began to forge an industrial economy, they were able to employ cheap, surplus rural labor at machines. Farm girls, for example, worked in the early factories at Lowell, Massachusetts. So it was that the agricultural surplus made rapid industrialization possible. This American experience was not unique, for a glut of distilled spirits has preceded industrial development in many modern nations. A mid-eighteenth-century craze for gin preceded England's Industrial Revolution, mid-nineteenth-century distilled spirits binges preceded the rapid transformations of Prussia and Sweden, and an upsurge in vodka consumption preceded the industrialization of Russia. In each of these cases, as in the United States, agricultural surpluses had created conditions favorable to rapid industrial development.[40]

The spirits glut also destabilized the traditional agrarian economy. By 1810, Americans were spending 2 percent of their personal income on distilled spirits, and, although this figure does not sound high, it represented a high proportion of discretionary income going to buy strong drink at a time when expenditures for food, clothing, and shelter absorbed most income. Furthermore, the money spent on alcohol had the potential for being a significant source of capital for investment. Money that went to buy alcohol, unlike money that was accumulated to buy major purchases or invested in long-range ventures, could be shifted suddenly into new channels. With the advent of industrialization, Americans switched from buying liquor to investing in industrial projects or purchasing other manufactured consumer goods. Rapid industrialization after 1830 was stimulated by lower liquor consumption.[41]

Cheap, abundant liquor also had consequences for society itself. People who continued to believe that alcohol was a 'good creature' were unwilling to impose restrictions that would reduce excessive consumption with its socially debilitating effects. And because society lacked traditional inhibitions against overindulgence, drinking had disruptive and destructive social consequences. During the period of peak consumption liquor induced wife beating, family desertion, and assaults, as well as payments from public funds for the support of inebriates and their families, increased. Such rising disorder alarmed a public that resented the expense and feared social chaos. As American leaders groped for mechanisms to control the socially disruptive results of drinking, they turned to an attempt to limit drinking itself.

The temperance movement was born during the market revolution, and I am convinced that its success would not have been possible without the decline in the number of distilleries. Before 1830, when numerous distillers who made small quantities of spirits served their neighbors by converting unwanted corn and rye into salable whiskey, it was difficult to organize much public opposition to distilling. It was hopeless to persuade even those Americans who did not need a distiller's services to condemn their neighbors, and, in that atmosphere, temperance advocates acknowledged that they were not "able to boast of great achievements." After 1830, the rise of the national grain market gave farmers an outlet for their produce, while the abandonment of local distilleries made it possible for reformers to challenge and change community attitudes. Spirituous liquor was no longer a local commodity but the manufactured product of an anonymous, remote entrepreneur. To men who lived in rural communities only recently touched by the market revolution, the far away distiller loomed as a frightening symbol. His enormous power, influence, and wealth seemed to be a consequence of his ability to manipulate and control the destinies of other men. It should not be surprising that the leaders of the temperance movement chose to play upon these fears by portraying the distiller as the devil's disciple.[42]

These were the sentiments of later years, long after the whiskey glut had passed. During its inception and development, the spirits surplus had been viewed quite differently. With drinking ingrained in the national heritage and whiskey a significant element of the American economy, corn liquor, during the first quarter of the nineteenth century, achieved the status of a cult. Americans believed that whiskey was healthful because it was made of a nutritive grain, that it was patriotic to drink it because corn was native, and that its wholesome, American qualities ought to make it the national drink. Wrote distiller Harrison Hall in defense of this sentiment, "The French sip brandy; the Hollanders swallow gin; the Irish glory in their whiskey; surely John Bull finds 'meat and drink' in his porter—and why should not our countrymen have a national beverage?" Kentuckians hostile to foreign ideas, or foreign spirits, promoted liberty by pledging "to drink no other strong liquor than whiskey." And Dr. James Tilton of Wilmington, Delaware, boasted that he had renounced foreign wine and spirits. "I indulge," he wrote, "in a cheering glass of spirits and water, once or twice a day. For this purpose, I prefer good rye whiskey or high-proof apple-brandy; for I scorn to go abroad for any thing that I can get better at home." The love of whiskey extended even unto death. Frontier Kentucky poet Tom Johnson penned this epitaph for his grave:[43]

> Underneath this marble tomb,
> In endless shades lies drunken Tom;
> Here safely moor'd, dead as a log,
> Who got his death by drinking grog—
> By whiskey grog he lost his breath,
> Who would not die so sweet a death.

Such romantic expressions showed the role that whiskey played in the national consciousness.

There can be no question as to the importance of the distilling industry to the American economy during the early nineteenth century. The whiskey trade had been one of the few links between the preindustrial East and West. It was a binding force, a reason for union, and the national whiskey market had foreshadowed the economic nationalism that the transportation revolution and the market economy would extend to all commodities. The development of the whiskey industry was an early attempt to rationalize the economy on a national scale. Whiskey was one of the first abundant and cheap products that American technology and exploitation of resources was bringing into being. In another sense, however, the corn liquor cult was less an economic than a psychological phenomenon. The worship of whiskey as a national drink can be viewed as an expression of national aspirations for distinction and greatness. The whiskey binge was not only an episode of euphoric intemperance; it was also a celebration of a waning reliance upon such foreign products as rum. Whiskey was truly the spirits of independence.

CHAPTER

WHISKEY FEED

"Have you any meat?" "No."
"Either cold or hot will make no difference to me."
"I guess I don't know."
"Have you any fowls?" "No."
"Fish?" "No." "Ham?" "No." "Bread?" "No."
"Cheese?" "No." "Crackers?" "No."
"I will pay you any price you please."
"I guess we have only rum and whiskey feed."

HENRY FEARON

1817

THE AVAILABILITY of cheap, plentiful whiskey was one key to the extensive use of spirituous liquor by so many Americans in the early nineteenth century; another key was the American diet. There were a number of ways in which the habits of eating and drinking at that time encouraged Americans to drink whiskey. But the preference for whiskey as a significant article in the diet was more than a matter of diet; that preference was also related to larger social questions. Dietary habits, as Claude Lévi-Strauss has pointed out, are good indicators of a culture's popular attitudes and social structure. Thus, an examination of the role of whiskey in the American diet in the early nineteenth century will both inform us about the use of whiskey in everyday life and broaden our understanding of the inner workings of American society in those years.[1]

To understand the great popularity of whiskey we have to consider, among other things, the shortcomings of other available beverages. To begin with, neither Americans nor Europeans of the period tended to indulge in refreshing glasses of water. This was not so much the consequence of an aversion to that healthful beverage as that the available water was seldom clear, sparkling, or appetizing. The citizens of St. Louis, for example, had to let water from the Mississippi River stand before they could drink it, and the sediment often filled one-quarter of the container. Further downstream, at Natchez, the river water was too muddy to be drunk even after it had settled. Instead, people drank rain water, which they collected in roof cisterns. During frequent droughts, however, the cisterns were empty. Rural areas often lacked good water because deep wells were expensive and difficult to build, while the water from shallow wells was usually cloudy. The purest water came from clear, free-flowing springs, but these were not always conveniently located. Although Kentucky and Tennessee had abundant low-lying springs, pioneers who feared swamp fevers or Indian attacks preferred to build their cabins on high ground. As a result, water had to be carried uphill in a bucket, as at Lincoln's birthplace at Hodgenville, Kentucky. Toting water lessened the frontiersman's enthusiasm for drinking it. So did the cold of winter, for then, recalled one pioneer, water had to be thawed.[2]

Water supplies were no better in the nation's largest and wealthiest cities. Washingtonians, for example, long had to depend upon water from private wells because of a deep-seated opposition to higher taxes to pay the cost of digging public wells. During the 1820s the capital city's only piped water was from a privately owned spring that supplied two blocks along Pennsylvania Avenue. Cincinnati was no better off. There, according to a concerned Dr. Daniel Drake, most people drank "often impure" water drawn in barrels from the frequently low and muddy Ohio. To escape beclouded river water, wealthy citizens dug their own wells, which provided an ill-tasting drink "slightly impregnated with iron, and . . . salts."[3] New York City was worse, for Manhattan's shallow, brackish wells made it certain that the drinker of water would not only quench his thirst but also be given "physic." It was this latter effect, perhaps, that caused New Yorkers to avoid drinking water and earned them a

reputation for preferring other sorts of beverages. One
resident who was asked whether the city's water was po-
table replied, "Really, I cannot pretend to say, as I never
tasted water there that was not mixed with some kind of
liquor." Conditions were so bad that New Yorkers
adopted a plan to dam the Croton River and transport its
water forty miles to the city. As soon as the aqueduct
opened in 1842, residents began to switch from spirits to
water. Two years later, on the 4th of July, teetotaling
Mayor James Harper shrewdly countered traditional holiday dram-drinking by setting up in the city hall park a
large basin of iced Croton water. It was only after the
improvement of public water supplies that temperance
zealots embraced the idea of 'Cold Water' as a substitute
for alcohol.[4]

During the first third of the century water was often
condemned on the ground that it lacked food value and
did not aid digestion. Indeed, many people believed
water unfit for human consumption. As one American
said, "It's very good for navigation." Others thought
water to be lowly and common; it was the drink of pigs,
cows, and horses. Or, as Benjamin Franklin put it, if
God had intended man to drink water, He would not
have made him with an elbow capable of raising a wine
glass. There were also those who thought that water
could be lethal, especially if drunk in hot weather. English immigrant Joseph Pickering, for example, so feared
the effect of drinking water on scorching days that he
resolved to drink only a concoction of water and rye
whiskey, a beverage he believed to be less dangerous.
Nor was Pickering alone in refusing to drink this insidious liquid. From Virginia, Elijah Fletcher assured his father in Vermont, "I shall not injure my health in drinking water. I have not drank a tumbler full since here. We
always have a boll of toddy made for dinner. . . ." In
the same spirit, John Randolph warned his son, "I see by

John B. Gough, the Cold-Water warrior.

the papers, eight deaths in one week from cold water, in Philadelphia alone." Randolph himself was unlikely to fall victim to water drinking, for he used none in mixing his favorite mint juleps.[5]

While water was eschewed, many Americans drank milk—when they could get it. Sometimes milk was excellent, cheap, and plentiful; at other times, especially on the frontier, it was not available or its price was as high as 12¢ a quart, more than whiskey. Costs were erratic and supplies spotty because each locality depended upon its own production. Bulk and lack of refrigeration made both transportation and storage difficult. During the winter poor fodder insured that the supply of milk was small, and in all seasons the needs of children often forced adults to forego this drink. Even when milk was plentiful, many did not drink it for fear of the fatal 'milk sickness.' This illness, which killed Abraham Lincoln's mother, was caused by a poison transmitted through milk from cows that had grazed on the wild jimson weed. Those who believed that it was better not to risk getting the milk sickness turned to safer beverages, such as whiskey.[6]

Americans also rejected tea, which was relatively expensive. During the 1820s, a cup of tea cost more than a mixed drink made with whiskey. As much as half the price of tea represented import duties, which had been set high because tea was imported from the British colony of India, carried in British ships, and drunk by the rich. Although tea's unpopularity was usually attributed to its high price, its popularity remained low even after temperance advocates succeeded in getting the impost halved. In 1832 annual consumption continued to average less than a pound—250 cups—per person. Even when its price was low, most Americans considered tea to be an alien 'foreign luxury.' To drink it was unpatriotic. While popular in anglophilic New England, imported teas were so disliked in the rest of the country that New Yorkers substituted glasses of wine at society 'tea parties,' and westerners, who disdained imports, brewed their own sassafras, spicewood, mint, and wild root teas. Frontiersmen believed imported teas to be insipid "slops" fit only for the sick and those who, like British Lords, were incapable of bodily labor. So rare was tea on the frontier that its proper method of preparation was not always known. Thus, when one English traveller presented an innkeeper's wife with a pound of tea and asked her to brew a cup, she obliged by boiling the entire amount and serving the leaves in their liquid as a kind of soup.[7]

Although tea was expensive, it cost less per cup than coffee, and before 1825 tea outsold coffee. At 25¢ a pound, the annual per capita consumption of coffee was less than two pounds or 100 cups. Imported coffee was then such a luxury that many Americans drank unappetizing homemade substitutes concocted from rye grain, peas, brown bread, or burned toast. Although coffee was imported, it did not share the scorn heaped upon tea. Perhaps coffee was more acceptable because it was imported from Latin America. Nor had there ever been a Boston Coffee Party. During the late 1820s, therefore, when the price of coffee fell to 15¢ a pound, imports rose, and consumption increased correspondingly. This development delighted those temperance reformers who wanted coffee to replace distilled spirits, and in 1830 they succeeded in persuading Congress to remove the duty on coffee. The price soon dropped to 10¢ a pound, a rate that brought the price of a cup of coffee down to the price of a glass of whiskey punch and pushed coffee sales ahead of tea to five pounds per person. By 1833 coffee had ceased to be a luxury and, according to the *Baltimore American*, entered "largely into the daily consumption of almost every family, rich and poor," prominent "among the necessaries of life." (See Chart 4.1.) But in the first third of the century it had been too expensive to compete with whiskey.[8]

Having found coffee, tea, milk, and water unacceptable for one reason or another, some Americans turned to fermented drinks, such as wine. Although its high price of $1 a gallon, often four times that of whiskey, limited annual per capita consumption of wine to less than a fifth of a gallon, its preference by the wealthy and their attempts to promote its use gave it a social importance out of proportion to its small sales. Many upper class oppo-

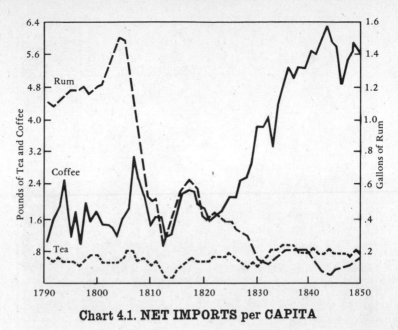

Chart 4.1. NET IMPORTS per CAPITA

nents of distilled spirits favored wine because they believed it to be free of alcohol, the chemical that a number of physicians and scientists regarded as a poison. While the presence of alcohol in distilled beverages had long been recognized, early nineteenth-century wine drinkers noted with satisfaction that no experimenter had found that compound in a fermented beverage. It was an unpleasant surprise when chemist William Brande succeeded in measuring the amount of alcohol in fermented drinks and not only proved that wine contained a higher percentage of alcohol than hard cider or beer, but also showed that the favorite American wine, Madeira, was more than 20 percent alcohol. After 1820, as temperance organizations disseminated Brande's findings, the number of wine advocates declined, although a few, such

Lady pouring wine for a gentleman.

as Dr. S. H. Dickson of South Carolina, insisted that the alcohol in wine was rendered harmless by its incorporation into the wine.[9]

Early wine connoisseurs included such men as Thomas Jefferson, Andrew Jackson, and John Marshall. At the executive mansion during Jefferson's presidency, diners enjoyed round after round of fine, light French wines, and at Monticello the Sage himself customarily drank three glasses of wine each day, a task facilitated by a dumbwaiter that carried wine bottles from the cellar to Jefferson's dining room. Another wine fancier was Jefferson's political rival Aaron Burr, who maintained New York's most impressive cellar. It was at a Burr dinner that Andrew Jackson was introduced to the subtleties and pleasures of the grape. He subsequently stocked the Hermitage in Tennessee with a selection that led to its reputation as the wine center of the West. Vinous drink, however, had no greater devotee than Chief Justice John Marshall. At the boarding house in Washington where the Supreme Court justices lived, the boarders permitted wine only in wet weather, for the sake of their health. Upon occasion, the chief justice would command Justice Story to check the window to see if it were raining. When informed that the sun shone brightly, Marshall would observe, "All the better; for our jurisdiction extends over so large a territory that the doctrine of chances makes it certain that it must be raining somewhere." The chief justice, observed Story, had been "brought up upon Federalism and Madeira, and he [was] not the man to outgrow his early prejudices."[10]

During the first quarter of the century, among society's upper classes, wine was central to the male dinner party. Wine provided both a chief topic of discussion and an excuse for late hours, which were spent sampling new and exotic varieties. A well-to-do Maine landowner, Robert Gardiner, has left a picture of one such party held in New York in 1803. "After the cloth was removed and the bottle had passed once around," he wrote, "Mr. Hammond asked what was the duty of the guests when the host opened for them a bottle of very choice wine." A voice replied, "To see the bottom of it." The servants then presented the party with a gallon bottle. "This, gentlemen," said the host, "is very fine old wine, the best I have, and as I open it for you, I expect you will finish it." Gardiner was forced, as a matter of propriety, to drink until he left the party with his head reeling. While the custom of holding these lengthy gentlemen's dinners gradually faded, it did not disappear before mid-century. As late as 1836 New York socialite Philip Hone, who often hosted such dinners, noted with satisfaction that his well-stocked cellar contained 672 gallons of Madeira and sherry.[11]

Although wealthy wine drinkers continued to indulge their palates, the Revolution's patriotic and democratic ideals had put these Americans on the defensive. Nearly all the wine Americans drank was imported, largely from Madeira, and to continue to purchase dutied, foreign beverages both worsened the American balance of payments and cast doubts upon the patriotism of the purchasers. Then, too, continuing to drink a refreshment priced beyond the means of the average citizen was considered elitist and undemocratic. On the other hand, few devotees of wine were willing to forego their beverage. To resolve these conflicts, wine drinkers promoted the planting of American vineyards in the hope that the United States could produce a cheap, native wine. Men such as Thomas Jefferson, John Calhoun, and Henry Clay experimented with grapes on their own land, encouraged others to do so, and invited European vintners to immigrate to America to establish vineyards. During the 1820s vintner's guides proliferated, and numerous periodicals printed recipes for making wine. Journalist Hezekiah Niles, one of the leaders of this movement, prophesied that in time the United States would produce all its own wine.[12]

This promotional campaign was not without results. In 1805, with Jefferson's blessing, Swiss vintners founded Vevay, Indiana, on the Ohio River below Cincinnati. Underfinanced and inexperienced in American agriculture, these vintners produced wine that was pronounced by visitors to be "of an inferior quality," "poor stuff," and "too sour to drink." After this experiment failed, another attempt was made by Nicholas Longworth, the great-grandfather of the man of the same name who married Theodore Roosevelt's daughter Alice.

Longworth, Ohio's wealthiest citizen, used much of his money to create an American wine industry in southwestern Ohio. He tried to avoid the mistakes made at Vevay, and while he imported European vintners to tend his vines, he shrewdly decided to graft European grapes onto native stock rather than to use European roots that tended to rot in the American climate. By 1850, his own Hamilton County accounted for 35,000 of the 150,000 gallons of wine produced in the United States east of California. But though his vines survived and he produced a modest quantity of passable wine, the venture was never a commercial success. The native stocks yielded poor quality grapes, and the vintners deserted his employ to establish their own vineyards and farms.[13]

Such failures did not deter perennial optimists like Georgetown's John Adlum, whose own wine was described by a connoisseur as "a fine palatable *liquor;* but . . . inferior to the weak clarets of Bordeaux, or the red wines of the Rhine." His vineyard's twenty-two varieties of grapes yielded little except complimentary bottles for high government officials. Although officeholders, embarrassed at serving foreign wines to the diplomatic corps, encouraged Adlum, he was unable to parlay gifts of his wine into congressional financial backing for a proposed book on wine making. Undaunted by this failure, he continued to declare that American viticulture would triumph, asserting that by 1900, when Virginia and the Southwest had as many acres in vineyards as France, they would produce as much wine as that country. Adlum was not the last publicist to seek the grail. As late as 1851 Senator Stephen A. Douglas stated enthusiastically that "the United States will, in a very short time, produce good wine, so cheap, and in such abundance, as to render it a common and daily beverage."[14]

Douglas aside, such rhetoric waned after 1830, as the well-to-do who had promoted American wine making began to recognize that the country was not destined for viticulture. People began to press for lower wine duties, some in the hope that cheap foreign wine would lure Americans away from distilled spirits; others, particularly farmers, in the hope that decreased tariffs would encourage overseas trade and increase the export of American foodstuffs to wine producing areas like the Canary Islands. After 1829, when Congress reduced duties from an average of 50¢ to an average of 30¢ a gallon, lower prices did combine with prosperity to stimulate wine consumption, which rose during the 1830s to a modest annual three-tenths gallon per person. This increase appalled those who had advocated wine in lieu of distilled spirits when they discovered that former whiskey drinkers were getting drunk on fortified wine. Purveyors were finding it profitable to mix expensive wine with cheap whiskey to create a fortified product that was 20 to 30 percent alcohol. This concoction was sometimes cut with water to produce a still potent beverage and large profits. Indeed, fortification, watering, and adulteration were so common that it was estimated that Americans drank five times as much 'Madeira' as was imported. The high potency and adulteration of the wine sold in America led antispirits crusaders to sacrifice it on the altar of teetotalism. In addition, temperance men who had preached that the poor should give up whiskey while the rich might continue to drink wine came to recognize the inconsistency of their position. Madeira drinkers, pointed out one democrat, "should not be so ready to deprive the laboring man of his drink." Reformers finally concluded that the wine-drinking upper classes had to set an example by renouncing their own drink. By the 1840s teetotalism had caused the consumption of wine to fall by half, and many Americans concluded that divine will had decreed the failure of their country's vineyards.[15]

Beer, like wine, was advocated as a substitute for distilled spirits. As early as 1788 Benjamin Rush had calculated that the best hope for his antispirits crusade was to persuade Americans who found wine too costly to drink beer, a beverage that could be brewed in America and that the masses could afford. The Philadelphia physician's argument that beer was more healthful than distilled spirits was popularized both by late eighteenth-century agricultural improvement associations and by agricultural guides, which were then a new and powerful force for modernization and change. One of the guides flatly called beer "the most wholesome beveradge" and went on to advise farm owners that if they replaced cider and spirits with beer their workers would be able to perform "double the labour, with half the fatigue."[16] Farmers were also told that a switch from rum to beer would improve morals, reduce imports, and create a new market for 2.25 million bushels of barley. This campaign received official support in the 1790s when the federal government levied duties and excises on wine and spirits but not on beer.[17]

Despite Rush's propaganda, agricultural guides, and tax incentives, little beer was brewed. Neither the manuals to instruct Americans in the art of brewing nor the encouragement of presidents Jefferson and Madison furthered the cause. In 1810, annual per capita consumption of beer was less than 1 gallon; today, it is more than 18 gallons. Furthermore, the little beer that was consumed was not distributed evenly around the country. In Philadelphia, the nation's premier brewing center, beer was "the common table drink of every family in easy circumstances." It was also popular in New York, Albany, Pittsburgh, and Cincinnati; indeed, the states of New York and Pennsylvania produced three-fourths of the nation's beer. Elsewhere the beverage was "not a fashion of the country." Lack of customers hampered the development of the industry because a low sales volume kept the price high, so high at times that beer cost more than whiskey. In Cincinnati 18¢ would buy either a bottle of beer or more than a half gallon of whiskey. On Long Island, New York, William Cobbett calculated that it cost 7 pence to homebrew a gallon of ale and about six times as much to buy a gallon of whiskey. Since drinks made with spirits were customarily diluted, whiskey would make a cheaper refreshment than beer.[18]

Although beer was expensive, the brewing industry was not particularly profitable. Breweries required a high capital investment, as much as $3000 being necessary to establish a brewery that produced only 4,500 gallons a year. One Washington brewer reported that such an operation would yield only a 50 percent return at the current, low level of sales, a poor use of capital. A retailer, by contrast, could realize a 100 percent return on his sales with little or no capital. Consequently, capitalists were deterred from investing in breweries and turned to other industries, including distilling. Furthermore, breweries required skilled labor, a major difficulty in a country where labor was expensive and maintaining a stable work force impossible; it took years of apprenticeship to become a skilled brewmaster, and, as foreigners observed, Americans lacked a sense of craft; and a brewery owner had no guarantee that his brewmaster would not leave suddenly for some other, unrelated, higher-paying job. Another problem was the American climate, which forced brewers who needed a cool brewhouse to close down during the long, hot summers. One reason that Milwaukee emerged as a brewing center was that it had relatively short summers. Then, too, beer was so bulky, expensive to transport, and difficult to store that it needed a concentrated market, and at the time most Americans lived on farms dispersed across the countryside. Finally, beer spoiled easily. Because of the high price of bottles, beer was usually sold in 16-gallon kegs or 31-gallon barrels, but few taverns could sell that much before the beer turned sour and flat.[19]

In addition to these economic handicaps, American brewers suffered from a technical difficulty. Before 1840 they employed an English method of brewing in which fermentation was produced by a yeast that floated on the top of a vat of barley malt. To the brewers' exasperation, this process did not work well in America. The yeast interacted with the air and produced a bitter brew that was ill-tasting, cloudy, and without sparkle. Contemporaries disputed the cause of the poor results. The problem, according to Yale scientist Benjamin Silliman, was that American breweries used smaller vats than their English counterparts. American vats exposed too great a proportion of their contents to the top-floating yeast and to the air that operated upon it. Others argued that the problem was the American climate. In any event, the difficulty was not solved until the 1840s, when German immigrants introduced a new kind of yeast that sank to the bottom of the vat and, hence, was not exposed to the air. This beer did not turn bitter. The Germans called their beer lager, because it was aged in a cool store room for several weeks. During the forties few native-born Americans drank this lager beer, but its popularity in the following decade led the protemperance *New York Times*, October 15, 1856, to warn that lager was "getting a good deal too fashionable." Its popularity continued to rise, especially after the Civil War, when the high taxes on spirits and nostalgic memories of wartime Union Army lager beer rations stimulated its sales. The German brewers, particularly those located in Milwaukee, exploited this new, larger market. Today's major breweries, such as Anheuser-Busch, Schlitz, Pabst, Schaefer, and Miller (originally Müller), bear the names of German immi-

German Beer Garden.

grants of the mid-nineteenth century. Of the older, pre-lager brewing tradition, little has survived, except the Ballantine Ale label and the college founded by Poughkeepsie brewer Matthew Vassar.[20]

During the early nineteenth century whiskey's only rival as the national beverage came from apple orchards. Trees planted on farms in Virginia, Pennsylvania, parts of Ohio and New York, and throughout New England produced a glut of apples. On the Erie Canal this fruit was "floating away on the Water;" in eastern Ohio apples lay "so thick that at every step you must tread upon them." Plentiful supplies inhibited local sales, while high shipping costs and spoilage, before the railroad era, prohibited sales in a distant market. Consequently, apples had such little value that they were usually free for the picking. The farmer found this annual crop to be an embarrassment of riches. He could dry his fruit, but that process was not popular, and he usually sent his apples to the cider press.[21]

Throughout the apple country, farmers pressed their fruit on wooden frames that stood in nearly every orchard. In contrast with brewing, which required substantial capital, skilled labor, and a local, densely populated market, cider making was so easy, cheap, and low skilled that a farmer could afford to press apples strictly for family use. Cider was not usually marketed because its bulk made its shipment unprofitable; hence, little was drunk in the South or in cities. Where the beverage was available, however, it was cheap, often selling for as little as 50¢ a barrel. Even at Pittsburgh, where it cost $3 to $4 a barrel, it was only half the price of local beer. Though inexpensive, it was highly alcoholic: to avoid spoilage it was fortified with distilled spirits until it contained at least 10 percent alcohol, twice as much as beer. There were even stronger forms: cider royal, which was hard cider mixed with distilled apple brandy or whiskey, and applejack, which was the 20 percent alcoholic liquor that could be poured off after cider had been set outside to freeze on an autumn night.[22]

The rural North loved cider. The beverage was "omnipresent," with a pitcher on every table and a jug in every field. During the winter, a typical New England family could be expected to consume a barrel a week. So prevalent was cider that it became a symbol of egalitarianism as "the common drink of . . . rich and poor alike." Even crusty John Adams, who railed against distilled spirits for a half century, drank a tankardful every morning. Cider was so popular that Americans tended to look askance at anyone who chose to drink imported wine instead. Americans heralded their sparkling amber beverage as a cousin to champagne, indeed such a close

Drinking Cider.

relative that cider had "oftentimes been passed on *knowing* Europeans." These visitors, alas, were no doubt those who denounced the nation's terrible, sour champagne.[23]

Cider and whiskey were America's most popular drinks. Both were cheap and plentiful where available, and because they were processed in the United States from home-grown products, both benefited from nationalistic sentiment. As we have seen, water was usually of poor quality, milk often scarce or unsafe, and coffee, tea, and wine imported and expensive. To have preferred cider or whiskey over these beverages seems natural enough. But why, when they had the choice, did Americans drink cider or whiskey rather than beer, which was also a domestic product and comparatively cheap? The answer, I believe, is that Americans preferred cider and whiskey because those drinks contained more alcohol than beer, which was too weak for American taste. As already noted, when Americans did drink wine, they drank highly alcoholic varieties, often fortified with distilled spirits, and seldom below 20 percent alcohol. One can only conclude that at the root of the alcoholic republic was the fact that Americans chose the most highly alcoholic beverages that they could obtain easily and cheaply.

The taste for strong drink was no doubt enhanced by the monotony of the American diet, which was dominated by corn. In the winter Americans ate dried, parched corn kernels; in the summer, roasted green ears; in the autumn, freshly boiled golden ripe ears dripping with melted butter. But it was corn pummeled into hominy or ground into meal that was ever present at all seasons. It appeared on the table three times a day as fried johnny cakes or corn bread, Indian pudding with milk and sugar, or the ubiquitous corn mush. Ordinary bread was baked with flour compounded of corn and rye; bread made with white wheat flour was a luxury for the rich or for special occasions. Corn was also fed to the hogs, and the hog meat was eaten in the form of salt pork, smoked ham, and lard. Each day, it was calculated, the typical adult American ate a pound of bread, most often made with corn meal, and a pound of meat, usually salt pork.[24]

This proportion of meat in the diet was probably the highest in the world. Americans were sufficiently prosperous that they could afford to raise stock or to buy meat, and meat was cheap because of open grazing amid sparse settlement, but the high consumption of meat also showed a preference for the taste of meat, especially salt pork. That Americans liked meat is clear from the fact that on festive occasions, when they might have been expected to indulge their whims, they chose to have barbecued pigs, beefs, oxen, or game birds, or burgoos, which were meat stews concocted of pork, beef, venison, and fowl. Although there were many species of fish in western rivers, most frontiersmen rejected even an occasional fish dinner in favor of a steady and continuous diet of salt pork. Similarly, many farmers who might have kept both hogs and poultry refused to be troubled with chickens, ducks, geese, or turkeys. There were a few who objected to so much meat. Among them was Dr. Benjamin Rush, who had observed that the healthy and robust Pennsylvania Dutch ate a varied diet that included large quantities of turnips, onions, and sauerkraut. One of Rush's dietary followers was Thomas Jefferson, who wrote that he ate "little animal food, and that . . . as a condiment for the vegetables, which constitute my principal diet." But Rush and Jefferson were exceptions. Most Americans believed so strongly in "the eternal hog meat" that slaveholders among them gave their slaves generous rations of pork fat as well as corn meal, and, until later in the century, prison officials fed inmates meat stews with their corn mush.[25]

The monotonous corn and pork diet of the average American was only occasionally varied. Sometimes frontiersmen had forest game such as deer or wild turkey, while those who lived near the ocean enjoyed local delicacies such as oysters. On holidays such as Thanksgiving there might be apple sauce, pumpkin pie, or plum puddings. In the summer the kitchen garden yielded onions, cabbages, and potatoes, but not tomatoes, which during the early nineteenth century were thought to be poisonous. Autumn brought peaches, pears, and apples. Seasonal fruits and vegetables were eaten fresh because of the difficulty of preserving them. While most farmers kept a cow, the milk usually went to the children. Adults had to be content with butter, which was at times so rancid that it turned black. One frontiersman recalled that "skimmed milk brought three miles to eat with hominy for a meal, seemed a luxury." Some families kept chickens either for the eggs or to honor occasional dinner guests. All these items were supplements to the basic diet of 'hog and hominy.' When the supplements were out of season or failed, people did without.[26]

In Jefferson City, the capital of Missouri, an astonished traveller found it impossible to "obtain any provisions except salt pork, biscuits, and whisky." The shortage of such items as milk, sugar, or fresh meat led to the use of substitutes. A lack of milk on the hardscrabble frontier meant that corn mush might be served with molasses, maple syrup, or even oil obtained from the blubbery fat of a bear. In the spring, before the corn crop came in, pioneers who were forced to turn from agriculture to hunting might call venison "bread" and bear flesh "meat." Erratic food supplies often led to odd combinations. One Ohio vagabond was spotted on the highway carrying a knapsack of bread and cheese and a canteen of distilled spirits, while Philadelphia railroad laborers were known to dine on watermelons, cucumbers, and whiskey. A Swedish visitor to the Alabama frontier was served a three-course dinner that began with pickled pigs feet, advanced to bacon and molasses, and concluded with a main course of milk and black bread soaked in whiskey. Foreigners who suffered through such experiences had no fondness for American cookery. "I had never undergone such gastronomic privations," wrote one, "as in the western parts of America."[27]

Even where food was abundant, its preservation was difficult or impossible. Before the middle of the century home canning was unknown, but even if the process had been developed, its widespread use would have been precluded by the high prices of glass jars and sugar. Nor was there cold storage except for primitive burial. Plentiful seasonal fruits, especially peaches and apples, had to be eaten fresh, dried, or, more commonly, converted into mild alcoholic beverages. Without refrigeration food spoiled very rapidly in the scorching American summers. Cheese melted into unappetizing blobs and morning-fresh cow's milk soured by mid-afternoon. Climatic conditions favored dry, salty foods that did not spoil readily, such as parched corn, smoked hams, or salt pork.[28]

Cooking techniques were primitive. Before 1850, for example, corn bread was usually fried in a skillet over a fire rather than baked because most households had no stove and no ovens except cumbersome, portable Dutch ovens that were placed over the open hearth. With rudimentary equipment and no way to control the temperature of the fire, it is not surprising that roasted meats, oven-baked bread, and cakes were rare. Such a simple baking aid as yeast was little known, and even the baking soda or pearlash methods by which heavy, hard to digest, 'salt risin' ' bread could be made were not universally known. One Illinois pioneer was quizzed by an ignorant neighbor on the pearlash technique. "They say," said the inquirer, ". . . you put a lot of nasty truck in your bread. It is what you keep in a bottle, purlass, I believe, is the name, and they say it is full of dead flies, and bugs, and cricket legs." With this challenge, Christiana Tillson produced her "little bottle of dissolved pearl ash, looking so clear and pure." Such neighborly exchanges were the principal means of spreading information about cookery. Recipe books were only beginning to appear, and they often advised the most primitive procedures. Amelia Simmons, for example, suggested that to prepared a 'syllabub' one should "Sweeten a quart of cyder with double refined sugar, grate nutmeg into it, then milk your cow into your liquor . . . [and] pour half a pint or more . . . of the sweetest cream you can get all over it."[29]

Without ovens for roasting and baking, American

cooks had to either boil or fry. Boiling, however, was never popular with American cooks, who tended to be in a hurry. They preferred the quicker method of frying food in pork lard or butter. Fried foods became the American gastronomic speciality, and the country's breakfasts, dinners, and suppers were soon floating in "extraordinary rivers of butter and oceans of grease." Everywhere, every thing that was cooked was fried. Fried fish, chicken, ham, salt pork, beefsteak, eggs, johnny cakes, and mush poured forth from the nation's kitchens. Never have so many sung the praises of lard. To one traveller who faced bread that arrived at the breakfast table already afloat "in a menstruum of oleaginous matter," it seemed that grease entered "largely into the composition of every dish;" it constituted "the sole ingredient of many." These remarks should sound familiar, for our love of grease persists, as shown by the success of Colonel Sanders' fried chicken and McDonald's hamburgers and french fries.[30]

Heavy, oily foods, especially fried corn cakes and salt pork, left Americans in need of a complementary beverage, and the commonest turned out to be whiskey. The strength of its flavor overcame the blandness of corn mush and johnny cakes, while its sweetness neutralized the unpleasant puckering effects of salt pork. Its high proportion of alcohol warmed the throat and cleansed the mouth of layers of clammy grease. Tradition taught that spirituous liquor aided digestion, and Americans who indulged in starchy fried foods needed an aid to digestion. In addition, whiskey was a refreshing potion that helped break the monotony of a corn and pork diet. Furthermore, in a country where food supplies were sometimes erratic, whiskey could, at 83 calories an ounce, provide a substantial part of an American's daily food requirements. Finally, whiskey shared with pork a common origin in the corn cult. Indian maize was a native, American grain that provided corn bread, corn-fed meat, and corn-made drink. These three were an American's "common necessaries."[31]

Taking strong drink to accompany a meaty, greasy, fat-laden diet was only one of the nation's peculiar eating habits. Americans also had a propensity for 'rapid eating.' Foreigners observed that Americans who ate in hotels and taverns often finished their meals in less than five minutes, before the visitors had been comfortably seated. This haste reflected a lack of interest in food; no one examined, smelled, or tasted it. At the table people neither drank nor talked, and the silence of the meal was broken only by the hurried passing of dishes and the rapid movement of dozens of jaws in unison. "As soon as food is set on the table," wrote one traveller, "they fall upon it like wolves on an unguarded herd. With the knife in the right hand, they cut and bring vegetables and sometimes meat as well to their mouths. With the fork in the left hand, they deliver meat without interruption to the teeth."[32] It was an honor for a man to be the first to leave the table, in order to rush to the bar for hours of leisurely drinking. No wonder Americans preferred spirits to food, an idea aptly expressed in a bit of doggerel sung to the tune of "Home, Sweet Home":[33]

> *Mid plenty of bacon and bread tho' we jog,*
> *Be it ever so strong, there's nothing like grog.*
> *A shot from the jug sends such joy to the heart,*
> *No eating on earth could such pleasure impart.*
> *Grog, grog, sweet, sweet grog.*
> *There's nothing like grog, there's nothing like grog.*

While eating in an American hotel, English phrenologist George Combe observed 150 people down breakfast in less than fifteen minutes. As he lingered over his own meal contemplating this scene, he was accosted. "You Europeans," said the American, "eat as if you actually

Rapid eating.

enjoyed your food!" The Englishman replied, "As-
suredly we do—and you Americans will never escape
from dyspepsia and headaches until you also learn to
enjoy your meals." It is doubtful that the American believed him, for few Americans thought that happiness
could be achieved through the pleasures of the table. Eating was a bodily chore, a burden of nature, an animal
function that was to be concluded as rapidly and pain-
lessly as possible. While this attitude resulted, at least in
part, from the prevalence of poorly prepared, ill-tasting
food, it also encouraged the kind of cookery that led to
such an attitude. Gastronomic satisfaction was further
reduced because the speedy ingestion of salt pork and
fried corn cakes tended to produce headaches, nausea,
and upset stomachs. Indigestion was very common and
was widely blamed on seasonal fevers, bad water, or
overexertion. Dyspepsia, like other illnesses, was commonly treated by drinking whiskey.[34]

These peculiar dietary attitudes and habits were essential aspects of American culture, and I believe that they were the result of underlying tensions within American society. This can be seen more clearly if we examine what happened to American eating habits after 1830, when they were attacked by temperance zealots. Benjamin Rush had advocated substituting vegetables for salt pork in order to reduce the intake of distilled spirits, but by the thirties a number of reformers had moved from Rush's moderate stand against meat to a vigorous vegetarianism. Furthermore, those opposed to liquor tried to root out wine and brandy from American cookery. Cookbooks published after 1830 had fewer recipes using liquor, and some became totally dry. Mrs. Sarah J. Hale, among the more fanatical, advised her readers, "I have not allowed a drop to enter into any of the recipes contained in this book." One of her later works did present some cake recipes that used alcohol, but everyone recognized that baking dissipated the liquor. Purists, however, stood firmly on principle, as when the Massachusetts Temperance Almanac banned brandy from its mince meat pies and labeled them 'temperance pies.' Hostility to alcohol evolved into attacks on tea and coffee. Finally, Oberlin College pursued dietary reform to an ultimate by proscribing not only alcohol, meat, tea, and coffee, but also gravy, butter, fish, and pepper.[35]

Dietary reformers banned articles that they regarded as stimulants. Such items as whiskey, meat, and coffee, they feared, would overstimulate the emotional faculties, unleash uncontrollable passions, and destroy the capacity for doing God's labors. Proper stimulation came from the Bible, not at the table. What man needed was a nutritional diet that would subdue passion. The belief that proper food was to be found in the vegetable rather than the animal kingdom may have followed from the belief that the eating of animal food made a man animalistic.

This idea was rooted both in experience, where fiery spirits were perceived to kindle burning passions, and in theory, where the notion of animal magnetism suggested that objects containing similar qualities were attracted to each other. The rejection of meat, however, was also symbolic: it signified the march of progress, since the grain-eating agriculturalist was perceived to be more civilized than the meat-eating hunter. Reformers wanted man to be a grain eater so he would be a replenishing creature, sowing his heavenly inspired good deeds across the earth. The quest for a godly diet culminated in Sylvester Graham's experiments with grain, as this one-time state agent for the Pennsylvania Temperance Society mixed a variety of grains to create a wholesome, nutritious, dark-colored flour that became the forerunner of the graham cracker. Three of the most prominent reformers of the era, Sarah Grimké and her sister and brother-in-law, Angelina and Theodore Weld, followed the Graham diet at their New Jersey commune.[36]

"In the creed of a Teetotal," wrote one opponent, ". . . abstinence is the grand specific for reformation." To deny use was to advance; to prohibit was to progress. Feeling and emotion must be subjugated to rules and ritual. In the emerging social order, everything not "needful or useful" was to be rejected. From drink to diet to all aspects of life the prohibitionist mentality spread. It was a time when "to be natural was next to being called a 'natural-born fool.' It was an age of pure art,—the art of walking *uprightly*, with *unbending* joints; the art of shaking hands after the 'pump-handle' formula; the art of looking inexpressibly indifferent towards every body and every thing."[37]

The severity of self-denial and the repression of emotion that were practiced after 1830 suggest the existence of strong underlying feelings that, in the eyes of the temperance reformers, had to be suppressed and controlled lest they threaten the social order. I believe that these same strong feelings and related tensions can be seen before 1830 in the rapidity with which Americans dispatched wretched food, in the rush from the dining room to the bar, and in the widespread preference for strong drink. Habits such as these indicate to me something more than the lack of adequate cooking equipment and good cooks: Americans had psychological needs that were met better by alcohol than by food. The disdain for food and the taste for whiskey were signs, just as vegetarianism was a sign in later years, of the currents of emotion that ran fast but submerged in American life.

THE ANXIETIES
OF THEIR CONDITION

The [drinking] habits thus acquired grew out
of the anxieties of their condition.

EDWARD BOURNE
1875

We have seen that Americans in the early nineteenth century had inherited a hearty drinking tradition, that an overabundance of corn on the western frontier had encouraged the production of cheap, plentiful whiskey, and that whiskey had become important in the American diet. While these circumstances provided Americans with the opportunity to consume great quantities of distilled spirits, they do not explain why so many Americans so readily availed themselves of that opportunity. The question of motivation cannot be answered conclusively, but some inferences can be made by examining in greater detail the drinking habits of those Americans who belonged to the heaviest drinking segments of society. Robust drinking often had roots in conditions peculiar to the early nineteenth century. It was, among other things, a period of unprecedented change for which, I believe, the traditional society of the time was institutionally, ideologically, and psychologically unprepared. Between 1790 and 1830 almost every aspect of American life underwent alteration, in many cases startling upheaval. The impact of change on some social groups was greater than on others, and it becomes apparent in a study of the period that those groups most severely affected by change were also the groups most given to heavy drinking.

The single most important change with the most far reaching consequences was the rapid growth of population. The number of inhabitants in the new republic was doubling every twenty-three years. Although this rate of increase was no greater than during the colonial period, its effects were much more pronounced because of the larger population base. Between 1790 and 1810, when the population rose from almost four million to more than seven million, the increase alone nearly equalled the total increase since European settlement began. Because America was an agrarian society, this growth in population had to be accompanied by proportionate gains in cultivated acreage in order to maintain the standard of living. Geometric population growth necessitated the cultivation of new land at a greatly accelerated rate. In other words, between 1790 and 1810 it was necessary to bring into production almost as many acres as had been planted in the preceding two centuries.[1]

The dispersion of a burgeoning population in search of arable land was socially destabilizing. Pioneers who needed acreage were forced to cross the Appalachian Mountains, and, as we have seen, whereas eighteenth-century settlers had been able to locate on rivers and streams that drained into the Atlantic, these migrants to the West found themselves cut off from eastern trade and markets. The economic, social, and political ties that had bound the seaports and the hinterlands into an Atlantic community could not reach across the Appalachians. For the first time, significant numbers of Americans lived apart from the influences of traditional society. In 1790 only one hundred thousand of four million Americans resided in the West; by 1810 one million of seven million did. In that year, before steamboats, canals, or railroads, more Americans lived in isolation and independence than ever before or since. It should not be surprising that these isolated and lonely western pioneers had a reputation for drinking more alcoholic beverages than residents of other sections of the country.[2]

During the early nineteenth century the vast majority of Americans worked on the soil, either as farm owners or as hired hands. Traditionally, the farm laborer was a young man who expected to become a farm owner. If he saved his pay from several seasons of harvest labor, he could buy animals and implements, marry, and purchase a farm or move west to clear and settle virgin land. It was this expectation of becoming a landholder, I believe, that enabled him to accept with equanimity the years of hard work and low annual earnings that he faced while he worked on other men's land. But after 1790, when the demand for land increased, the price of land in settled areas must have increased. Frontier settlement also became more difficult, because settlers had to cross the Appalachians at great effort and expense. At the same time, increases in land speculation and title disputes in the West must have discouraged people from migrating. The principal effect of all of these circumstances was to diminish the chance of a farm laborer from acquiring his own farm.[3]

The lot of a farm hand was very different from that of his employer. The owner of a farm was rooted in the soil, tied to his community, a family patriarch, and a faithful observer of the seasons. Nature's rhythmic cycles assured him that what he sowed in the spring and nurtured through the summer he would reap in the autumn. Harvest was the culmination of a seasonal cycle that made his rural world secure in a pattern of continuity. The farmer had "comfort and freedom from anxiety." To the farm laborer, on the other hand, nature's rhythm meant little. He reaped only what others had sown, and harvest to him was only a brief period of exhausting

labor with good pay whose transitory nature confirmed his view that life was chaotic. After harvest he faced a long, inactive, uncertain winter. Is it any wonder that farm hands turned to strong drink? They were among the greatest consumers of alcohol; farm owners, at least in the North, were among those least likely to drink heartily or to excess.[4]

Rapid population growth was accompanied by unprecedented urban development. From 1790 to 1830 the number of cities with at least 5,000 people increased from eight to forty-five. While in 1790 cities of this size were all Atlantic seaports, by 1830 a number of such cities were in the interior, and some, such as Cincinnati, had not even existed in 1790. The inhabitants of these new cities tried to copy the culture of the older seaports by instituting colleges, theaters, literary guilds, and daily newspapers, but they could not create the established families, endowed institutions, and settled economies that only time and a slower rate of growth could bring. Perhaps more important than the rise of so many small cities was the rapid growth of the largest urban centers. From 1790 to 1830 the population of greater Philadelphia leaped from 40,000 to 160,000; that of New York from 30,000 to 200,000. People who lived in these huge cities suffered from inept government, poor sanitation, chaotic social conditions, and a sense of alienation. Colonial seaports had been governed through informal channels by a commercial elite that had provided aid to the poor and funds for the construction of public docks, warehouses, and other community improvements. As urban population grew, the proportion of the old, wealthy elite lessened, their influence waned, and nineteenth-century cities found it difficult to maintain order and suitable living conditions. With the collapse of elitist paternalism, the loss of guild controls, and the decline of neighborliness, city dwellers were increasingly bewildered, frustrated, and isolated amid a sea of strange faces. And all the available evidence suggests that Americans who lived in cities and towns drank more than their rural neighbors.[5]

Dramatic changes also occurred in transportation. Steamboats, canals, and, later, railroads created a new, national economy: these innovations lowered shipping costs, and thereby destroyed local markets by encouraging people to buy cheap goods manufactured in distant places rather than more expensive goods produced locally. As Americans began to participate in a national market economy, they discovered that custom and tradition became less important and that they were subject to such indeterminate forces as outside competition and fluctuations of the business cycle. The development of a national market spurred manufacturing, which between 1810 and 1840 tripled in the value of its output. Increased production was accompanied by a change in in-

New York's Five Points in 1829. By permission of Alfred A. Knopf, Inc.

dustrial methods. Whereas farm families had once spun yarn or woven cloth at home during seasonal lulls, by 1840 textiles were more often than not made in factories. Large-scale mills and factories also made machinery, sugar, paper, glass, pottery, drugs, paints, and dyes. While these new establishments were widely praised as symbols of progress, factory workers who had previously lived on farms found the discipline of factory work to be new and unsettling. Long, regular hours and dull, unvaried work away from home were in contrast to agricultural labor, with its extensive family contact, variety of tasks, slower pace, and periods of comparative leisure alternating with periods of frenzied activity. It appears that many factory workers met these new conditions by turning to heavy drinking.[6]

Skilled craftsmen were also adversely affected by the upheavals of the early nineteenth century. The authority of master craftsmen over journeymen and apprentices eroded, the growth of cities made it easier for apprentices to desert and escape successfully, and the booming cities of the West attracted workmen who became disgruntled with their employers. The most significant change, however, was the rise of the factory system, which destroyed customary relationships among craftsmen. Apprentices observed that masters employed more youths than they could properly train to become journeymen with the intention of exploiting cheap, unskilled labor rather than training workmen. And journeymen discovered that the amount of capital needed to establish a shop was becoming so large that they had no expectation of ever becoming their own masters. In the printing industry, for example, the introduction of new equipment raised the price of setting up a shop from less than $1,000 in 1817 to $4,000 by 1841. While an industrious, prudent journeyman might be able to save $1,000 over several years, it was unlikely that he could save $4,000. A man who wanted to open a shop found it necessary to obtain loans or political subsidies, to accept capitalists as partners, or to form a corporation. Thus was the traditional route from apprentice to journeyman to master blocked with many men stimied at the middle level.[7]

As the interests of masters and journeymen diverged, masters exploited their employees, while the journeymen themselves, having lost their expectations of becoming masters, became disillusioned and frustrated. William E. Channing warned that seeing the wealth of others provoked "a tendency to self-contempt and self-abandonment among those whose lot gives them no chance of its acquisition." Shoptime drinking, which had been traditional, began to increase. The occasions for having a drink increased from the customary 11:00 A.M. refreshener and afternoon break to a long list of celebrations: the shop must drink when a new man arrived, or an old one departed; when a man married or had a child; or when an apprentice came of age. There were numerous fines, levied in alcohol, "for the breach of certain by-laws enacted for the express purpose of obtaining liquor." Nor was imbibing limited to business hours. Each shop had its favorite spot for "midnight revelry," and on payday the workmen often were compensated in a tavern or bar, where they were encouraged to spend their earnings.[8]

Masters were alarmed. Whereas they once had been able to limit drinking on their premises through personal pleas, they now found that "noxious habits continued to increase in many places with unabated ardour, until the evil had become so great as scarcely to be endured." Some employers, usually hearty drinkers themselves, won the confidence of their thirsty workmen by providing liquor, but businesses operated that way often failed from inept and besotted management. Masters more

often tried, though with little success, to persuade work-men not to drink on the premises. When this failed, and desperation drove owners to prohibit spirits on their premises, dramshops would spring up at nearby sites. Journeymen then turned to cajoling apprentices to smug-gle liquor into the shop. "One man was stationed at the window to watch," recalled a baker, "while the rest drank."[9]

Economic adversity could whet a man's appetite for strong drink; so could startling gains and prosperity. Consider, for example, the newly wealthy cotton planters. Though it is true that a small number of colo-nial slaveholders had enjoyed a luxurious standard of liv-ing, a much larger number of them had lived at a level only moderately higher than that of their slaves. King

Cotton did not improve the lot of slaves, but it did greatly increase the number of rich planters. By 1830 thousands of newly minted overlords occupied baronial estates from the Carolinas to the Mississippi. Although these planters had unprecedented leisure and wealth, their backgrounds provided them with little training in ways of spending their time and money. They had no knowledge of the arts and sciences, no enthusiasm for manufacturing and technology, no customary pattern of spending, no cultural refinement or well-developed taste.[10]

These rich planters tried to copy the traditional manners of the colonial elite, but theirs was a pale imitation. Whereas the eighteenth-century upper class had modelled its plantation life on quasi-feudal lines, educated its most promising youth abroad, and organized its social life after the style of English gentlemen, the social life of this nouveau riche aristocracy was built on display, conspicuous consumption, and crude materialism. In one frontier Alabama town, for example, the ladies paraded through the streets in showy clothes to impress people with their husbands' wealth. It was by such ostentatious means as extravagant dress, magnificent barbecues, and palatial mansions that a southern gentleman of this order established his place in society. However, when he was not engaged in display, he returned to the pursuits of his early rural existence and spent his private life riding, hunting, and racing horses. He extolled the virtues of rural life, deplored cities and merchants, and damned his cotton broker.[11]

There were those who found this mode of life frustrating. Slaveholders were discouraged from labor by their own haughty ideal that only slaves or poor whites should work, but American tradition provided no satisfying role for idlers. The consequence was that idleness led to boredom, and boredom led the planters to seek excitement.

But excitement of the kind they craved was rare on plantations isolated from neighbors, professional entertainers, or even daily newspapers. "We have," wrote a Florida planter, "nothing . . . but whiskey." Drinking accompanied gaming, horse racing, dueling, and the pursuit of black women. "The style of manners amongst the young Virginia gentlemen," recalled one observer, "was that of riot and dissipation." Thus did planters turn the fruits of King Cotton into a new lifestyle. In the emerging southern way of life the wooden columns that ornamented the facades of the Big Houses were not all that was hollow.[12]

Amid this economic upheaval a tradition of social hierarchy was also dying. Although colonial Americans had never fully subscribed to the English class system, they had preserved class distinctions. A Virginia gentleman had been distinguished by his powdered wig and gilded carriage; a Massachusetts man's station had been indicated by whether or not he was called 'mister,' and key political offices, such as the Virginia Council of State, had been reserved for members of the upper class. The Revolution had overturned these marks of distinction and lessened the importance of caste. Because so many of the upper class had been Tories who had fled—one-quarter of the attorneys, for example—, many new people rose into the ranks of the elite, and this new elite could not very effectively argue that hierarchical status was fixed and rigid. More important, the Revolution's libertarian and egalitarian rhetoric discouraged class distinctions. The war, however, had not entirely destroyed a consciousness of classes, for inequality of mind and substance continued to separate the well-educated and wealthy from the ignorant and impoverished. During the early nineteenth century Americans were torn between the reality of inequality and the ideal of equality, and they became ambivalent about matters of class and rank.

This ambivalence can be observed in the custom of bestowing upon adult white males honorary military titles such as 'General,' 'Colonel,' 'Major,' or at the very least 'Captain.' All were to be gentlemen and officers, although some might have a higher rank than others.[13]

Physicians, ministers, and attorneys particularly suffered from the decline of social hierarchy. During the colonial period, professional men had been securely entrenched at the pinnacle of society, but the Revolution had eroded their position, and after the war they found that their elite professionalism clashed with post-Revolutionary egalitarianism. For doctors, there were other difficulties: their reputations suffered because they cured so few patients. The failure of either Benjamin Rush or his professional rivals to control the Philadelphia yellow fever epidemic of 1793 caused a widespread loss of confidence in all physicians. Declining trust in the authority and ability of orthodox medical men led to the overthrow of state licensing and the rise of new medical theories that competed with orthodox views. Vermont farmer Samuel Thomson, for example, proposed that true democrats should learn to treat themselves. This Jeffersonian, a jealous rival of the local arch-Federalist regular doctor, held that all disease was caused by an insufficiency of body heat, which he believed should be treated with hot baths, hot pepper, and brandy. While these remedies were not efficacious against most diseases, they were probably less harmful than Rush's practice of bleeding.[14]

Clergymen of the old-line sects also faced a threat to their standing. In the South after the Revolution the loss of Anglican subsidies left a void that was not easily filled. The Congregational Church was disestablished in Connecticut in 1818 and in Massachusetts in 1833, and the informal arrangements by which many Vermont and New York towns had used tax money to maintain a single orthodox church also disappeared. Traditional denominations suffered financial strains and lacked the funds to supply the 8,000 additional ministers that the country was estimated to need. On the eve of the Second Great Awakening, a series of religious revivals that occurred after 1800, many churches, in a break with the eighteenth century, refused to provide salaries that would enable ministers to live in their accustomed stylish comfort. The educated clergy discovered that they served an ever decreasing proportion of their communities and correspondingly that they were losing much of their former power and authority. The passing of the old order caused gloom and apprehension. "Our habits," wrote Congregational minister Lyman Beecher, ". . . are giving way. So many hands have so long been employed to pull away foundations, and so few to repair the breaches, that the building totters." The erudite leaders of the older denominations faced competition both from Methodist circuit riders, whose ignorance and lack of refinement often embarrassed the educated clergy, and from advocates of deism, disbelief, and other unorthodox tenets. ". . . the Unitarians in this quarter," wrote one distressed evangelical, "neither believe nor think any thing about Jesus Christ, whether he be man, angel or very God."[15]

Both ministers and physicians faced popular contempt for authority. When frontier neighbors learned that Daniel Drake was being apprenticed to a doctor, they cautioned him "against getting proud." Such public sentiments weakened the idea of a profession as a body of enlightened experts, undermined the ability of a profession to discipline its members, and compelled trained professionals to compete with untrained self-proclaimed democratic rivals, such as Thomsonians or Methodist itinerants. Physicians, not only frustrated by the dismal failure of their treatments but also incessantly invited to drink wherever they called, were reputed to be among the greatest sots. Dr. David Hosack of New York estimated that in his city 40 of 100 physicians were drunkards. "I often hear the people saying," wrote Dr. Joseph Speed of Virginia, "that they scarcely know of a single sober doctor but myself." The clergy were hardly more temperate, drinking daily for health and on Sundays to relax before preaching. Alas! One Sunday when the poor Rev. Dodge of Pomfret, Connecticut, rose to speak he collapsed on the pulpit "overcome with drunken sickness." So ended the career of one graduate of the liberal Harvard Divinity School. His experience was scarcely more embarrassing than that of a Tennessee parson who was so intoxicated at a corn husking that when asked to serve the chicken he plunged his fork into the table. Clergymen, like other mortals, fell victim to the stresses of their time.[16]

I believe that the stress of change was felt most keenly by the rising generation, that is, by those Americans born during or just after the Revolution, who came of age about 1800. Nowhere was that stress greater than on the nation's college campuses. College students, an admittedly elite minority, had to face crises that were both institutional and intellectual. Although colleges continued to emphasize curriculums designed to train youths to be ministers, students found that religious retrenchment meant that their degrees no longer entitled them to positions in the ministry. The proportion of graduates entering the ministry declined from one-third in the half century before 1770 to one-sixth in the decade after 1800. This decline in positions for graduates was accompanied by a growing belief that the college's traditional role, that of educating an elite class, was in conflict with the Revolutionary concept of equality. Students steeped in ideals of liberty and equality had contempt for institutions whose outmoded curriculums, old-fashioned teachers, and predilection for training clergymen were survivals from colonial times. Tom Paine's irreligious radicalism was the height of fashion among the idealistic young. The trouble was that many of Paine's doctrines were alien to American tradition and offered students no mechanism for realizing the Revolutionary ideals of equality and liberty. Before Thomas Jefferson's election to the presidency in 1800, some students found that his ideas expressed their idealism; at liberal Harvard, Benjamin Tappan became an ardent democrat. After Jefferson succeeded to the presidency, his political maneuverings made him less useful as a hero for the young; perhaps that was why Tappan's younger brother William had no idealism and became a drunkard.[17]

This post-Revolutionary generation of students indulged in unprecedented lusty drinking. One spirits-loving collegian informed the president of Dartmouth "that the least quantity he could put up with . . . was from two to three pints daily." Worse than the amount of imbibing was the atmosphere that surrounded it, for students mixed their daily bouts of intoxication with swearing, gaming, licentiousness, and rioting. Consequently, college officials strengthened rules against the consumption of alcohol. Whereas the College of William and Mary in 1752 had warned students to drink hard liquor with moderation, after 1800 most colleges banned spirits altogether. At Union College, for example, the fine for bringing spirits onto campus was set at $1 in 1802, raised to $3 by 1815, and altered to a fine or suspension in 1821. Such regulations proved ineffective because students resisted the authority of college officers whom they no longer respected. A series of disturbances at the University of Virginia led one irate gentleman of the Old Dominion to suggest that "the place ought speedily to be burnt down as a horrible nuisance." Perhaps this Virginian got the idea from Princeton, where the students were suspected of setting fire to the main college hall. In any event, drunkenness and rioting had become ways for students to show contempt for institutions that failed to provide them with a useful, up-to-date, republican education.[18]

Among the lustiest consumers of alcohol were stage drivers, lumberjacks, river boatmen, and canal builders. Men engaged in these occupations shared one common trait: they were members of a new, mobile class without customs, roots, or social ties. They lacked the means by which other, better organized men could lessen the impact of change. When members of a cohesive group, such as journeymen artisans, were threatened by economic dislocation, the group could at least protest as a body. Social solidarity made it easier to identify a target to attack; if they failed, their unity provided some solace, for 'misery loves company.' And men in a traditional, cohesive group could respond creatively. Journeymen artisans, for example, became so class conscious during the 1830s that they formed unions, published periodicals, and created a political organization, the Workingmen's Party. For artisans, the rise of factories had enhanced group identity and encouraged organization for the purpose of trying to control the destiny of the group. For mobile laborers, on the other hand, life was more chaotic. They were restless, rootless men who led lonely and unstructured lives. They had no way of joining together to help one another; they had no group identity; no social identity; they were 'nowhere men.' As a consequence they expressed their frustrations outside social channels. This anomic existence, lawless and alienated from society, gave rise to acute drinking.[19]

Consider the plight of stage drivers. A driver's life was miserable, often boring, for much of the time he waited in the tavern for sufficient cargo or passengers to make a trip. When on the road he drove over bumpy tracks through the woods, splattered by mud, chilled by wind, and often soaked by rain or snow. Although he might live in a town, he worked alone on the road, under wretched conditions, remote from family and friends. His work was detached from society, except for his passengers, many of whom were rude and unreasonable people who cursed him for jostling them. They were strangers he would never see again. Not surprisingly, the driver turned to alcohol. He had a drink whenever he stopped to water the horses at a wayside inn, and often he travelled with a whiskey bottle on the seat beside him. While journeying from Nashville to Alexandria, Virginia, one passenger noted that only one driver had not drunk on the road. "It was well," concluded the traveller, "the horses were sober!"[20]

Like stage drivers, lumberjacks were rootless. They lived in jerrybuilt camps in remote forests; when the timber was gone, they moved on. In the early nineteenth century the growth of population and business activity created an ever greater demand for lumber, and logging increased. As timber cutting spread to remote parts of Maine and Pennsylvania, lumberjacks became increasingly isolated. Alone in the forests, they turned to liquor. It was said that enough rum was consumed in one Maine lumber town annually "to float the whole village off." The drinkers of this town had a 'temperance society' that pledged "every one who should get drunk to treat the rest all around." Such incessant drinking by the lumberjacks enabled timber barons to increase their profits by paying their workers in liquor rather than cash. No matter that the lumberjacks lost a part of their wages; they reveled in spirits. A drunken timber cutter on a spree forgot the dangers of his work and the disadvantages of his rootless, anomic state. One observer of lumberjacks wrote, "He never planted; he knows not its pleasures. A tree of his own planting would be good for nothing in his estimation, for it would never during his life be large enough to fell. It is by destruction he lives; he is a destroyer wherever he goes."[21]

Then there were the boatmen who plied the western rivers with keelboats and rafts. For a generation, from the beginning of western river commerce to the arrival of the steamboat after the War of 1812, they held sway over the main trade routes. While they had seized the initiative in western trade, they were incapable of maintaining their preeminence when the modes of transportation changed. It is easy to understand why. The typical boatman combined mobility with frontier exuberance, cockiness, restlessness, and daring. These qualities were accompanied by deficiencies that insured his doom, for the boatman's independence made him overconfident and unreliable; his individualism inhibited him from organizing with other boatmen to protect himself; and his ignorance barred him from effective participation in the increasingly complex economy. Underlying these characteristics was the boatman's lack of age-old tradition and social ties to other groups in society, his inability to view himself as part of any group or tradition, in short, his anomie. On the river he literally floated outside society.[22]

The boatman lacked a well-defined place in American culture, and I believe that as a consequence he suffered doubts about himself, his role, and his worth. Since he did not have the usual, customary ways of expressing his fears, he developed ways of his own. One mechanism was boasting, by which the insecure boatman sought reassurance about his own importance from his listeners. He might claim, as one did, "I'm the very infant that refused its milk before its eyes were open and called out for a bottle of old Rye! W-h-o-o-p! I'm that little Cupid!

. . . Cock-a-doodle-dedoo! . . . I can . . . keep soberer than any other man in these localities!" Perhaps his fears are clearer in his songs, which were always restless, romantic, and mournful. He sang such lines as:

> *Here's to you, and all the rest,*
> *And likewise her that I love best;*
> *As she's not here to take a part,*
> *I'll drink her health with all my heart.*

His songs and boasts reveal a mixture of loneliness and anxiety that was most often, as the words suggest, drowned in alcohol. The boatman drank heartily, lustily, frequently, excessively. In whiskey was solace for the uncertainty of his condition, confirmation of his independence, and fellowship that reassured his empty soul.[23]

Like the river men, canal laborers lacked traditions and stability. Their alienation from society, however, was greater because almost all were Irish immigrants. From the Emerald Isle they came, at first in a trickle, later in hordes, always impoverished and famished, often spiritually broken and bewildered. America offered them menial jobs digging canals or building railroads; no native American would work so hard for so little. Although the immigrants were better paid, housed, and fed than in their home land, they suffered. They were happy to get three meals a day, but not every man liked what he got. Complained one Irishman about American potatoes, "O, murther!—shure what they call pratees here is all *wather, and melts in your mouth, no maley taste at all!*" Such cultural shock exemplified the dilemma of these newcomers. Although they lived in America, they continued to think of themselves as Irish; yet they could not be Irish, because they were not in Ireland but in America. Bewildered by separation from native church and tavern, ancestral hearths, and the fabric of Irish culture, they found life in an alien and sometimes hostile land difficult and confusing. Wrenched from their past, unhappy in the present, the Irish responded with fanciful if unrealistic hopes that they would be able to go home to die.[24]

Dreams of having an Irish wake and burial could not sustain men in this life; the immigrants became aggressive and violent. Canal laborers were notorious combatants. Deadly fights and brawls usually originated in petty disputes that escalated when laborers unleashed against each other rage engendered by their situation. More frequently, they reduced their tensions with strong drink, which they consumed exuberantly and in great quantity. A number of observers of drinking among adult male Irish immigrants concluded, independently, that within a few years a majority had drunk themselves to death. Others resolved their anomic problem more dramatically. Sam Patch, a penniless Irishman driven to despair by life in the United States, plunged 70 feet into the chasm at the Passaic River's Grand Falls. Miraculously, he survived. Observing that his jump had attracted a large crowd, Patch began to jump into rivers for money. At Genesee Falls, near Rochester, New York, in 1829 he mounted a 25-foot platform, bowed to the thousands of spectators, and plunged 122 feet to his death. He was drunk. Witnesses disagreed as to whether the intoxicated Patch had miscalculated or had planned this jump to be, as advertized, his last.[25]

Finally, there were some groups of Americans of whom it can be said that while they drank heartily, they drank no more heartily during the early nineteenth century than they ever had. The most conspicuous of these were soldiers and sailors, who had age-old drinking rites. So common was inebriation among the tars that some drunkards, when dismissed from other jobs, went to sea in order to get liquor, to have drinking companions, and to assure themselves that their habits were normal. Among these high consumers of long standing the oddest

and often the saddest were the schoolmasters. Although skilled and sometimes educated, teachers indulged themselves with liquor as zestfully as ignorant, unskilled laborers. The profession, if it can be so dignified, attracted mainly misfits. Keeping school repulsed most Americans, for it combined low pay, irregular work, much moving about, and low status. Poor Ichabod Crane. He existed apart from the community, boarding 'round, uncertain of his tenure, certain only that school would end when planting or harvest called his charges to the fields. The life of a schoolmaster was lonely and unrewarding.[26]

Between 1790 and 1830 the United States underwent not only a period of unprecedented heavy drinking but also a period of unprecedented and extremely rapid change. We have seen that the segments of society affected adversely, in one way or another, by these rapid changes were also the segments of society most attracted to alcohol. This correlation, while it does not prove a causal relationship, strongly suggests that such a relationship existed. And one further point can be made. Social scientists who have studied drinking in a variety of cultures have agreed with Donald Horton, who wrote in 1943 that the primary reason people drink is to relieve anxiety. A corollary of this theory would seem to be that where there is heavy drinking there is significant underlying anxiety. There certainly seems to have been much cause for anxiety in the early American republic. Perhaps Edward Bourne was correct when he wrote of American drinking habits during those years that they "grew out of the anxieties of their condition."[27]

6

THE PURSUIT OF HAPPINESS

Life, Liberty, and the Pursuit of Happiness

DECLARATION of INDEPENDENCE
1776

No one would seek artificial excitement
when in a happy frame of mind.

Dr. N. R. SMITH
1829

Dᴜʀɪɴɢ the first quarter of the nineteenth century Americans not only drank a lot of alcohol, but they drank it in distinctive, even peculiar ways. The patterns of drinking that prevailed in those years are important, because each pattern can tell us something about life in the young republic and about various facets of its culture. Then, too, the popularity of some drinking patterns increased while the popularity of others waned, and the reasons for these changes are also important. To know how Americans drank is as necessary for an understanding of the times as to know how much they drank.

In colonial days there were two clearly differentiated patterns of drinking distilled spirits. One way was to drink small amounts with daily regularity, often alone or in the family at home. Drams were taken upon rising, with meals, during mid-day breaks, and at bedtime. Americans who took their spirits in frequent but comparatively small doses did not become intoxicated; indeed, social scientists tell us that such drinking leads drinkers to develop a tolerance to alcohol's intoxicating effects.[1] Coexisting with this pattern of drinking, but in sharp contrast to it, was the communal binge. This was a form of public drinking to intoxication that prevailed whenever groups of Americans gathered for elections, court sessions, militia musters, holiday celebrations, or neigh-

Communal drinking.

borly festivities. Practically any gathering of three or more men, from the Mardi Gras to a public hanging, provided an occasion for drinking vast quantities of liquor, until the more prudent staggered home while the remainder quarreled and fought, or passed out. One observer estimated not long after the Revolution that a typical American indulged in such mass celebrations ten or fifteen times a year.[2] Although both dram drinking and communal binges continued into the nineteenth century, I have found that by the 1820s a distinct shift in customs was taking place: the taking of daily drams waned, and participation in group binges increased.[3]

After 1800, drinking in groups to the point where everyone became inebriated had ideological overtones. For one thing, such drinking became a symbol of egalitarianism. All men were equal before the bottle, and no man was allowed to refuse to drink. A guest at an evening party might be dragged to the sideboard and forced against his protests to down glass after glass. A refusal to drink under such circumstances was viewed as proof that the abstainer thought himself to be better than other people. He would not be invited to another party. Similarly, after one English-born schoolmaster offended Americans by declining to drink with them, they so ostracized him that when he took ill and died suddenly it was several days before his absence from the scene was noticed and his death discovered. It was expected that a man attending a southern barbecue would follow the 'barbecue law,' which required that everyone drink to intoxication. The only excuse for refusing a round was passing out. In Mississippi, recalled Henry Foote, drinking to excess had become so fashionable that "a man of strict sobriety" was considered "a cold-blooded and uncongenial wretch." To refuse to imbibe gave "serious offense," suggesting a lack of respect and friendship. It was sometimes dangerous. A gang of lusty Kentuckians angry with an abstinent comrade is reputed to have roasted him to death.[4]

While drinking in a group made the participants equals, it also gave them a feeling of independence and liberty. Drinking to the point of intoxication was done by choice, an act of self-will by which a man altered his feelings, escaped from his burdens, and sought perfection in his surroundings. Because drinking was a matter of choice, it increased a man's sense of autonomy. To be drunk was to be free. The freedom that intoxication symbolized led Americans to feel that imbibing lustily was a fitting way for independent men to celebrate their country's independence. It was surely no accident that one

early temperance society adopted a pledge that allowed
its members to become intoxicated on Independence
Day. During the 1820s no holiday had more import than
the 4th of July, a date that evoked "a national intoxication." On that day liberty triumphed, at least in the
heads of the overzealous patriots who lined the nation's
gutters.[5]

Another occasion when Americans drank was at elections, when candidates were expected to treat the public,
voters and nonvoters alike. Treating at elections had been
a colonial custom borrowed from England. In 1758, for
example, when George Washington sought a seat in the
Virginia House of Burgesses, he was determined that
sufficient liquor be provided. "My only fear," the candidate wrote his election agent, "is that you spent with
too sparing a hand." Washington had reason to be concerned, for a failure to treat had led to his defeat in a
previous campaign. To win this new contest, he gave
away £38-7-0 of rum, punch, wine, hard cider, and beer.
For his 144 gallons of refreshment he received 307 votes,
a return on his investment of better than 2 votes per
gallon. Such electoral practices did not change significantly after the Revolution. The most important facet of
treating was never the dispensing of strong drink, which
was expected as a matter of course, but the manner and
style of dispensing it. The candidate had to demonstrate
his generosity and hospitality without a hint of stinginess
or parsimony. An illustration is in order. The favored
aspirant in one Mississippi election poured drinks for the
voters with so much personal attention that it seemed
clear he would win. After his liquor was gone, his opponent, a Methodist minister, announced to the crowd that
he also had whiskey to dispense, but that he would not
be so stingy as to measure it out. "Come forward, one
and all," he invited, "and help yourselves." The generous
parson won. That liquor elected incompetents and the

County Election. By George Caleb Bingham. Engraved by John Sartain.

lack of it defeated able men was widely conceded. "I guess Mr. A. is the fittest man of the two," said one South Carolina woman, "but t'other whiskies the best."[6]

While liquor at elections provided voters with a good time, I believe that it also served symbolic purposes. A candidate could use alcohol to indicate his stand on the issues. Consider, for example, this 'account' of a Kentucky campaign:

To the expences of the election of 1799—To 225 half pints of whiskey at different times and places, as introductory to declaring myself a candidate, . . $28 12 5

To 100 do. purchased during the summer, merely for the purpose of shewing that I was attached to diets of domestic growth and manufacture, and was disposed to encourage them, ... 12 66

*To ten bottles of wine at different times among
merchants, for the purpose of shewing that I was
a gentleman and fond of the importation of foreign
luxuries, ...*   20

Whiskey drank at my house, 41 *gallons*   20   50

Expenses of election days in whole, ...   80   00

Liquor also had more subtle symbolic functions. An office seeker who furnished strong beverages to the voters was expected to drink freely with them, and, by his drinking, to prove the soundness of his democratic principles, that he was independent and egalitarian, indeed truly republican. Many an aspirant for office became inebriated in order to show the voters that he was an autonomous, independent being. At the same time, a candidate's good nature and congeniality in his cups demonstrated his respect for his peers, the voters, and thereby confirmed his egalitarianism. Thus it was that a Pennsylvania tavern crowd stated that one popular contender's election was certain because he could and would "get drunk with any man."[7]

Drinking at elections may also have been evidence of deep-seated frustrations with the political system. Before the rise of democratic politics in the 1820s, Americans who believed in the Revolutionary ideals of equality and freedom could hardly fail to note that those values clashed with electoral reality. The voter in most places had to declare his choice publicly. This subjected him to economic and social pressures and created resentment at the lack of true independence. Often, too, the voter had to choose between a patrician Jeffersonian or a patrician Federalist. Perhaps the Federalist was the more arrogant, but the election of either put the country under the domination of a wealthy, powerful elite that might have left the average voter feeling impotent. Records for the period show that only a small percentage of eligible voters cast ballots, and we should not be surprised that many of those who did go to the polls chose to turn elections into farces by selling their votes for liquor. In a world where equality was sometimes mocked and freedom often illusory, a drink was at least tangible, a pleasure, and something that gave a feeling of personal liberty.[8]

The communal binge was exploited not only by election candidates but also by entrepreneurs in the fur trade. Liquor played such an important role among Americans who roamed the mountains trapping beaver that it is worth discussing at some length. But first, by way of contrast, let us consider how the British and French used alcohol in their conduct of the fur business. The British obtained pelts, primarily beaver, from trade with the Indians through a highly organized chartered monopoly, the Hudson's Bay Company. The officers of that company believed in stability, which they sought to secure by encouraging the loyalty of employees and trading partners to the company, by cooperation with the Indians, and by conservative trapping policies. Hudson's Bay was organized with the idea of obtaining modest profits over a long period of time. Accordingly, its officers sought to give an appearance of permanence to the company's outposts by bringing their British wives to live in the primitive forts, by fitting their residences with silver tea sets and white table cloths, and by living as far as possible as at home. Wherever a Briton went, there was civilization. Although these officials occasionally drank imported wine, they often banned distilled spirits from their territory because they believed that alcohol, by making the Indians quarrel and fight among themselves, discouraged them from trapping. In Oregon during the 1830s the company went so far as to purchase all the distilled liquor that was brought into the country, warehoused it, and dispensed it sparingly for medication.[9]

In contrast to the British, the French Canadians were trappers rather than traders. They adopted Indian manners, mingled with the natives, and often took Indian wives. When they married Indian women, they sought tribal acceptance by living in the Indian camps, eating Indian food, and learning the language and customs. Some were adopted as brothers. They frequently moved with the tribes, taking along their wives and half-Indian children. They seldom travelled alone and often trapped in groups. They were unassertive, noncompetitive, and self-indulgent, gorging themselves with food and drink whenever possible. Although these men were never sufficiently organized to pose a direct threat to the hegemony of the Hudson's Bay Company, their cohabiting with the Indians and their willingness to trade beaver for liquor undermined the company's control over fur trading and lessened its profits.[10]

The American fur trade was carried on differently from that of either the British or the French. American trading companies suffered from a disadvantage, because the Indians preferred well-made British blankets, knives, and other industrial goods to shoddy American ones. Consequently, the Americans turned to trading with liquor, the one commodity they had that the Indians wanted. While alcohol was indispensable to the American fur merchants, it threatened to ruin the natives. Liquor not only encouraged Indian wars and accelerated tribal disintegration but, as the British had anticipated, discouraged trapping. Intoxicated Indians sought few furs, and the resultant shortage of pelts in the mid-1820s led American traders to hire white American trappers who trapped more aggressively with increased profits to the traders. Although the companies recognized that overtrapping would soon destroy the fur supply, they were not deterred because they believed that in the long run it was inevitable that the West would be depleted of beaver, depopulated of Indians, and settled by pioneer farmers. Consequently, the American fur companies were operated solely for the rapid exploitation of both men and resources. We should not be surprised to learn that one leading trader, William Ashley, cleared $80,000 in three years and retired.[11]

The American fur companies had no difficulty in hiring white trappers. The occupation appealed to Americans for a variety of reasons. A few trappers had a need to escape from the law, some saw prospects for instant wealth, and many who had been raised on the rapidly disappearing frontier yearned for an exciting challenge. Although trapping beaver was adventurous, it was not dangerous: hostile Indians killed few trappers, and most lived to old age, a greater testament to their hardiness than to their daring. The numerous diaries, memoirs, and travel accounts written by trappers indicate that they had a higher than average intelligence and that they were conscious of the historical significance of their role in the West. While catching beaver, they explored the wilderness and, in the process, named rivers, valleys, and mountain peaks for themselves. Yet neither vanity nor the hope for riches were the main attractions. It is my view that what lured Americans to trapping was the mountain man's opportunity to live by the Revolutionary ideal of the 'independent man.'[12]

The trapper believed in the myth of perfect, natural freedom. The independent man needed no one, for he was complete in and of himself. He lived in Rousseauian harmony with nature, coaxing her to yield up her treasures, making her do his bidding. He savored his freedom, which he jealously guarded from others, and he concentrated his powers of body, mind, and soul on making himself strong enough to resist the temptations of civilization, on being self-confident enough to care for himself, shrewd enough to handle any emergency. For

friendship he had a horse, for companionship an Indian wife whom he had purchased and who was required to reside in his house, remote from her people. He absented himself from that dwelling for months at a time, living alone, trapping. Because he had to compete with other trappers, he tried to avoid them, staking his own territory in a remote place, where he set his traps, collected his animals, skinned them, and cached his furs. For food he lived off the land, with his knife and rifle, like Natty Bumppo, somehow surviving. His spartan style included abstinence from alcohol, which he could not afford to carry with him. Once a year, at the season's end, in

June, he brought his pelts to sell to the fur company. With the proceeds he planned to retire, take his Indian wife east, buy a farm, and live as a virtuous republican.[13]

So much for the myth of independence. In reality the trappers were controlled and manipulated by the fur companies. Each summer from 1824 through 1839 the American companies hosted a rendezvous of traders and trappers in the Rocky Mountains. Ostensibly, these meetings were organized in order to collect all the beaver, bear, and buffalo skins in one place to facilitate their shipment to the eastern market. However, the trappers themselves favored the rendezvous because it brought them together for several days of story telling, gambling, fighting, and drinking. Throughout, there was inebriation. The companies delighted in trading whiskey for beaver, and after the rendezvous many a trapper awoke from his binge to realize that for a few days' drunk he had traded away the profits that might have bought a farm. When this happened, he could do little but curse his luck, resolve to do better next year, and return to the mountains in search of more beaver. It was said that every trapper who died in the mountains was in debt to one of the companies.[14]

The sale of spirits to trappers at the rendezvous and trading liquor to the Indians for pelts throughout the year accounted for all the fur companies' profits. In 1817 and 1818, for example, John Jacob Astor's American Fur Company sold the Indians at Mackinaw 'whiskey' made of 2 gallons of spirits, 30 gallons of water, some red pepper, and tobacco. This concoction cost 5¢ a gallon to make and sold for 50¢ a bottle. The fur companies treated white trappers in the same fashion. Whiskey that cost 25¢ a gallon in Missouri was hauled to the rendezvous, cut ten to one with water, and sold for $4 per 4-ounce glass, a price increase of more than 5,000 to one. Without liquor sales, the fur companies would have

Rendezvous.

made no profits. It is fair to state that Astor's wealth
came from selling liquor rather than from buying furs, a
fact that may explain why later, with a touch of conscience perhaps, he gave money to the temperance movement. As for the trapper, that independent man's mode
of life encouraged his exploitation. During most of the
year, in heroic isolation, he strived hard to gather furs; in
the rendezvous binge he gave away his earnings in a
frenzied period of communal conviviality.[15]

The drawing of the trappers to the rendezvous, like fil-
ings to a magnet, shows that the mountain men did not
completely act out the myth of the independent man.
The human spirit is seldom capable of the detachment

from society that the myth demanded. In the lives of the trappers ideals and reality rarely, if ever, coincided. Although they were driven by a determination to live the life of the independent man, their lapse at an annual festival revealed a high degree of ambivalence: they denied being lonely or wanting companionship, but they rushed to the rendezvous for a bout of intoxication in the society of others. Not that they came together in a spirit of comradeship. To have treated one another with warmth and friendliness while sober would have shown too painfully the split in their own lives between their need for company and their ideal of detached independence. Inebriation, however, allowed them to maintain consistency, because they believed that their behavior while drunk was involuntary and hence meaningless.[16] Thus was their camaraderie enjoyed and denied. They remained loyal to their values as they wandered across the West, trapping beaver and themselves, in a trek of loneliness.

I believe that the mountain man used communal binges not only to relieve his loneliness but also, like other Americans, to relieve his anxieties. When he was sober, his inability to realize his aspirations engendered an acute sense of frustration that increased during long periods of abstinence. A drunken spree enabled him to turn his thoughts away from the failure of his own life, to perpetuate his illusory hopes, to deny the contradictions between his ideals and reality. This refusal of an American to see the fact that his values were at odds with everyday human experience limited self-understanding and stunted intellectual and moral growth. Oscillating between abstinence and binges, he blurred reality, lessening simultaneously his understanding of his frustrations and his hope of ever ameliorating his condition.

The mountain man's failure to understand himself sometimes led him to express his fears in roundabout ways. Old Bill Williams, so called because of his prematurely gray hair, was typical of the mountain men, flaunting his independence and spurning the company of other trappers. But he was not totally independent. Old Bill begged his fellow trappers to abstain from shooting elk after his death, because, he believed, he would be reincarnated as a buck. This request was as close as Williams would ever come to an admission of dependence upon human society.[17] One of the few Americans to comment frankly on the disappointments of the independent man was William Marshall Anderson. Although not a mountain man himself, which may explain why he was able to write as candidly as he did, Anderson was well acquainted with that way of life because an enlightened doctor had sent him West to cure his tuberculosis. That Anderson understood the problem of the independent man is shown in this entry in his western journal, September 11, 1834:

"Why is it that I am not satisfied? I have always had some place in advance, to reach which, I intended to be contented—I expected, when I arrived at the fort on Laramee's fork, I should feel entirely free from personal alarm—perhaps I did, yet another engrossing desire took possession of me, I reckoned, & found myself a great way from the big river in hope, a place of rest. I next was all anxiety to be at the forks of the Platte, where I knew I should be only three hundred miles from the mouth—There—I wished myself at the Bluffs. Now here, my calculated figures tell me I am 900 miles from Louisville, my home—Restless being! I fear I shall never be settled & happy—Now for St. Louis, then for Kentucky & again, for,—God Knows—where! for a man that cant be satisfied there—ought to roam 'toujours.'—We passed by the ruins of the old Council bluffs. Emblem of human fortunes—! One day—all a wilderness—another day— the strong-place of strong men—the next, a heap of rubbish—So with man—One minute, a child a helpless, puking child, In a little while, a proud strong man—lord of creation! and, yet, a little while a carcass, a rattling skeleton of dry bones—"[18]

Such sentiments reveal the underlying frustrations and fears that led a number of Americans to self-destructive drinking. What seems to have been essential to the would-be independent man was not the communal nature of the binge but the fact that it was episodic. Apparently he needed to punctuate his detached, rational independence with periods of frenzied, forgetful intoxication; to stupefy himself with liquor; to escape from himself. And he discovered that his bouts did not require participation in a group. During the early nineteenth century, for the first time, a sizeable number of Americans began to drink to excess by themselves. The solo binge was a new pattern of drinking in which periods of abstinence were interspersed every week, month, or season with a one to three-day period of solitary inebriation. It was necessary to devise a name for this new pattern of drinking, and during these years the terms 'spree' and 'frolic' came into popular usage.[19] Solo binge drinking has seldom occurred in other countries. It is rare in Europe, except in countries such as Finland where society is hostile to drinking and the binge is a form of deviant behavior. There is no binge drinking in France or southern Europe. Although the French are, per capita, among the highest consumers of distilled spirits, they drink their brandy not in binges but in small amounts taken frequently and consistently, a practice that all but disappeared from the United States about 1825. There are a few primitive societies in which spirituous liquor is taken for the sake of a psychic experience of one kind or another, but in most societies alcohol is a social drink taken in company with others for relaxation and conviviality.[20]

To show how solo sprees met the needs of some Amer-

Solo drinking.

icans of this period, the case of David Bacon will be helpful. David was born in 1813, the youngest of a large
brood. Fatherless at four, by the age of twelve he was so
wild and undisciplined, drinking with the village's rowdy
boys, that his mother sent him to live with an older
brother, the Rev. Leonard Bacon. Here there was more
authority than affection, and David learned to be resent-
ful as well as righteous. Although intellectually gifted, he
was not studious and passed in and out of several appren-
ticeships before he became a schoolmaster. Like other
teachers, he was a hearty drinker, so hearty that his
school folded when alarmed parents withdrew their children. After this failure he aspired even higher, studied
medicine, and in 1835 used his brother's influence to obtain a position in Liberia as a physician. That African
country's heat, fevers, and inept officials discouraged and
demoralized Bacon and shattered his vision of a messianic
mission. Between bouts of intoxication he quarreled with
the blacks, badgered officials, and expressed, in the

words of one observer, an "apparent discontent with every thing which he witnessed."[21]

David Bacon's inflated expectations and disillusionment were not unusual in those times. It is true that his father's death, his mother's inability to manage him, and his brother's righteous authority probably affected him adversely, but another consideration must be taken into account. He grew up during the 1820s, a decade during which rapid economic change created unparalleled opportunities for material gain, and everyone expected to 'go ahead' in triumph. At that time prosperity seemed to offer Americans a chance to build a society that would enable them to realize their idealistic hopes for liberty and equality, which hitherto had been only Revolutionary abstractions. The young, in particular, were enraptured by the period's optimism, self-confidence, ideological faith, and high aspirations. It is not surprising that Bacon's hopes, like those of many young Americans, far exceeded what he could possibly achieve.

After Bacon's ambitions failed in Africa, his idealism was shattered. His disillusionment was similar to that of others of his generation who came from emotionally intense and fervently religious backgrounds. The illustrious families that produced the self-confident, zealous leaders for the nineteenth-century moral crusade also produced spectacular failures. David's life was in contrast to that of his brother Leonard. The latter was the pastor of New Haven's First Church from 1825 to 1865, wrote essays for the reform movement, consulted regularly with the Yale faculty, and circulated in the upper echelons of society. Among Leonard's burdens, in addition to David, was Delia, a sister whose obsessions with proving that Francis Bacon, a distant relative, had written Shakespeare's plays drove her to insanity. There was the same kind of overwrought intensity in other prominent families. We have already made a passing reference to the Tappans, where success in business and politics was matched by one brother's migraine headaches and another's habitual drunkenness. In the family of Lyman Beecher three daughters took the water cure for nervous disorders, son Henry Ward suffered migraine headaches, and son James went insane and committed suicide. So did another son, George, of whom it was written that "at the end it seemed to him as if Satan controlled him, and he lived in dread of himself and his actions." And daughter Harriet Beecher Stowe had a son who drank excessively.[22]

David Bacon did not have migraine headaches; nor did he commit suicide. But he did periodically retreat from reality in a bout of solitary drinking. Such a spree, which was quite common among so many young Americans of that period, might have been a way for Americans who were frustrated in achieving idealistic goals of freedom and independence to relieve those frustrations. And drinking alone was a logical outgrowth of the cult of individualism. The inebriated man felt and insisted that he was free, that "liberal drinking denotes a liberal mind." Because alcohol released inhibitions, it imparted a temporary sense of freedom from responsibility, restraint, or social custom. A man who drank alone could feel not only free but independent and self-sufficient. Although such considerations no doubt encouraged Americans to drink in solitary sprees, they cannot entirely explain the episodic nature of so much American drinking.[23]

Why, we might ask, did so many Americans repeat the binge cycle over and over? Consider how the cycle worked. During the abstaining phase a man faced contradictions between his ideals and reality; his unwillingness to modify his ideals combined with his inability to alter reality created frustration, stress, and anxiety. The contradictions did not disappear, and the anxieties increased until the man turned to liquor. He took a drop of whiskey. He felt better, as the alcohol began to relieve his anxiety. Then he took another drink. He felt even better, and as his anxieties diminished, he felt that he was free. Drink followed drink, and the man enjoyed his spree. Yet even as he indulged himself, the man knew that his riotous intoxication would lead to a hangover. The agony of a hangover was the price that a man had to pay in order to enjoy a short, sweet binge. Why were so many Americans willing to pay so much for so little? The answer, I suspect, is that Americans who drank to intoxication felt that their drunkenness was an act of self-manipulation in which pleasure had been engineered for personal benefit. And American culture rejected such hedonism. The consequence was that overindulgence made Americans feel guilty, and the hangover became a kind of deserved punishment that purged the guilt. Feelings of guilt were exploited by fervent evangelical protestants. Americans like the Rev. Leonard Bacon preached that every man was a sinner, that he caused his own failure, that he was responsible for himself, and that only the Lord's grace could purify him. This message was empty for nonbelievers such as David Bacon. American culture, however, did not make it easy to ignore the preacher's warnings of damnation, and many heard inner voices that constantly badgered them until they sought escape, even through self-destruction. For many guilt-ridden Americans the solitary binge provided the only way for them to play out their lives as a form of suicide.[24]

This cyclical pattern of abstinence and sprees was also consonant with the needs of an emerging industrial society. During the sober phase, work-crazed Americans sacrificed their emotions to production, their ambitions overriding their concerns for liberty and equality. Americans were, in the words of one Briton, "wofully ignorant of the difficult art of being gracefully idle." By working hard and intensely they hoped to buy freedom, in the form of a farm where they could live as free and as equal as any man. Foreign observers were astonished at American vigor and enthusiasm for long hours and hard work. However, with the economic changes that were taking place many cherished goals were becoming more and more difficult to attain. Therefore, frenzied activity was accompanied by doubts of success and feelings of frustration. The resulting anxiety frequently led to a binge, during which the American retreated from heroic attempts to implement his ideals into a realm of fantasy. That was why an intoxicated man lying on a tavern floor could earnestly proclaim, "I am as independent as the United States of America." Even though he could not raise himself from the floor. The binge gave a temporary sense of achievement. That the achievement was illusory mattered little, for during that brief spell alcohol dissipated building tensions. After the hangover, the drinker, fallen from grace, was spurred by guilt about his indulgence to work harder than ever.[25]

Episodic drinking was in line with another new American cultural development: compartmentalization. In the early nineteenth century every thing began to have its proper place: e.g., men worked away from home; women in the home. Children learned reading, writing, and arithmetic at school; they played at home, the boys with wagons and the girls with dolls. I suspect that this categorical ordering of people's lives served to reduce uncertainties in a society beset increasingly by contradictions between its ideals and reality. To maintain sanity and social cohesion, it was necessary to assign inconsistent elements of the culture to separate and appropriate compartments or spheres of influence. The development of a drinking pattern based on oscillation between abstinence and binges can be viewed as one attempt at compartmentalization. But the episodic pattern was unstable, for each period of indulgence failed to dissolve all the abstaining phase's tensions. For many the solution was to quicken the frequency of their binges. "My sprees," said Thomas Marshall, nephew of the chief justice, ". . . came so uncommon close together, that there was considerable danger of their completely running into each other in one continual stream."[26]

By the 1820s there were noticeable changes in drinking patterns. While many men continued to treat together in taverns, the old custom of drinking small amounts of alcoholic beverages regularly and frequently throughout the day was declining, and binges, whether communal or solitary, were increasing. It was the changing patterns of drinking rather than the increased consumption of alcohol that alarmed so many Americans; indeed, a principal reason for the organization of the temperance movement was the desire to eliminate solitary bouts of drinking, which were viewed as destructive both to the drinker and to society. But the antiliquor reformers only succeeded in discouraging daily dram drinking and communal binges. Thus, by 1840, the most benign and least disruptive patterns of imbibing had almost disappeared, while the private, solo binge remained. Even during the 1850s the leaders of the prohibition campaign could not succeed in eradicating the solo spree, which has endured down to the present.[27]

One phenomenon that seems to have appeared for the first time in America during the 1820s was the alcoholic delirium, a malady that is still common today. Delirium tremens—often called the D. T.'s—affects a heavy drinker after a binge, an illness, or a withdrawal from accustomed portions of alcohol. The disorder begins with a period of irritation and anxiety, frequently accompanied by muscle spasms called 'the shakes.' There ensues a period of paranoid hallucination, during which the subject commonly reports being chased by people or animals, usually either tiny or huge. During this highly excited phase restraints may be needed to prevent the subject from injuring himself. Finally, the victim falls into a deep sleep and enters an acute alcoholic depression. Either death or complete recovery follows. In the early nineteenth century many doctors treated this disorder by inducing sleep with spirits or opium. Unfortunately, opium often caused blood pressure to fall so low that the patient died.[28]

Delirium tremens does not appear in all societies; social scientists have found that it is associated with particular cultural patterns. Since the disorder is most commonly caused by sudden withdrawal of alcohol from people physically addicted to its use, it occurs most often among those who drink distilled rather than fermented beverages. Undoubtedly one reason the incidence of deliriums increased in America during the 1820s was that the consumption of hard liquor, especially whiskey, increased. However, heavy drinking of distilled spirits does not necessarily lead to delirium tremens. One observer discovered an Indian village in Mexico where the natives daily drank spirits to intoxication without any cases of delirium being noted. Indeed, none of the intoxicated villagers ever vomited, got headaches, or showed any signs of hangovers. (The observer was not so lucky.) People in that culture drank for the purpose of getting drunk; intoxication had taken the place of aesthetic expression, intellectual pursuits, games, conversation, and companionship. It appears that because liquor was so well integrated into the culture, it had no detrimental social or physical effects. The importance of the cultural context in which the drinking is done has been demonstrated in a German study, where heavy drinkers who suffered deliriums were found to have different social and cultural backgrounds from those of other heavy

Delirium Tremens.

drinkers. Thus, it seems likely that the emergence of alcoholic deliriums in America during the 1820s was due not only to increased consumption of hard liquor but also to the presence of new cultural conditions conducive to the disorder.[29]

The hallucinations of the victims of this disorder may suggest what some of these conditions were. Fortunately, a number of physicians recorded their patients' hallucinations and reported them in the medical journals. These reports are suggestive. One man, for example, envisioned a rattlesnake chasing him as people tried to shoot it; another was convinced that those present in the room were attempting to shoot him; a third imagined at various times during his hallucination that his fellow steamboat travellers were plotting to kill him, that a tavern landlord had the same intent, and that his wife wanted to poison him. Yet another was afraid that mice "had come to eat his library." He was distraught because they had already ruined $100 worth of books. Others feared that their beds were infested with rats, that the walls of the room would fall in, or that the devil had come to take their souls.[30]

What is most striking in these hallucinations is the realism, the absence of hobgoblins, unicorns, leprechauns, or monsters from the deep. What seems significant is the fact that delirious patients invariably believed that they were being persecuted. One, James Gale, later wrote, "I imagined to myself enemies, where I doubtless never had any." Such a paranoid view could easily develop in a culture that rejected paternalism and stressed autonomy and where great competitiveness was encouraged and lauded. One problem, I think, was that trying to live up to the ideal of the independent man was a burden too heavy for many people to carry. At a time when American values stressed the virtue of competition, it is not surprising that delirious drinkers who felt endangered by rivals imagined themselves to be threatened by snakes, mice, or rats as well as by travelling companions or landlords. Moreover, the doctors who prepared these case studies sometimes mentioned that the spree that had led to the delirium had begun with a bankruptcy or business failure. In the case of the mice-infested library, the idea of financial loss became a part of the hallucination. In any event, the anxieties evident in the hallucinations were probably the same anxieties that prompted the drinking.[31]

These hallucinations appear to be rooted in a sense of guilt. People blamed themselves for failing to implement their own goals, and American society taught them to accept that responsibility. Although most outwardly conformed to this cultural norm, not all could keep their rage at failure inward or channel their anxieties through the accepted religious institutions. For many, strong

drink appeared to offer an escape from the weight of responsibility. Liquor, however, was not capable of absolv-
ing the guilt that accompanied failure, and the consequence of turning to drink was sometimes a delirium in
which guilt caused a man to turn against himself. It was
guilt that made the drinker's hallucination a hellish world
in which American ideals were inverted: thus did the
striving for autonomy become a fear of others, the belief
in equality a fear that others were superior—like a giant
rat. Even the desire to exploit the material world became
an impotent rage in which men felt themselves to be manipulated by the devil. These guilt-laden and paranoiac
deliriums may reveal underlying fears that gripped
Americans. There is, to my mind, little psychological
difference between a drunkard's hallucinations and an
Anti-Mason's hysteria.[32]

Another important drinking pattern was the preference
for distilled spirits over other types of alcoholic beverages. Although whiskey and rum were cheaper and more
readily available than beer or wine, it can be argued that
these stronger beverages were selected for psychological
rather than economic reasons. If Americans had wanted
to drink fermented beverages, most could have afforded
them. As one observer put it, distilled liquor was preferred "not because it is so much cheaper, but because it
is so much more powerful." That this choice of the most
potent beverages was not merely economic can be seen in
the hostility to the whiskey tax. If distilled spirits had
been less popular, Americans would have accepted that
excise, given up whiskey for beer, and planted barley
rather than corn. Such changes did occur in Great Britain in the mid-eighteenth century after the government
there imposed high duties on distilled spirits. The stub-
bornness of American opposition to the whiskey tax indicates a thirst for strong drinks, and I find this penchant
worth exploring in the light of a recent study which

suggests that the choice of a particular type of alcoholic beverage is related to certain personality characteristics.[33]

Let us speculate a little. Social scientists have found that anxiety arises from a variety of circumstances. Two are salient here. One source is a function of aspirations, and the anxiety comes from trying to attain ambitious goals. People who have high aspirations set themselves difficult, perhaps impossible, targets, fail to meet their own expectations, suffer disappointment from their failure, and thereby become susceptible to anxieties. A second source of anxiety is a function of the motivation for achievement, and the anxiety comes from the failure to try to fulfill aspirations. People who have low motivation lack the confidence and drive to succeed, are unable to accept moderate risks necessary to try to reach goals, are disappointed at their failure, and suffer from anxieties. Thus, anxieties depend upon both the level of motivation for achievement and the level of aspirations. These ideas can be linked to drinking in a specific way. If Horton's theory that drinking allays anxiety is correct, then we would expect the most potent alcoholic beverages to be used to cope with the greatest anxieties. And even though the strongest distilled beverages such as whiskey or rum are often drunk in diluted form, these diluted drinks usually contain more alcohol than nonspirituous beverages such as wine or beer. Thus, a person's choice of alcoholic beverage can be related to the level of his anxieties and, by inference, to the level of motivation for achievement and the level of aspirations. Among high aspirers the highly motivated have the ability to strive toward goals, suffer some anxiety from the attempt, and drink wine; those with low motivations have less confidence in their ability to reach targets, suffer greater anxiety, and drink whiskey. Among low aspirers the highly motivated find it easy to try to gain minimal expectations, are free of anxiety, and abstain; the lower motivated find it difficult to attempt to reach even low goals, suffer some anxiety, and drink beer.[34]

What do these ideas suggest about the United States during the 1820s, when so much distilled spirits was being consumed? America, it appears, was a society in which people combined high aspirations with a low motivation for fulfilling goals. This conclusion is supported to some extent by the remarks of foreign travellers. They found Americans to be boastful, overly sensitive to criticism, and frank in expressing their yearning for national greatness. Thomas Hamilton, for example, reported that Americans had "a restless and insatiable appetite for praise, which defied all restraint of reason or common sense." Henry Fearon wrote that they suffered from an "excessive inflation of mind." These are the traits that one would expect to find among people who combined desires for greatness with a limited motivation to achieve those desires. Fearon's comments are particularly revealing; he wrote, "As a people, they feel that they have got to gain a character, and, like individuals under similar circumstances, are captious and conceited in proportion to their defects. They appear to aim at a standard of high reputation, without the laborious task of deserving it, and practise upon themselves the self-deception of believing that they really are that which they only wish to be."[35]

The American aspiration for greatness was the kind of state of mind that had the potential to alter society drastically, and, in fact, that potential was realized through the Industrial Revolution. I noted earlier that grain surpluses had led to distilled spirits binges prior to many of the world's great industrial expansions, in Britain, Germany, Sweden, and Russia as well as the United States. In each case the surplus grain had been turned into distilled beverages rather than fermented ones. If my remarks about beverage choice are correct, then in each of these countries the popularity of distilled spirits at particular times signified high aspirations combined with low motivation for achievement. Motivation was low because these were traditional societies. High aspirations, however, could lead to changes that would raise motivation, and high motivation, as social psychologist David McClelland has stated, is an indicator of future economic growth. I would hypothesize that when industrial expansion begins, motivation to succeed is necessarily low, rooted in peasant values that stress the virtue and safety of tradition. As economic development leads to success in meeting targets, confidence in the ability to attain goals grows. This increase in motivation, combined with a narrowing of the gap between aspirations and achievement, reduces anxieties, at least for those social and economic classes that achieve success. Consequently, many people who have drunk distilled spirits become abstainers. After 1825, when the United States enjoyed accelerating economic growth, the temperance movement flourished, particularly among the middle classes that were the principal beneficiaries of prosperity. Similar developments can be observed in the industrialization of Great Britain and Scandinavia. It might also be noted that in the United States after 1840, as factory workers whose dead-end jobs discouraged both motivation and aspirations became more numerous, the consumption of beer increased.[36]

If the preference for distilled spirits over fermented beverages reflected American needs, so did the rejection of other available euphoric drugs, such as opium. During the 1820s it was estimated that there were a thousand liquor drinkers for each opium user, a hundred drunkards for each opium addict. The use or non-use of opium was a matter of choice, for the drug could have been supplied easily and cheaply by American merchants who were the principal buyers of the Turkish crop. They did not sell opium at home, however, but in the Orient; most of the small amount that was imported into the United States was used medicinally. Because opium's addictive properties were not recognized, it was dispensed rather freely. However, its classification as medicine insured that it was controlled by prescription, that it was not sold competitively on a free and open market, and that it was more expensive than home-distilled alcohol. Because most Americans seldom visited a doctor, access to the drug was limited. Its use was greatest among physicians, pharmacists, doctors' patients, and the wealthy.[37]

In those days, opium was one of the most important drugs in the pharmacopoeia. It was used for a variety of treatments: to soothe drunkards during delirium tremens, to reduce or regulate the pulse rate of patients suffering from fast or irregular heart beats, and to relieve the pain of those with broken bones, acute infections, or chronic ailments. It was also employed to quiet children, who were given the drug in the form of laudanum, which was opium dissolved in alcohol. This pacifier appealed especially to hired nurses, although its use was probably more common in England than in America, where there were fewer children's nurses. Physicians prescribed opium principally as a sedative, and it was often the active ingredient in sleeping pills given to troubled, anxious adults of the upper class. By the middle of the century the drug's tranquilizing properties had led to its inclusion in many patent medicines, where it soothed purchasers who suffered from anxiety—or from opium addiction.[38]

I believe that Americans considered opium to be a medication rather than an euphoric agent because they found that its particular mind-altering qualities did not give them the kind of pleasure or escape that they sought. For one thing, American society was free and fluid, even chaotic, and Americans were fervent believers in the ideal of the independent man. Such social conditions and values are not those of opium eaters. Social scientists have found that opium appeals to people who live in a highly structured culture that lacks socially approved channels for individual escape from social control. Under those conditions, so alien to America in the early nineteenth century, opium provides a more certain escape from oppressive social controls than does liquor. Then, too, alcohol is a drug conducive to conviviality and group activity. In a society where communal drinking has been customary, as it was in America during the 1820s, the private act of taking opium is a form of deviancy, a rejection of society, in this respect similar to the solo binge. That the few who did use opium were disproportionately upper class Americans who were most likely to reject their country's egalitarianism suggests the validity of this analysis. Another difference between alcohol and opium is the way in which they affect individuals. A man who has failed to achieve his aspirations may react to his failure either by lowering his goals or by increasing his efforts. In this situation opium acts to reduce drive and thereby deflate ambitions. Alcohol, on the other hand, enables a man to strive harder by decreasing inhibitions. Liquor is in this way more closely associated with the unleashing of aggression, a quality that was abundantly evident in the young republic.[39]

Alcohol's link to aggression can also be observed by comparing its effects with those of another drug, marijuana. Although the use of marijuana is not indigenous to Anglo-American culture, the plant did grow in America, and some Indian tribes apparently dried it and smoked it. Americans borrowed corn and tobacco from the Indians, but they did not choose to cultivate marijuana. The reason seems clear in the light of a 1954 study that contrasted the use of marijuana and distilled spirits in a province of India. There the priestly caste smoked cannabis, which they praised as a promoter of contemplation, an aid to insight, a stimulant to thought, and a help in attaining inner peace. Spirits they condemned for producing violence and sexual promiscuity. The warrior caste, on the contrary, drank distilled liquor, which they heralded as a reviver of sagging spirits, an invigorator of sexual desire, a stimulant for the brave warrior, and the promoter of a more zealous, active life. Marijuana they condemned for producing apathy and lethargy. In other words, a group's preference for a particular drug and appreciation of its properties were determined by the group's ideology, values, and psychological set. The caste that valued aggressive behavior drank alcohol.[40]

The rejection of nonalcoholic intoxicants, the preference for distilled spirits over fermented beverages, the prevalence of delirium tremens, the solo binge, and the communal binge—each of these patterns of drinking has been associated with one or more social or psychological traits. This investigation has suggested that Americans were highly anxious, aspiring, and aggressive, that they combined ideals of liberty and equality with guilt, a desire for compartmentalization of their lives, and little faith in their ability to attain their high goals. We have already discussed anxiety, freedom, and equality at length, and few would doubt that Americans were aspiring and aggressive. But did Americans have little faith in their ability to attain high goals? Let us concentrate on this trait. At first glance, low motivation for achievement contradicts a common impression about American character, for it would seem to deny the self-confident, go ahead, entrepreneurial spirit that we are frequently told built the country. Although only one of the drinking patterns, the preference for distilled spirits over other alcoholic beverages, is related to low motivation for achievement, the probability that that trait prevailed in early nineteenth-century America is suggested by other social science research. For one thing, social psychologists have shown that low motivation for achievement is related to high aspirations and to high anxiety, both of which we have found in early nineteenth-century America. Researchers have explained this connection by noting that high goals can be self-defeating, since they are unlikely to be fulfilled and hence discourage efforts to succeed. Social scientists have also found that low achievement motivation occurs in cultures where people do not believe in social stratification, and it is clear to me that Jacksonian Americans were fervently egalitarian. Furthermore, theorists have related an unwillingness to strive for success to the desire to take great risks, to gamble for long odds. And the new republic was rampant with land speculations, wildcat banks, lotteries, and high stakes card games—the river boat cardsharp became legendary. Finally, social scientists have identified low achievement motivation with economic stagnation, and economic historians report that from 1790 to the 1820s American per capita gross national product showed little real growth.[41]

This interpretation of early nineteenth-century America as a low motivated society stands, until we examine what social psychologists have written about child rearing. The theorists have related high aspirations and low achievement motivation to dependency in children, high motivation to independence. These findings are in contrast with the American experience, where low motivation for the whole of society was combined with independence for children. The available historical evidence suggests that parents were determined to instill independence in their offspring in order to produce free and independent republican citizens. They encouraged their children to be autonomous, to express a "spirit of republicanism." To a great extent these independent youngsters did as they pleased; they were saucy and impudent. When they abused a schoolmaster, that unfortunate wretch was often forbidden by parents to correct his charges. Only years later did masters attain more than a modicum of authority. Such child rearing practices were the consequence of the unwavering devotion of American parents to the Revolutionary ideals of liberty and equality.[42]

It is my conclusion that low motivated parents were raising a generation of high motivated children. The validity of this interpretation is supported by several indications of an early nineteenth century shift in values. One study of American school readers found that in books published after 1830 the proportion of stories stressing the importance of achievement increased substantially. Accordingly, children born after 1820 who read these books were subjected to an influence that motivated them toward success. High achievement motivation has also been related to parental instillation of protestant values in children. The protestant belief that a man must act as his own agent to save himself, the stress on attaining educational skills in order to read and understand the Bible, and the turning of guilt about one's inadequacies into a driving mechanism to achieve both success and visible proof of one's worthiness are all conducive to striving for goals. Early in the nineteenth century protestant ideals were boosted by a series of religious revivals that swept across America. In my judgment, the greatest impact of this Second Great Awakening must have been upon the young, who would have been the most malleable. The moral values of American youths were transformed, and their motivation to succeed was raised.[43]

In the years following 1800 children were more likely to be taught by their parents to be assertive, aggressive, and aspiring. Not surprisingly, this younger generation, which was beginning to come of age in the 1820s, led the country into unprecedented industrial growth, technological innovation, and westward expansion. Their material success should not startle us, since social scientists have shown that high motivation for achievement leads to high economic growth. These young Americans became the exuberant and self-confident go ahead men whose entrepreneurial spirits and materialistic hopes dominated the industrial boom that occurred after 1825. But their penchant for this world's goods was tempered by an interest in religion and reform. This younger generation also led the temperance movement, promoted revivals, and went on to organize Bible societies, Sunday schools, and antislavery organizations. In so doing, they harnessed the old Revolutionary ideals of equality and liberty to more manageable yokes, and in the process they sacrificed the ideals of the independent man to a vision of national, industrial greatness.[44]

Young Americans, I think, dismissed the older generation's views of equality and liberty as impractical abstractions, rejected the independent man's quest for those elusive ideals, and placed their confidence for attaining happiness in a combination of enterprise and evangelical religion. That the aspiration to be an independent man gave way to materialism may not have represented an ascent of the human spirit, but I believe that it did show an appreciation of practicality and reality. After all, the independent man's more visionary ideals too often had led only to delusion, despair, and drink. Furthermore, their materialism was coupled with spirituality, and young Americans of the 1830s were determined to build a society based on both elements. Today, it is difficult for us to understand that attempt, for while we retain the belief in materialism, we find it difficult to comprehend nineteenth-century revivalism fully. We have lost an appreciation for that half of their ethos that concerned hopes, ideals, and values. We are jaded by materialism and cut off from the saving grace of the Second Great Awakening, and because we find those mid-nineteenth-century values so alien, we look back with envy to the earlier, holistic aspirations of the independent man. Although the simplicity of his ideals of liberty and equality continues to appeal to us, we ignore his unhappiness over his failure to realize his idealistic yearnings. We are less committed but more comfortable.

CHAPTER

DEMON RUM

The devil had an efficient hand
in establishing, perfecting, and sustaining
the present system of making drunkards.

Rev. HUNTINGTON LYMAN
1830

During the 1820s per capita consumption of spirituous liquor climbed, then quite suddenly leveled off, and in the early 1830s began to plummet toward an unprecedented low. This decline marked a significant change in American culture, as a zestful, hearty drinking people became the world's most zealous abstainers. Just why this dramatic change took place is not entirely clear, due at least in part to the fact that historians who have studied the temperance movement have not analyzed it adequately. In the late nineteenth century historians such as Daniel Dorchester and Henry Scomp sympathized with the temperance cause, viewed it as an overdue reform, heralded its progress, and traced its rise to the discovery of alcohol's harmful effects upon the human body. The problem with this interpretation is that in the late eighteenth century, when Benjamin Rush had noted those harmful physiological effects, his widely circulated warnings had little influence upon the consumption of alcohol. Consumption actually rose in the years following the doctor's largely unsuccessful crusade. Recent historians, such as J. C. Furnas and Frank Byrne, though not in sympathy with the temperance cause, have been overly influenced by the twentieth-century controversy surrounding prohibition, and they have been no more successful than their predecessors in explaining the triumph of antiliquor sentiment in the 1820s and 1830s. John A. Krout, the most perceptive scholar to study the problem, emphasized the fact that temperance was merely one of many early nineteenth-century reform movements. But Krout's *The Origins of Prohibition* is principally a narrative, and it does not explain why reformers chose to pursue that particular cause when they did.

A fresher and more analytical approach was adopted by sociologist Joseph R. Gusfield in his book, *Symbolic Crusade*. He argued that the clergymen and the middle class who embraced the temperance cause did so because they believed their status to be threatened by new, powerful industrialists. While this theory may hold true for the prohibition movement during the late nineteenth century, it fails to explain the antiliquor movement in its earlier phase. For one thing, Gusfield emphasized the clash of nativist and immigrant values in fomenting antiliquor activity, although the temperance movement began twenty years before mass immigration. For another thing, Gusfield identified the movement as middle class because its leaders were middle class; he ignored the fact that temperance was a mass crusade with participation from all levels of society, particularly from lower class Methodists. And finally, Gusfield suggested that industrialization led factory owners to advocate abstinence to improve the efficiency of their labor force, whereas the temperance movement actually preceded industrialization by at least a decade. In addition to these errors, Gusfield's theory does not explain why people who felt that their status was threatened chose to express that fear through the particular vehicle of the temperance movement. Indeed, the principal difficulty with all of the investigations of temperance is that they have not considered fully what motives, rationales, fears, and hopes drove so many Americans during the early nineteenth century to organize against alcohol.

I believe that the temperance movement was a logical response by early nineteenth-century Americans to the conditions of their times. The movement was a reaction to the prevailing patterns of drinking, especially the solitary binge. It served to perform the same psychological functions as did liquor, and for most people it did so in superior ways. Perhaps some examples are in order. When the market revolution caused a loss of local autonomy and social cohesion, some men turned to drink; others created village temperance societies to combat the importation of spirits from outside their own community. In an age of unprecedented prosperity some people found that the increasing availability of new commodities, including food and drink, was bewildering; others narrowed their choices by voluntary restriction through abstinence from meat or strong beverages. Some men sought camaraderie at the tavern, others in their local temperance organization. While rapid change produced anxieties that encouraged many to drink, others, who listened to sermons that denounced liquor, developed even higher anxieties about the devil's brew, and these anxieties were relieved by their participation in temperance organizations.

Since drinking and abstinence performed many of the same functions in people's lives, we must consider why so many found abstinence more appealing. A partial explanation is the fact that users of alcohol rapidly develop a tolerance to the drug; that is, Americans who drank alcohol found that they had to drink larger and larger amounts to get an intoxicating effect. High dosages, however, had adverse physical consequences, such as nausea, vomiting, delirium tremens, or even death. As a result, drinkers who found that the large amounts necessary to bring euphoria also brought discomfort and pain were ripe for conversion to some other means of relieving anxiety and acquiring happiness. And as the consumption of alcohol rose, many saw that it harmed society. The solitary drinker was detached from society and its constraints; he was likely to become antisocial, to fight, steal, or otherwise indulge in malicious mischief, to be sexually promiscuous or beat his wife, or to squander on liquor money needed to feed his hungry children. Such behavior rent the social fabric. Society even suffered from the escapist drinker, whose anomie was conducive to isolation, alienation, and self-destruction. Liquor, therefore, was widely perceived to provide neither happiness for the individual nor stability for society.[1]

Another explanation for the success of the antiliquor movement, provided by social theory, is that American society was essentially healthy. Theorists have argued that every society has institutions that shape its social structure and an ideology that enables people to resolve institutional frictions. Societies are vigorous and healthy when their institutions and ideologies reinforce one another. When a culture undergoes rapid, disruptive change, its social structure is altered, some of its institutions are weakened, its ideology loses vitality, and stress develops. How a society responds to these conditions determines its future. If a society eases its stress in nonideological ways, such as the consumption of alcohol, institutions will be weakened further, and the structure of society may, as in many primitive tribes, disintegrate. If a society handles its stress by developing ideological responses, such as a temperance movement, old institutions can be reinforced, new ones created, and the social structure maintained.[2]

The turning from alcohol to abstinence in the late 1820s, therefore, signified the vitality of American society. As long as anxieties and fears were relieved by drinking, they were destructive both to individuals and to society, which was beginning to crumble under the pressure. I would argue that the process of social disintegration was slowed, however, by the creation of new attitudes, beliefs, and values that helped relieve anxieties, frustrations, and stress in general. When stresses were reduced by the new ideology, Americans could devote new energy to strengthen old institutions, such as organized religion, or to create new ones, such as temperance societies. These renewed and new institutions, in turn, were the building blocks of a new social order. The temperance movement, then, was one element in a social process by which Americans, during the 1820s, were adopting an ideology that would shape for a hundred years the country's social, economic, political, and moral development. That ideology opened some routes and foreclosed others, linked industrial expansion to human needs in specific ways, gave birth to a peculiarly pragmatic ethical system, cut off the influence of competing ideologies, and threw many forms of experimentation into the ashcan.

The antiliquor campaign was launched about 1810 by a number of reform-minded ministers, who were evangelical Calvinists associated with the newly founded Andover Seminary. Indeed, it appears that the movement began at one of a series of Monday night gatherings where Justin Edwards, Moses Stuart, Leonard Woods, and Ebenezer Porter met in the latter's study to discuss social questions. Early fruits of this Andover meeting were a number of militant antiliquor articles in Jeremiah Evarts' *Panoplist*, a Boston religious periodical with strong Andover ties. These articles were followed in 1814 by a seminal temperance pamphlet issued by Andover's New England Tract Society. This pamphlet was widely used by ministers to prepare sermons opposing the use of alcohol. The founders of the movement soon discovered that their cause had broad appeal, and when the Massachusetts Society for the Suppression of Intemperance was organized in 1812, its leaders included not

Temperance was serious business.

only the Andover crowd but such prominent figures as
Abiel Abbot, Jedidiah Morse, and Samuel Worcester.
Within the next two decades these clergymen and others
who subsequently joined them spread their message
across the country.[3]

Militant moral reformers succeeded in attracting public
attention. A populace that had not responded to Benjamin Rush's rational warnings that spirits brought disease and death was captivated by emotional, moral exhortations warning that the drinker would be damned.
The success of this emotional appeal shows clearly that
Americans were more receptive to a moral argument
against liquor than to a scientific argument. To persuade
people to quit drinking, temperance leaders used two
techniques. On the one hand, they advocated religious

faith as a way for people to ease the anxieties that led to drink; on the other hand, they made drinking itself the source of anxieties by portraying liquor as the agent of the devil. Those Americans who were persuaded that Satan assumed "the shape of a bottle of spirits" found that liquor did more to increase anxieties than to lessen them. Such people preferred abstinence to alcohol.[4]

The leaders of the temperance crusade created a significant socializing institution, the temperance society. These "moral machines" were established in many villages and towns following a visit from an agent of a state or national temperance organization. An agent commonly wrote ahead to the ministers of a town to seek support for the cause. He then visited the town, gave a public address in one of the churches, and urged the clergymen and leading citizens to form a temperance society. The agent furnished a model constitution for such an organization, blessed the project, and proceeded to the next town. If successful, he left behind a concern about drinking and a group of prominent local people who would organize a society, adopt a constitution, write a pledge against drinking intoxicants, and undertake to get members of the community to sign it. Copies of the pledge were circulated among friends and neighbors, and new signers were initiated at monthly meetings where members congratulated themselves on the strength and vigor of their organization. When a temperance society had gathered sufficient popular support, it might plan to celebrate a holiday, such as the 4th of July, with a dry parade, picnic, or public speech designed to counter traditional wet festivities. These celebrations did not always succeed. Sometimes rival wet and dry programs sparked controversy, and at least one temperance group fought a pitched battle with its opponents. What is more surprising is how often temperance societies came to dominate the life of a town. Perhaps the best indication of their

Signing the Pledge.

strength and influence is the fact that in some localities
drinkers felt sufficiently threatened to form antitemperance societies.[5]

One reason for the popularity of temperance societies
in the 1820s was that they satisfied many patriotic longings. Antiliquor reformers asked Americans to draft temperance society constitutions, sign pledges, and celebrate
their dry oaths on the 4th of July. These actions were
analogous to those that the Founding Fathers had taken a
half century earlier. The symbolism was explicit, as
shown by the frequent references that temperance advocates made to the struggle for independence. They
argued that abstinence from liquor required as much virtue as had fighting the British during the Revolution,
that it demanded the same kind of sacrifice as renouncing
British tea in 1773, and that the early temperance movement, though a failure, had prepared them for the

present struggle just as the French and Indian War had prepared the colonists to fight the Revolution. Some reformers drew a closer parallel to the Revolution. At one 4th of July celebration, a speaker declared that when future generations assembled to honor the Founding Fathers, they would be able to say, "On this day, also did our fathers, of a later generation, declare and maintain a SECOND INDEPENDENCE. . . ." Another group of abstainers read a version of the Declaration in which George III was replaced by Prince Alcohol. Uses of symbolism and analogy were particularly popular in 1826, during the celebration of the fiftieth anniversary of the nation's birth. Americans apparently felt the need to be reborn, to be baptized anew in a struggle for liberty and equality, to be reassured by each other that they were worthy descendants of the Founding Fathers. They, too, needed a Revolution; so they pledged their lives, their fortunes, and their sacred honor in the war against Prince Alcohol.[6]

Antiliquor men employed various means to combat the power and influence of people who had an interest in the consumption of alcohol. For one thing, temperance reformers tried to cajole grain growers, distillers, tavern keepers, and drinkers into renouncing liquor. Often they succeeded, but when persuasion failed, they sought to overthrow the Demon Rum by novel means. After tavern keepers had explained that hotels could only show profits if they sold liquor, temperance reformers used subsidies to establish dry public houses. By the 1830s many American cities had temperance hotels. They were quasi-religious; some refused to serve people who travelled on the Sabbath, many held daily worship services, and most provided guests with moral tracts—especially temperance pamphlets. Another innovation was dry boat lines on canals and rivers. Since steam boats, like taverns, depended upon their bars for profits, such lines required financial subsidies. Abstainers also encouraged businessmen to ban spirits from the premises of their factories or stores, to require their employees to sign pledges, and to work cooperatively with other concerns that supported the cause. Insurance companies were persuaded to offer 5 percent discounts to ships manned by abstaining sailors. Finally, some antiliquor men pledged themselves to vote only for candidates who would abstain and work for the banishment of taverns and distilleries.[7]

Temperance reformers also flooded America with propaganda. By 1851 the American Tract Society reported the distribution of nearly five million temperance pamphlets; thirteen tracts had been issued in quantities in excess of one hundred thousand copies. Widespread dissemination of temperance literature depended upon the invention and perfection of cheap printing and the creation of an efficient distribution system. Both were necessary to insure that people who lived in remote places were exposed to the most advanced ideas about liquor, as presented in pamphlets, magazines, and newspapers. One wealthy New York landowner, Stephen Van Rensselaer, paid to have a copy of one tract delivered to every post office in the country, and retired Albany merchant Edward Delavan circulated a temperance broadside to every household in the state of New York. With Delavan's financial support the New York State Temperance Society, between 1829 and 1834, circulated 4,551,930 copies of its publications. Delavan had other projects. He once rushed 2,000 copies of a pamphlet to a meeting of the Virginia Temperance Society, and on another occasion he asked former presidents James Madison and John Quincy Adams and incumbent Andrew Jackson to sign the pledge abstaining from hard liquor. He succeeded in obtaining their signatures, which were published in facsimile on the back cover of the *Temperance Almanac* (1837). Perhaps most important to the success of

AN

ESSAY

ON

TEMPERANCE,

ADDRESSED PARTICULARLY TO STUDENTS,

AND THE

YOUNG MEN OF AMERICA.

BY EDWARD HITCHCOCK,
Professor of Chemistry and Natural History in Amherst College.

PUBLISHED UNDER THE DIRECTION OF THE AMERICAN TEMPERANCE
SOCIETY.

IT BEING THE ESSAY TO WHICH A PREMIUM WAS AWARDED.

SECOND EDITION.

AMHERST.

PUBLISHED BY J. S. & C. ADAMS;
JONATHAN LEAVITT, NEW YORK; PIERCE AND WILLIAMS,
BOSTON.
1830.

AN

ADDRESS

TO THE

YOUNG MEN OF THE UNITED STATES,

ON THE SUBJECT OF

TEMPERANCE.

BY THE

NEW-YORK YOUNG MEN'S SOCIETY FOR THE PROMOTION OF
TEMPERANCE.

Published under the Direction of the Board of Managers.

NEW-YORK:

JONATHAN LEAVITT, No. 182 BROADWAY.
Clayton & Van Norden, Printers.

1830.

AN ADDRESS

DELIVERED BEFORE

THE TEMPERANCE SOCIETY OF BATH, N. H.

JULY 4, 1828.

ALSO,

AN ADDRESS DELIVERED BEFORE THE

AMERICAN TEMPERANCE SOCIETY,

AT ITS SECOND ANNUAL MEETING,

HELD IN BOSTON, JAN. 28, 1829.

BY JONATHAN KITTREDGE, ESQ.

Boston:
T. R. MARVIN, PRINTER, 32, CONGRESS STREET.
1829.

AN

ADDRESS,

DELIVERED AT

NORTH-YARMOUTH, APRIL 28, 1830,

BEFORE THE

CUMBERLAND CO. TEMPERANCE SOCIETY.

BY SOLOMON ADAMS,
Cor. Sec. of the Society.

SECOND EDITION.

PORTLAND:

SHIRLEY, HYDE AND COMPANY.

1830.

the temperance cause was the wide circulation of the annual reports of the American Temperance Society,
1828–1836, and the American Temperance Union,
1837–1854, and the national distribution of the Andover
Journal of Humanity, 1829–1833, and Delavan's Albany
Temperance Recorder, 1832–1843. These publications
reached large numbers of clergymen, professionals, and
business leaders, many of whom became disciples of the
antiliquor scribes.[8]

Temperance propaganda came in a variety of forms
designed to evoke a number of moods with different audiences. It could be a song ("Cold Water is King, cold
water is lord, And a thousand bright faces now smile at
his board.") or a poem ("Our temperance efforts we must
never cease, Till from Rum's curse we do our land re-
lease."). It could be a humorous story. One anecdote told
of a drinker who mistook the swine hut for his house. He
stumbled into the trough and dozed off. When the pigs
came to investigate, the partially wakened man said,
"Wife, do leave off tucking up, and come along to bed."
Temperance literature instructed parents how to raise
their children. "If you must some times scare them,"
pleaded William Hines, "in the room of telling them that
bears will catch them, that hobgoblins or ghosts will
catch them, tell them that *Rum* will catch them. . . ."
At other times antiliquor pamphlets were self-congratula-
tory ("temperance societies have . . . much of the wis-
dom, virtue and talent of the community"), optimistic
("It is . . . an age singularly prolifick in schemes for
doing good to men."), or lurid ("The drunkard . . .
cleaves . . . like a gangrenous excrescence, poisoning
and eating away the life of the community.").[9]

The most memorable pieces that the temperance forces
published were stories and anecdotes in which the antiliquor message was implicit rather than explicit. No one
could fail to understand why an influential village squire

in New York joined the local temperance society after he found that in a public debate all of his arguments against the pledge were echoed by the town drunk. And a reader could not help but be moved to disgust and outrage upon reading a sensational account of how a drunkard father of a thirteen-year-old boy who had lost his leg in an industrial accident carried the leg to a surgeon, to whom he sold it for 37½¢, a sum that enabled him to carouse for several days. Most pathetic was a more probable story recorded by a man in Maine. "As I was riding in my sleigh I came up with a lad about 16 years old, very raggedly clothed—although an utter stranger to me, I was prompted to give him an invitation to get into my sleigh, which invitation he gladly accepted. No sooner had he taken a seat, than he commenced relating a tale which touched the very fibres of my soul. Said he, 'I am an abused child'—the tears gushed from both his eyes— What is the matter? said I. 'My father' he replied 'is a drunkard—he spends all he can get for rum—he returns home from the stores, fights with mother, who is as bad as my father—he has licked me (to use his own words) till gashes have been cut by the lashes of a green hide, till the blood has run all down over me. I have got no learning. I can't write any, and read but a very little—my father won't let me go to school, but keeps me all the time to work, and then beats me for doing no more.' "[10]

Most temperance propaganda was less realistic and more rhetorical. It usually employed the kinds of devices that preachers used to hold audiences. Occasionally, as in the following example, a romantic form was used to attack romanticism itself. William Goodell wrote, "*Why is it* that sober reasoning is well nigh banished from our Senates? *Whence* these inflammatory *harangues?* *Why* is it that history and biography have lost their interest and charms? *Why are they* displaced by quixotic romance and demoralizing fiction? Why are the classic models of the last century delivered to the moles and to the bats, while the ravings of insanity are admired? Why has the inspiration of the poet degenerated into the vagaries of derangement? Lord Byron will answer. He confessed that he wrote under the influence of distilled spirits. Here the disgusting secret is developed. Authors drink and write: readers drink and admire." Goodell's shock at the modern age is expressed in a form that is scarcely less than an 'inflammatory harangue' itself. This apparently self-contradictory result was the consequence of blending the rational themes that were at the core of the temperance movement with an emotionally charged presentation that during those years was necessary to win converts. At the same time, emotional presentation restricted the development of rational temperance thought. Temperance propaganda was highly repetitious and stressed themes that were linked to basic American values.[11]

Much of this literature sought to persuade Americans that the temperance cause promoted American ideals. Drinkers had claimed that to become intoxicated was their right as free men. Now, as Anthony Benezet had suggested years earlier, that idea was challenged and freedom redefined. A man no longer had the right to seek personal indulgence, to attain selfish gratification, to act alone and apart from others. The drinker, explained the reformer, was not free, for he was chained to alcohol, bound to the Demon Rum. He boasted of "independence and wealth, in the midst of disgrace and rags." Only self-delusion and self-deception made him feel free. To be free, it was necessary to curb appetites, to subordinate passions to reason, to control animalistic impulses through the development of moral ideals. Man could attain liberty only through self-control, self-examination, vigilance, the development of high moral values, and integration of himself into a moral society. Freedom, then, was autonomy exercised within a moral code. "Nothing can be more respectable," wrote John Randolph, "than the independence that grows out of self-denial." That kind of liberty could only be achieved within society, when a man sacrificed his personal interest to the social good. Only through devotion to social action and reform could a man gain liberty; to be free it was necessary to be socially effective; to be socially effective it was necessary to organize. Thus, freedom demanded that a man act in concert with others for the social good, as, for example, through temperance societies.[12]

Temperance advocates also attacked the traditional concept of equality. Drinkers had the idea that communal drinking bouts were proof of egalitarianism. Now equality was to be seen differently, no longer as the right to demand that all men drink together in holiday frolics. The members of the drunken mob, warned the antiliquor men, were not worthy of equality, for they were driven to the lowest level, sunk in degradation, mired in the devil's muck. The conviviality of the moment made them feel equal to all men, but equality at such an immoral level was destructive to one and all. The only equality worth having was the equal opportunity for all Americans to uphold high moral principles. The concept of equality must encourage the immoral to raise themselves to the highest level, it must not pull down the virtuous; the righteous must set an example, and moderate drinkers must be willing to renounce liquor in order to persuade drunkards to abstain. This egalitarianism required abstinence.[13]

Although we may find these arguments contorted and specious, they were the arguments that moved Americans to accept the idea that alcohol was destructive, dangerous, and evil. The vigorous and powerful intellects who fed the temperance presses created a moralistic climate that discouraged drinking and fostered the formation of temperance organizations. These societies in turn produced more tracts that encouraged more people to join the movement, and greater participation led to the publication of even more tracts, which brought about the conversion of even more people. An accelerating national campaign strengthened temperance institutions and propagated the new, antiliquor ideology. By 1831 the American Temperance Society reported more than 2,200 local organizations with more than 170,000 members; in 1834, 7,000 groups with 1,250,000 members. By 1839 a majority of the physicians and 85 percent of the ministers in the state of New York were reported to have become teetotalers.[14]

While the movement's ability to develop an ideology and to build organizations accounted for much of its success, I would argue that the essential source of the cause's dynamism was its accordance with two central impulses of the era: an appetite for material gain and a fervent desire for religious salvation. The prosperity that the market revolution had brought to the United States turned many Americans to materialism. Americans preached equality, but they worshipped success, by which they meant wealth. This pursuit of wealth ran parallel to a rising interest in evangelical religion. Ever since the turn of the century, ministers had found that people had an increasing concern for salvation. Materialism and devotion to religion were two contrasting sides of American culture, the former a cool, detached rationalism, the latter a highly charged emotionalism. The temperance movement, in my judgment, was a balance wheel which made it possible for these two principal and often conflicting elements of the national ethos to work together.

Americans expressed materialism in a number of ways. They believed that time should not be wasted, that it must be used productively because, in a sense, it was money. Americans adopted a hurried, harried pace. Now they gulped down their food not to rush to the bar but to rush to work; they raced to complete tasks; they dared not pause for polite conversation. "An American," wrote one traveller, "is born, lives, and dies twice as fast as any other human creature." Or as one immigrant who had still not adjusted to the pace of life after eighteen years in the United States marvelled in his diary, "How they rush around, these Americans, afraid they will die before they can finish what they have begun. And so they do die, worn out. They try to save time, but what do they do with that Time when they have it saved?" This obsession concerning time led one New York bank to print its currency with the slogan "Mind your business" encircling a sundial labelled "Fugio." No manner of idleness was approved, and in rural America in particular social pressure was applied to make sure that men carried on useful, gainful employment, even if they did not need the money. Leisure was expected to be employed productively. It could be used properly to learn new work skills, to study religion, to read moral tracts or other serious literature, to rest in order to regain one's strength for fresh labors, or to attend an illustrated lecture at the Lyceum. It was not proper to read novels, to go to the theater, or to tarry in taverns or groceries. Warned one pamphlet, "Intemperance and idleness usually go together."[15]

The concern for time was primarily a concern for money. "Making money," one observer declared, was "the all-powerful desire." Or as a jaded Scot said, Americans were "so keen about money, that . . . they would skin a flea for lucre of the hide and tallow." An American tried to gain as much wealth as possible, to get more than his neighbor, to acquire enough to be able to join the rich who ruled fashion, controlled politics, and received the adulation of the masses. Most Americans did not resent the rich and powerful but respected them and the visible evidence that gave a measure of their success. Americans confidently believed that equal opportunity, freedom, and hard work guaranteed that they or their children could also rise to such positions of prominence. They deferred to the rich not as their betters but as those whose achievements mirrored their own expectations. To people imbued with the go-ahead spirit, having money was a proof of virtue and acquiring it a measure of success.[16]

Men who chased dollars naturally disapproved of liquor, because a drinking man poured his money down his own throat, dissipating and destroying wealth for selfish, nonproductive ends. He was unable to accumulate capital, to invest for profits, or to save money for protection against misfortune. Drinking, declared temperance reformers, squandered capital. While this line of argument helped persuade the middle class to abstain, it held no appeal for the man who had little or no capital. A poor man would be tempted to spend his modest savings of 25¢ to $1 for refreshment in a tavern or grocery. Accordingly, reformers advocated the establishment of savings banks that would accept accounts as small as 5 or 10¢. Such institutions were opened in Boston and New York, and in Newton, Massachusetts, the temperance society itself operated a bank. Although many people could save only modest amounts, not exceeding a few hundred dollars after several years, these interest-bearing funds gave the poor an alternative to spending their money on liquor and at the same time provided a new source of capital that helped stimulate industrial development.[17]

Production was considered the only way to create wealth. Those hostile to liquor argued that alcohol inhibited industrial output and hence destroyed 'National Wealth.' This view was persuasively set forth by Horace Mann in a pamphlet urging rural grocers to quit selling liquor to their farm customers. A retailer's sales and profits, he claimed, were limited by his customers' incomes. Therefore, the nonproducing grocer could only attain greater prosperity if his customers produced more goods. However, increased production was possible only if farmers and manufacturers worked more diligently, gained new skills, or made capital improvements. If they bought spirits at the store, they would be unhealthy, wasteful, and nonproductive. Their low productivity would mean low profits for themselves, little money to spend, and a small income for the retailer. If, on the other hand, customers were unable to buy liquor at the grocery, they would be encouraged to use their savings to improve their education and to finance capital improvements. Better work habits and health would stimulate output, raise productivity, and increase the grocer's profits. It was in every retailer's self-interest, therefore, to quit selling liquor. Mann's analysis had only one flaw: many grocers found that spirits were their most profitable commodity. Still, what is important about this pamphlet, as well as others expressing the same view, is not the validity of its claims but the theme of its argument. Americans were, to put it simply, obsessed by an urge to produce and thereby create wealth.[18]

While the campaign against alcohol was of benefit to expansionary industrialism, it also met the needs of a growing religious movement. In the last quarter of the eighteenth century the influence of religion on American life had declined, the victim of Revolutionary chaos, a loss of English subsidies to the Episcopal church, popular distrust of authority, and the prevailing ideology of Reason. After 1800 the situation changed, and Americans, particularly those on the frontier, began to take a new interest in religion. The preachers soon saw that the Lord intended them to lead a great revival, to cleanse the nation of sin and to prepare for judgment, which might well be at hand. Some, especially the Methodist preachers, organized camp meeting revivals, where hordes of people pitched their tents, gathered for days on end, listened to numerous exhortations from a host of ministers, and were converted by the dozens amid frenzy and emotion. At one such meeting in Tennessee, "hundreds, of all ages and colors, were stretched on the ground in the agonies of conviction. . . ."[19]

Camp meetings became one of the focal points of frontier life, attracting not only those who sought salvation but also curiousity seekers, scoundrels, and scoffers. Troublemakers often crept along the edges of the camp, threatening to steal provisions, shouting obscenities, and drinking. These intoxicated scoffers presented the leaders of a revival with a dilemma. If they posted sentinels to protect the camp and bar entry, the rowdies would taunt them from the darkness of the forest. Moreover, such a policy precluded what could be the highlight of the meeting, the dramatic and inspiring conversion of a drunkard. On the other hand, if half-drunk rowdies were admitted, they might heckle or even try to force whiskey down the throat of an abstaining minister. In either case a preacher must be ever vigilant, like the incomparable Peter Cartwright. Once that pious Methodist swung a club to knock a mischief-maker off his horse; another time he stole the rowdies' whiskey. On a third occasion he drove off troublemakers by hurling chunks of a camp fire at them. As he threw the burning wood, he shouted that fire and brimstone would descend upon the wicked. Sometimes, however, the antagonists had their joke. The Reverend Joseph Thomas was horrified when several intoxicated men, having joined the celebration of the Lord's Supper, produced a loaf of bread and a bottle of spirits.[20]

These conditions led frontier revivalists to preach sermons contrasting the defiant, unrepentant drinker with

Camp meeting.

the pietistic, humble churchgoer. The consumer of alcohol was portrayed as a man of depravity and wickedness, and this idea was supported both by the presence of rowdies at camp meetings and by the emergence of a religious doctrine that demanded abstinence. Although most denominations had long condemned public drunkenness as sinful, it was revivalistic Methodists who most vigorously opposed alcohol. After 1790 the Methodist Church adopted rules that imposed strict limitations on the use of distilled spirits. In 1816 the quadrennial general conference barred ministers from distilling or selling liquor; in 1828 it praised the temperance movement; and in 1832 it urged total abstinence from all intoxicants. A similar rise in opposition occurred among Presbyterians. In 1812 their official body ordered ministers to preach against intoxication; in 1827 it pledged the church to sup-

port the temperance movement, in 1829 expressed regret that church members continued to distill, retail, or consume distilled spirits, and in 1835 recommended teetotalism.[21]

This increased hostility to drink showed the impact of the camp meetings and revivals upon all sects. Even conservative Congregationalists and Presbyterians were, in the words of one evangelical, moving "from the labyrinth of Calvinism . . . into the rich pastures of gospel-liberty." Ministers of these denominations were relieved, after a long period of religious quiescence, to find people thirsting for salvation. Although theological conservatives tried to bend the enthusiasm for revivals to their own interest, they were less successful than the Methodists, whose feverish, anti-intellectual, nondoctrinal spirit was most in harmony with the national mood. To compete in winning converts, conservative ministers were compelled to adopt an evangelical style that the public demanded and to subordinate doctrine to the task of winning hearts.[22]

Ministers of many denominations followed the lead of the Methodists, who preached that a man was saved when he opened his heart unto the Lord. This simple doctrine appealed to millions of Americans, but it also endangered religious authority, for the concept of personal salvation meant that it was impossible for an outsider, even a preacher, to know whether a man had actually received saving grace. A man might either claim salvation falsely or believe it mistakenly. The possibility of deceit or delusion so haunted evangelical clergymen that most came to believe that salvation was only likely when inner feelings were matched by outer deeds. When a man claimed grace, the preacher looked for a visible proof of conversion, an indication of true faith and allegiance, a token of the renunciation of sin and acceptance of the Lord.[23]

One visible outward sign of inner light was abstinence from alcoholic beverages. A man reborn of God had no need to drink spirits, since his radiant love for the Lord would fully satisfy him. Conversely, concluded one minister, "we may set it down as a probable sign of a false conversion, if he allows himself to *taste a single drop*." In the same vein it was held that a drinking man could not give himself to God; his drinking confirmed his hardness of heart; he was damned of God, because he would not save himself. Warned one clergyman, "Few intemperate men ever repent." This view led evangelicals to see alcohol as the devil's agent, the insidious means by which men were lured into Satan's works, such as gaming, theft, and debauchery and, worse still, trapped and cut off from their own eternal salvation. Said one preacher, "From the United States, then, what an army of drunkards reel into Hell each year!"[24]

Not all Americans adopted the view that abstinence signified holiness and that drinking was damnable. Among the most prominent opponents of the temperance cause were the primitive Baptists, sometimes called Hard Shells or Forty Gallon Baptists. They were antinomians who believed that faith alone insured salvation and that the demand for proof of faith, such as requiring abstinence, was blasphemous. Indeed, some held that abstinence was sinful, because "God gave the spirit in the fruit of grain, and the ability to extract and decoct it, and then he gave them the inclination to drink." Furthermore, they believed that temperance organizations, like home missions, Sunday schools, and moral tract societies, threatened the purity of religion by involving the church in social problems that were best left to secular authority. Doctrine, however, may not have been the most important reason for this sect's opposition to temperance, for it was claimed that their illiterate preachers were "engaged largely in making and selling whisky." In any event, many primitive Baptist congregations expelled a member either for public intoxication or for joining a temperance society. This bifurcated policy led one exasperated man to bring a flask before his church board and ask, "How much of this 'ere critter does a man have to drink to stay in full fellership in this church?"[25]

Most Americans, however, did accept abstinence as a sign of grace. During the late 1820s religious fervor peaked in a wave of revivals that swept across the country, that brought large numbers of new members into old congregations, and that led to the establishment of many new churches. This period of rising interest in religion coincided with the first popular success of the campaign against alcohol. The two were inexorably linked. In many localities revivals were held, church rosters bulged, and then six months or a year later temperance societies were organized. If this pattern had been universal, we could conclude that antiliquor sentiment was an outgrowth of religious enthusiasm, that the signing of a pledge was nothing more than proof of conversion, a symbolic act with no significance of its own. In some places, however, the establishment of temperance societies preceded the revivals, a pattern that suggests a different interpretation of the relationship between abstinence and holiness. It appears that some Americans rejected liquor for secular reasons and only afterward turned to religion. The prevalence of both patterns indicates that temperance and revivalism were not causally connected. I would argue, rather, that they were interwoven because both were responses to the same underlying social tensions and anxieties.[26]

We have already seen how the stresses of rapid change had made Americans anxious, how the failure to implement Revolutionary ideals of equality and liberty had heightened that anxiety, and how the decay of traditional institutions had left citizens of the young republic with few orderly outlets for their emotions, few acceptable means of satisfying their emotional needs. Under such circumstances many Americans had turned to strong drink, but they found alcohol emotionally unsatisfying. Then came the revivals and the temperance movement, which offered Americans new ways to resolve tensions, reduce fears, and organize their emotional impulses. The camp meeting, the evangelical church, and the temperance society were institutions that provided new mechanisms for coping with frustrations and for controlling, structuring, rationalizing, and channeling emotions. "It is *religion*," declared one tract, ". . . which alone contains in it the seeds of social order and stability, and which alone can make us happy and preserve us so." Both evangelical religion and the temperance cause encouraged people to subordinate emotions to rational, institutional processes. In my view the inexorable link between holiness and abstinence was that both called for emotions to be expressed and controlled, and at times repressed, within an orderly, institutional framework.[27]

This control of emotions meshed with the needs of the developing industrial complex. The process of industrialization required the accumulation of capital. This meant that current gratification had to be sacrificed in order to provide resources for future economic expansion. Workers were told that efficiency and self-discipline would increase productivity, which would lead to higher wages, promotions, and the chance to own their own businesses and factories. Capitalists were encouraged to forego the consumption of luxuries in order to reinvest profits in their enterprises. The new emphasis on rationality and discipline also led businessmen to adopt more orderly methods. They began to exercise more caution in the extension of credit, to promote efficiency by encouraging specialization of the labor force, to make more scientifically calculated investment decisions, and to keep better financial records. One is struck, for example, by a significant improvement in the precision of the business ledgers in Harvard's Baker Business Library for the years after 1820. Concern about the reliability of trading associates led New York's reform-minded Lewis Tappan to use his connections with the temperance movement in order to found the first national credit rating service, the forerunner of Dun and Bradstreet. And the abstinent Harper brothers built the country's first publishing empire through a combination of technological innovation, evangelical salesmanship, and a continuous demand for Methodist Bibles.[28]

Let me state the argument further. By the 1830s Americans had created a new culture that appears to have enabled them to prosper amid the upheaval of the Industrial Revolution. The rising tide of anxiety unleashed by the failure of the old order, the ideological beliefs in equality and liberty, and the high aspirations for national glory and success had receded as the old traditions and unrealized ideals were replaced by a new ideology within a new institutional framework. Central to the new culture were the subordination of emotion to rationality, the postponement of gratification, and an orientation toward the future. These were the principal means by which Americans reconciled the contradictions between their two key and sometimes contrary impulses, a drive for material gain and a desire for religious salvation. The former was institutionalized in business enterprise, the latter in evangelical religion. These two impulses were connected by certain cultural assumptions which dictated that efficient, rational enterprise must dominate emotion-charged religion, that religion itself must be orderly and structured, and that failure to realize goals in the present must be accepted as the price for success in the future.

Some Americans could not accept a society based on

such a delicately balanced, jerry-built ethos. People who found that evangelical religion could not meet their emotional needs sometimes turned to new, unorthodox denominations such as the Mormons or to a fervent belief in the immediacy of the Second Coming. Millennial hopes and prophecies increased under the stresses of rapid change and culminated with the rise of the Millerites, a group that gathered to await the world's end on October 22, 1844. Their expectation was but the crudest manifestation of a feeling that began to pervade the country after 1830. Most people, I am persuaded, recognized that they were living at the beginning of unprecedented social and economic upheaval and accepted the transitory nature of their times. Unlike the Millerites, however, the majority expected changes for the better to take place on earth. They believed that the quality of life was improving and that life would be more rewarding for future generations. Although Americans had not yet adopted a cult of progress, they were hopeful, even panglossian.[29]

It appears, however, that the more intelligent and shrewd saw contradictions between the materialistic and the religious aspects of the new American ethos. What they saw were, on the one hand, soft-headed hysterics and mystics who preached that evil and the fears it caused would be washed away by the apocalypse; on the other, hard-hearted materialists whose repression of their feelings enabled them to believe that all difficulties would be resolved in time through orderly industrial development. Neither vision seemed complete to thoughtful men who accepted industrial progress, but respected tradition, and held that man's needs were both of this world and another. Men who believed that salvation required faith, that good deeds could be signs of holiness, and that man was God's agent on earth turned to a religion that preached social reform. They believed that America could only become a vigorous, moral republic if society were organized to combat existing evils. While endorsing American ideals, they insisted that those ideals could only be attained by devotion to the cause of reform.[30]

The impulse for reform that grew out of concern for both material and moral well-being led to a variety of social movements, including the crusade to abolish slavery. It should not be surprising that many of the people opposed to alcohol were also opposed to slavery, for both intemperance and slavery were considered economically wasteful as well as immoral. Northern reformers such as William Lloyd Garrison and Theodore Weld embraced both movements. Indeed, Weld had travelled throughout the country as an agent for the American Temperance Society before he undertook similar labors on behalf of abolition. Among Weld's converts to temperance was James Gillespie Birney, who organized the movement in Alabama; a few years later Weld returned to the South and persuaded Birney to renounce slavery. The connection between abolition and abstinence weakened the temperance crusade in the South, especially after southern subscribers to northern temperance periodicals received unsolicited antislavery literature.

More interesting than the overlapping of these two movements, however, is the fact that the early reformers considered temperance to be the more crucial reform. They argued that while slavery encouraged the master to idleness and vice and the slave to ignorance and religious indifference, the effect of drink was worse: a slave had only lost control of his body, a drunkard lost mastery of his soul. The chains of intoxication, declared one reformer, "are heavier than those which the sons of Africa have ever worn." That men in the 1830s emphasized abstinence over abolition seems grotesque today. We find the equation of a liquor store with a slave market absurd. Nor is our revulsion lessened because it was moral con-

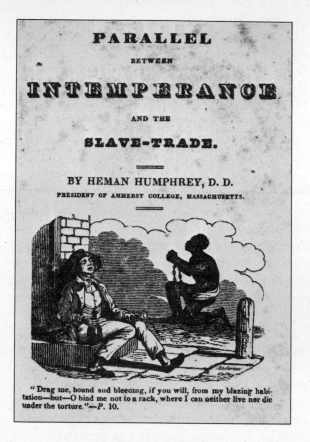

"Drag me, bound and bleeding, if you will, from my blazing habitation—but—O bind me not to a rack, where I can neither live nor die under the torture."—*P.* 10.

Temperance and Slavery.

cern that caused reform-minded men to reach the conclusion that alcohol was the greater evil. The tragedy of the early temperance movement was that men who believed in the American experiment, who accepted the value of industrialization, and who also tried to revitalize religion, were led to battle against liquor harder than against the other, greater evil.[31]

Misdirection of energies is common among moral crusaders, since principled and well-intentioned leaders are often self-deluded and unable to perceive their goals objectively. Temperance advocates did not comprehend their own arrogance in attempting to impose their views upon segments of the populace that were hostile, nor did they understand that effective moral codes must develop out of a social consensus, that they cannot be dictated by an elite group that seeks reform. The cry for abstinence was an attempt to cement the broken fragments of American society, but the leaders of the temperance movement could never gain the kind of unanimous consent that would have been necessary for the success of the cause. In another, broader sense the failure of the reformers to persuade all Americans to forego alcoholic beverages voluntarily was inevitable because of a peculiarity of evangelical religion. Since abstinence was the creed of those converted to godliness, universal salvation would have insured its triumph. Such unanimity, however, would have undermined revivalistic religion, whose vitality demanded a steady flow of repentant sinners. The damned drunkard was essential to the cause. On the other hand, if abstinence were not universal, this failure to achieve complete success would show that evangelical religion was not able to improve public morals greatly and would doom the idea of temperance as a consensual social value.

Antiliquor crusaders never understood these contradictions. Instead, they emerged from each bitter clash with their enemies determined to escalate the war against alcohol in order to achieve final success. And, of course, in one sense they were right; only escalation of their efforts could keep attention focused on their goal of a dry America and obscure the contradictions inherent in their position. During the 1830s, when new pledges began to fall off, reformers turned to attacking beer and wine and proving that the wine used in the biblical accounts of the Christian sacrament was the unfermented pure wine of the grape—i.e., grape juice. Not everyone was convinced. The failure of exhortation to procure universal teetotalism led to a campaign for legal prohibition, which brought about local option licensing in the 1840s, state prohibition in the 1850s, and, ultimately, in 1919, the national constitutional prohibition of all intoxicating liquor.[32] Each effort failed to achieve the universal abstinence that reformers sought. Again and again it was demonstrated that those who believed in abstinence could not succeed in imposing their own view of morality upon that portion of the population that did not share their vision. In 1838, when Massachusetts outlawed the retail sale of distilled spirits, Yankee ingenuity triumphed. An enterprising liquor dealer painted stripes on his pig and advertized that for 6¢ a person could see this decorated beast. The viewer also got a free glass of whiskey. Such ploys spurred a hurried repeal of the nation's first prohibition law.[33]

The moral of the striped pig was that a belief in temperance was only one component of the American ethos. This moral was lost on antiliquor zealots, who attempted to transcend the contradictions within American society with a combination of religious fervor, postponed gratification, and promises of heavenly rewards. While the faithful found these ideas appealing, others chose to forego religious commitment for the pursuit of economic gain. They were led to a kind of pragmatism that stressed industrialization, materialism, and progress. As worldly success became the counterweight to reform, the chance for Americans to develop a consensual, holistic ethos that would serve them during the period of industrialization was lost. Some, such as abolitionist John Brown, would lapse into self-deluding fanaticism; others, such as Wall Street stock manipulator Daniel Drew, into self-destructive cynicism. Most Americans would be content with a contradictory mixture of morality and materi-

Death on the Striped Pig. Broadside reprinted by permission of the Rhode-Island Historical Society.

alism that would be mindlessly played out in the years ahead. The heroes of the next generation would be entrepreneurs like Cornelius Vanderbilt, who had so few scruples that he could ignore his avaricious and rapacious pursuit of millions and without embarrassment deliver public lectures on virtue. Somehow, despite his utter baseness, Vanderbilt was more admirable than a hypocritical Henry Ward Beecher, who preached against sin while facing charges of adultery. In the years after the Civil War the hope for financial gain overshadowed the search for righteousness, although neither quest could express all the contrary desires of Americans. The times favored men such as Vanderbilt, who ignored principles, followed instincts, and subordinated both his head and his heart to his gut.

In my view the kind of society that Americans built in the nineteenth century resulted both from the way that ideology and institutions interacted with changing contemporary conditions and from the way in which society itself evolved as a consequence of those interactions. Just as historical circumstances and economic developments had led to the opportunity for increased drinking in the 1820s, the binge itself created another opportunity; the impulses toward materialism and evangelicalism dictated the shape and contour of the response to that opportunity. The campaign for abstinence and the transformation of alcohol from the Good Creature into the Demon Rum were a logical outgrowth of prevailing attitudes, values, and institutions. As drinking declined, as society was reshaped, as the framework for modern capitalism developed, and as the churches organized their moral campaign, the chance for a holistic ethos disappeared.

America was left as a culture dominated by an ambivalence that could be transcended only through an anti-intellectual faith. The potential for powerful intellects to influence American life had diminished; a unified moral code was no longer possible. By 1840 the pattern that would dominate the country for a century was set. Entrepreneurial capitalism, the corporate structure, the cult of private enterprise, and the glorification of profit were to dominate the rational, hard, masculine, and efficient side of the culture; evangelical religion, the voluntary reform society, the cult of Christian charity, and the glorification of God were to dominate the emotional, soft, feminine, and inspirational side. Institutions representing the two sides were to work in tandem to build the country. Important among those institutions were temperance societies. They were, in many ways, the crucial link between the two contrasting sides of American culture. A majority of the participants in the early temperance movement were women, but, in contrast to a later era, the leaders were men, mostly evangelical clergymen. These ministers were to be the bridge between the two sides of American culture, the men who connected the masculine and feminine, hard and soft, rational and emotional aspects. Or as one American said in the 1830s, clergymen were "a sort of people between men and women." This remark has a second, deeper meaning. Being neither men nor women, the clergy were clearly impotent, and, ultimately, incapable of sustaining a coherent, holistic, living culture.[34]

The result was predictable. America would remain materialistic, evangelical, volatile, and adrift. America, as it turned out, was not balanced; rather, she had only the illusion of balance, and her natural imbalance, like that of an airplane sailing across the skies, was overcome only by the speed of her material progress. The illusion of a tranquil and cohesive society could be maintained only so long as the materialist appetite could be fed by an increasing exploitation of men and resources. This process could not continue indefinitely. When Manifest Destiny reached its natural limits at the Pacific Ocean, the expansionist solution to social tensions lost much of its momentum. Soon afterward, when geographical barriers and northern economic and political power combined to threaten to strangle the expansionist Cotton South, she erupted with hysteria. The nation survived by turning from the acquisition of lands for republican farmers to the exploitation of immigrant labor and natural resources in order to build the world's foremost industrial economy. More was better, and the god of success was appeased by the increasing pollutants that poured forth from the nation's smokestacks. Later, when the Great Depression of the 1930s idled those factories, the lack of material progress disillusioned Americans and destroyed many of the assumptions that underlay the social order. The nineteenth-century ethos began to collapse. It was no accident that the Crash that obliterated the probusiness euphoria of the 1920s also brought an end to the noble experiment of prohibition.

It is now more than forty years since the repeal of prohibition, twenty since the Beat generation challenged the old morality, ten since hippies and yippies rocked and rolled across the American consciousness. Three-quarters of the way through the twentieth century both the temperance ideal and the culture that produced it have all but vanished. While that culture was imperfect, leaving in its wake a great civil war, the exploitation of the frontier, the ruin of America's first native inhabitants, and the squandering of natural resources, it also produced a vigorous and free industrial society. It raised living standards for all people and created a sufficient national consensus to allow the United States to grow and develop. Its self-deluding and sometimes hypocritical ability to bridge the gaps between desires and reality, between reason and feeling, and between modern industrialism and traditional religion effectively stimulated orderliness, hope, and rapid economic development. The disappearance of the temperance ideal has robbed American society of some of the grease that kept the machinery of society running smoothly. Today we Americans see too clearly and too painfully the contradictions between what we are and what we believe we ought to be. Institutions seem incapable of fulfilling our old ideals of liberty and equality, our belief in perfection torments us even as it drives us to greater efforts, and our failures bring us to methods for coping with life that are scarcely different from those of the alcoholic republic. So we remain what we have been.

APPENDICES

NOTES

INDEX

APPENDIX ONE

Estimating Consumption of Alcohol

How MUCH did Americans drink? This question is difficult to answer for much of the past because of the scarcity and poor quality of sources. There is no single source that could indicate consumption; indeed, records generally have reported production rather than consumption and frequently have stated only the production of one particular beverage. Information for the colonial years is so limited that per capita consumption could not be calculated. I have been able to use a few estimates of consumption for the early period to establish an upper limit for the consumption of distilled spirits in 1710, and I found that literary sources that consistently reported an increasing use of rum during the eighteenth century enabled me to draw a rising trend line from 1710 to 1770. Unfortunately, it was necessary to consider the intake of beer, cider, and wine in 1710 to be the same as for later periods. By 1770 there were more and better data, especially in the import records for 1768–1772. Using these records as well as reports of molasses and rum production and exports from the West Indies, economic historian John McCusker has been able to calculate per capita rum consumption for 1770. At the time, little grain or fruit spirit was drunk. Official records also suggest that little wine was imported; beer and cider intake was estimated to follow the pattern of later times. For 1785, rum consumption was calculated from a variety of sources. The absence of data about whiskey, however, compelled an attempt to guess the extent of the use of that relatively new beverage. As late as 1774 Anthony Benezet had felt obligated to define whiskey when he used the word

in an antiliquor tract. Whiskey must have held a minor role in
1785, for even in the 1790s, when its share of the market was
rising, it accounted for less than a third of all the spirits that
were drunk. For 1785, the consumption of wine, cider, and
beer was presumed to be at the 1790 level.[1]

Sources for the years after 1784 are somewhat better. Accordingly, it was possible to prepare more detailed and more
reliable estimates for 1790–1860. Customs accounts did provide
a way to assess wine consumption, since almost all the wine
that Americans drank was imported. These records also established long-range trends for imported rum and domestic
rum manufactured from imported molasses. Rum, however,
was losing its market to whiskey, and tracing the use of whiskey was more difficult. The only federal liquor taxes before
1862 were two haphazardly enforced excises on distilled spirits
covering 1791–1801 and 1814–1817. The first was Alexander
Hamilton's 'Whiskey Tax,' from which only limited information could be derived. For one thing, rural distillers, unlike
their urban counterparts, paid the tax not on the gallons of
their production but on the capacity of their stills. While some
farmers distilled full time, others did not, and, hence, it was
not possible to calculate rural production. Then, too, except
for New England's highly visible, large-scale distilleries, the
tax was widely evaded. Hostile Kentuckians prevented the organization of their state as a tax district for many years, and
western Pennsylvanians engineered the 1794 Whiskey Rebellion when a serious attempt was made to enforce the law in
that area. Even in the capital city of Philadelphia illicit production was common. The records for the 1814–1817 levy are, if
anything, less reliable.[2]

Early censuses failed to measure alcohol production (1790,
1800, 1830) or, when they did (1810, 1820, 1840), they were
incomplete and inaccurate. The best of these tallies was taken
in 1810, when census director Tench Coxe sought to demonstrate the strength and vitality of American manufactures
through reports of the production of beer and distilled spirits.
Distilling was then one of the nation's principal industries.
Even this report was imperfect: one New Yorker suggested
that only half of that state's manufactures had been counted,
and a South Carolinian asserted that his state's liquor produc-

tion was substantially underreported. Nevertheless, the 1810 census reports of spirits production were so much higher than private estimates that when the census was published in 1814, the announcement helped launch the temperance movement. Reformers widely disseminated the 1810 data. Although the 1820 census was organized similarly, the results were less accurate. The rise of textiles and iron works drew the attention of census takers from small-scale distilleries, and increasing hostility to liquor must have made distillers reluctant to report their production. During the 1830s an attempt was made to obtain commercial and industrial data from local authorities, but these fragmentary returns could not be used to estimate the consumption of alcohol.[3]

When the government again measured the production of beer and spirits in the 1840 census, that tally was incomplete. In South Carolina, for example, a census supervisor confessed that officials "omitted many an house either purposely or otherwise." Even the reasonably complete census of 1850 was imperfect, for minor but annoying discrepancies in the amount of alcohol production appeared in the various published volumes of that count. The information published in the latest volume was presumed to be the most accurate. Because a similar problem existed for 1860, I used the reports of alcohol consumption contained in the U.S. Census, *Statistical Abstract* (1921). The 1850 and 1860 census reports of alcohol production suffered from another difficulty. By that time production of distilled spirits was no longer a reliable guide to consumption. After 1830 alcohol gradually became a popular fuel, industrial solvent, and lighting fluid, and by 1860 as much as one-third of the nation's distilled liquor was not drunk. One indication of the rising industrial use of alcohol was that a number of census takers in 1860 distinguished between the production of industrial and beverage alcohol.[4]

Business records were not very helpful for measuring consumption. Tavern licenses could not be used to compute per capita consumption of alcohol because many houses were unlicensed and, more important, because a recent investigation has established that the number of taverns per capita is unrelated to consumption. Nor could much be gained from the ledgers of distillers, brewers, and retailers. Few manufacturers left records that have survived, and it could not be determined if the extant accounts were representative. The poor quality of existing records reflects the fact that brewing and distilling were dominated by thousands of small operators whose ledgers, if they ever existed, have long since vanished. As for retail sales, so many people distilled or brewed at home, bartered with neighbors, or bought directly from the manufacturer that the limited information in retail account books could not be employed to calculate total per capita consumption.[5]

For the consumption of distilled spirits, a number of private estimates were located. I used Alexander Hamilton's calculations and information that appeared in travel accounts, statistical compendiums, economic surveys, and the press, especially *Niles' Register*.[6] Most significant were the more than 200 references covering 1814–1840 in the early temperance literature. Information from the antiliquor movement was used cautiously, after it was tested for reliability. Signs of its credibility are the agreement among independent temperance estimates, the faith in these claims demonstrated by widespread borrowing, the lack of opposition to these statements, and the negligible differences between temperance estimates and those from other sources. Another sign of the validity of these reports is that the stated gallonage is usually specific. Temperance reformers appear to have prepared their calculations of spirits consumption conscientiously.[7] In Concord, Massachusetts, for example, local reform leaders visited the town's tavern keepers and grocers to elicit sales information. Most vendors candidly reported the quantity and value of their sales, but some refused to talk, and the reformers then sought the opinions of employees and competitors. These interviews enabled the investigators to prepare their statistical analysis. During the 1820s this kind of inquiry was possible because the clergymen who led the reform cause had good contacts with the liquor merchants, many of whom were religious men who had not yet left the trade. After 1835 consumption estimates disappeared from the temperance literature, for by then the crusade against spirits had deprived ministers of their sources.[8]

It was necessary to follow different procedures to estimate consumption of other alcoholic beverages. Since the 1810 and

1840 censuses show little beer production, intake prior to 1840 was considered to be negligible. This conclusion was supported by the observations of foreign travellers. Census reports were used to calculate consumption for 1810 and 1840–1860. For wine, low domestic production insured that customs records provided an accurate measurement. For hard cider, which was neither taxed nor included in a census, use was made of a few scattered references. Cider consumption was estimated based on these sources, the population of cider producing areas (defined as New England [except Maine], New York [except New York City], New Jersey, Maryland, Ohio, and half of Pennsylvania and Virginia), and an alcohol content of 10 percent, the minimum needed to prevent spoilage during storage.[9]

To calculate per capita consumption levels for each beverage from 1790 to 1860, estimates from all sources were considered for five-year periods. Within each interval, both median and mean consumption values were tabulated from the various estimates. For spirits intake, median and mean tables were constructed. A comparison of these tables with impressionistic information from literary sources, primarily travel accounts, indicated that the mean table gave the better fit. It was, however, considered desirable to smooth the table using three-point moving averages. Mean tables were then calculated for the other beverages.

One methodological problem was how to compare consumption of beverages that contained different amounts of alcohol. Social scientists usually prefer to measure alcohol consumption by calculating the quantity of alcohol present in all beverages consumed. This procedure can hide important information, for alcohol ingested from different kinds of drinks can produce various effects. While, for example, a can of beer has the same amount of alcohol as a jigger of whiskey, the former has nearly twice as many calories. Furthermore, low-proof beverages are less likely to lead to intoxication. To provide the maximum amount of information concerning changing patterns of beverage consumption, intake has been calculated for both the different beverages and the total amount of alcohol. For 1710–1860, I used the following values for the proportion of alcohol in various drinks: spirits, 45%; wine, 18%; cider, 10%; beer, 5%.[10]

A second problem concerned population values. Some recent investigators have restricted their studies to the drinking population, in order to prevent distortions due to varying proportions of abstainers. Inadequate data made it impossible to use this technique. Another method, which most recent estimators of per capita consumption have employed, is to measure intake only for the adult, drinking-age population, defined as age fifteen and above. Since children seldom drink much, this technique has been valuable when comparing societies which have low birth rates and few children with those which have high reproduction rates and many offspring. Because the proportion of children under age sixteen in the United States has declined from one-half of the total population in the early nineteenth century to one-quarter in 1970, it can be argued that this concept is applicable to the present study. On the other hand, during the past 150 years there have been radical changes in drinking customs, including a marked increase in the age at entry into the drinking population. Under these circumstances, to use an arbitrary, constant age of entry across such a long time span may be inappropriate.[11] Because the measurement of per capita consumption for total and drinking-age populations may be useful for different purposes, estimates were calculated according to both procedures. For 1710–1785 population estimates were drawn from the U.S. Census, *Historical Statistics of the United States* (Wash., 1975), 2:1168; age distributions were based on the ratios in the 1790 census. For 1790–1860 the census was used for population values; mid-decade intervals were interpolated.[12]

Information for 1865–1975 has been computed from the U.S. Census, *Statistical Abstract* (1952), 791; (1965) 797; (1976) 5, 6; (1977) 6, 811; U.S. Brewers Assn., *Brewers Almanac* (1971), 57, 59, 61, 63; (1972) 57; (1973) 57; *Wines and Vines*, 57 (1976), 38. For consumption during prohibition, I followed Clark Warburton, *The Economic Results of Prohibition* (N.Y., 1932), 71. (See Tables A1.1 and A1.2.)

It must be emphasized that these estimates are approximations, a compilation of personal judgments rather than scientifically verified measurements. Indeed, their presentation in tabular form tends to suggest a precision that is lacking. Certainly these figures should not be used in sophisticated statistical computations, where a far greater accuracy would be needed. On the other hand, these estimates do suggest major changes in drinking patterns, rising and falling trends, and the magnitude of change, e.g., doubled or tripled. The validity of the figures is confirmed in part by the comments of contemporary observers, many of whom were cited in chapter one. During the first portion of the nineteenth century Americans lamented that alcohol consumption had been rising since 1800; foreign travellers were shocked by the nation's drinking habits. After 1830 Americans noted a decline in drinking; visitors reported little imbibing and even less intoxication.

The general trends suggested by these estimates were confirmed by information in tavern and general store account books. A study of six tavern ledgers for 1810–1835 indicated that a typical customer frequented the tavern once a week and regularly bought distilled spirits in small amounts, most commonly a half pint. (See Table A1.3.)

At that rate annual per capita adult male consumption of distilled spirits at taverns was 13 quarts, one-fifth of total estimated consumption. This proportion seems reasonable considering that much hard liquor was taken at home.

Because of high home consumption, we would expect to find higher spirits sales in general stores than in taverns. An examination of account books for three concerns did show this pattern. (See Table A1.4.)

These purchases, however, even when added to drinks bought at taverns, would not account for the total amount of spirituous liquor that we have estimated to have been consumed. Explanations for this apparent discrepancy are that many farmers shopped in several different establishments, made their own whiskey or peach brandy, purchased directly from a manufacturer, or bartered for these goods with neighbors. Finally, a study of hard liquor sales in general stores showed not only that spirits were the most important product sold but also that in the case of the Frost Store, the one concern for which information could be obtained for a long period, the value of such sales peaked during the early 1820s.

Table A1.1. ALCOHOLIC BEVERAGE CONSUMPTION
absolute alcohol for each beverage,
per capita of total population, in U.S. gallons

| Year | SPIRITS | | WINE | | CIDER | | BEER | | TOTAL |
	Bev.	Abs. Alc.	Bev.	Abs. Alc.	Bev.	Abs. Alc.	Bev.	Abs. Alc.	Abs. Alc.
1710	2.0	.9	.1	<.05	18.	1.8	-	-	2.7
1770	3.7	1.7	.1	<.05	18.	1.8	-	-	3.5
1785	3.0	1.4	.3	.1	18.	1.8	-	-	3.3
1790	2.7	1.2	.3	.1	18.	1.8	-	-	3.1
1795	3.1	1.4	.3	.1	18.	1.8	-	-	3.3
1800	3.8	1.7	.3	.1	17.	1.7	-	-	3.5
1805	4.3	1.9	.3	.1	16.	1.6	-	-	3.6
1810	4.6	2.1	.2	<.05	16.	1.6	.7	<.05	3.7
1815	4.4	2.0	.2	<.05	16.	1.6	-	-	3.6
1820	4.7	2.1	.2	<.05	15.	1.5	-	-	3.6
1825	5.0	2.2	.2	<.05	15.	1.5	-	-	3.7
1830	5.2	2.3	.3	.1	15.	1.5	-	-	3.9
1835	4.2	1.9	.3	.1	8.5	.8	-	-	2.8
1840	3.1	1.4	.3	.1	2.	.2	1.3	.1	1.8
1845	2.1	.9	.2	<.05	-	-	1.4	.1	1.0
1850	2.1	.9	.2	<.05	-	-	1.6	.1	1.0
1855	2.2	1.0	.2	<.05	-	-	2.7	.1	1.1
1860	2.3	1.0	.3	.1	-	-	3.8	.2	1.3
1865	2.1	.9	.3	.1	-	-	3.5	.2	1.2
1870	1.9	.9	.3	.1	-	-	5.2	.3	1.3
1875	1.7	.8	.5	.1	-	-	6.2	.3	1.2
1880	1.5	.7	.6	.1	-	-	6.9	.3	1.1
1885	1.4	.6	.5	.1	-	-	11.4	.6	1.3
1890	1.4	.6	.4	.1	-	-	13.3	.7	1.4
1895	1.2	.5	.4	.1	-	-	15.2	.8	1.4
1900	1.2	.5	.4	.1	-	-	15.5	.8	1.4
1905	1.3	.6	.5	.1	-	-	17.3	.9	1.6
1910	1.4	.6	.6	.1	-	-	19.8	1.0	1.7
1915	1.2	.5	.5	.1	-	-	20.2	1.0	1.6
1920	1.4	.6	-	-	-	-	-	-	.6
1925	1.4	.6	-	-	-	-	-	-	.6
1930	1.4	.6	-	-	-	-	-	-	.6
1935	1.1	.5	.3	.1	-	-	10.9	.5	1.1
1940	1.0	.4	.7	.1	-	-	12.9	.6	1.1
1945	1.1	.5	.8	.1	-	-	17.9	.8	1.4
1950	1.1	.5	.8	.1	-	-	17.6	.8	1.4
1955	1.1	.5	.9	.2	-	-	16.2	.7	1.4
1960	1.3	.6	.9	.2	-	-	15.2	.7	1.5
1965	1.5	.7	.9	.2	-	-	16.0	.7	1.6
1970	1.8	.8	1.3	.2	-	-	18.4	.8	1.8
1975	1.8	.8	1.6	.2	-	-	21.4	1.0	2.0

Different versions of Tables A1.1 and A1.2 appeared in W. J. Rorabaugh, "Estimated U.S. Alcoholic Beverage Consumption, 1790–1860," *Journal of Studies on Alcohol*, 37 (1976), 360–361.

Table A1.2. ALCOHOLIC BEVERAGE CONSUMPTION
absolute alcohol for each beverage, per capita
of drinking-age (15+) population, in U.S. gallons

Year	SPIRITS Bev.	SPIRITS Abs. Alc.	WINE Bev.	WINE Abs. Alc.	CIDER Bev.	CIDER Abs. Alc.	BEER Bev.	BEER Abs. Alc.	TOTAL Abs. Alc.
1710	3.8	1.7	.2	<.05	34.	3.4	-	-	5.1
1770	7.0	3.2	.2	<.05	34.	3.4	-	-	6.6
1785	5.7	2.6	.6	.1	34.	3.4	-	-	6.1
1790	5.1	2.3	.6	.1	34.	3.4	-	-	5.8
1795	5.9	2.7	.6	.1	34.	3.4	-	-	6.2
1800	7.2	3.3	.6	.1	32.	3.2	-	-	6.6
1805	8.2	3.7	.6	.1	30.	3.0	-	-	6.8
1810	8.7	3.9	.4	.1	30.	3.0	1.3	.1	7.1
1815	8.3	3.7	.4	.1	30.	3.0	-	-	6.8
1820	8.7	3.9	.4	.1	28.	2.8	-	-	6.8
1825	9.2	4.1	.4	.1	28.	2.8	-	-	7.0
1830	9.5	4.3	.5	.1	27.	2.7	-	-	7.1
1835	7.6	3.4	.5	.1	15.	1.5	-	-	5.0
1840	5.5	2.5	.5	.1	4.	.4	2.3	.1	3.1
1845	3.7	1.6	.3	.1	-	-	2.4	.1	1.8
1850	3.6	1.6	.3	.1	-	-	2.7	.1	1.8
1855	3.7	1.7	.3	.1	-	-	4.6	.2	2.0
1860	3.9	1.7	.5	.1	-	-	6.4	.3	2.1
1865	3.5	1.6	.5	.1	-	-	5.8	.3	2.0
1870	3.1	1.4	.5	.1	-	-	8.6	.4	1.9
1875	2.8	1.2	.8	.1	-	-	10.1	.5	1.8
1880	2.4	1.1	1.0	.2	-	-	11.1	.6	1.9
1885	2.2	1.0	.8	.1	-	-	18.0	.9	2.0
1890	2.2	1.0	.6	.1	-	-	20.6	1.0	2.1
1895	1.8	.8	.6	.1	-	-	23.4	1.2	2.1
1900	1.8	.8	.6	.1	-	-	23.6	1.2	2.1
1905	1.9	.9	.7	.1	-	-	25.9	1.3	2.3
1910	2.1	.9	.9	.2	-	-	29.2	1.5	2.6
1915	1.8	.8	.7	.1	-	-	29.7	1.5	2.4
1920	2.1	.9	-	-	-	-	-	-	.9
1925	2.0	.9	-	-	-	-	-	-	.9
1930	2.0	.9	-	-	-	-	-	-	.9
1935	1.5	.7	.4	.1	-	-	15.0	.7	1.5
1940	1.3	.6	.9	.2	-	-	17.2	.8	1.6
1945	1.5	.7	1.1	.2	-	-	24.2	1.1	2.0
1950	1.5	.7	1.1	.2	-	-	24.1	1.1	2.0
1955	1.6	.7	1.3	.2	-	-	22.8	1.0	1.9
1960	1.9	.8	1.3	.2	-	-	22.1	1.0	2.0
1965	2.1	1.0	1.3	.2	-	-	22.8	1.0	2.2
1970	2.5	1.1	1.8	.3	-	-	25.7	1.2	2.5
1975	2.4	1.1	2.2	.3	-	-	28.8	1.3	2.7

Table A1.3. SURVEY of TAVERN LEDGERS

Name and Location	Date	Frequency of Visits	Proportion of Those Visiting a Median No. Times Who Purchased Distilled Spirits	Median Amount of Distilled Spirits Purchased
Brewer Tavern Ledger Annapolis, Md., Md. Hall of Records	Apr. 1810	2/month	NA	NA
Robinson Tavern Ledger Eatonton, Ga., GU	Dec. 1826	4/month	NA	NA
Patrick Store Day Bk. Morgan Co., Ga., GU	Feb. 1822	1/week	6/21	½ pt.
Lanier Store Day Bk. Antioch, Ga., GU	Feb. 1824	1/week	13/21	½ pt.
Madison Hotel Ledger Madison, Ga., GU (regular customers)	Mar. to Apr. 1823	1/month 4/month	NA 8/8	NA ⅓ pt.
Stubbs Tavern Acct. Bk. Macon, Ga., G-Ar	Jan. 1835	NA	NA	½ + pt.

Location symbols: Georgia State Archives (G-Ar); University of Georgia (GU).

Table A1.4. SURVEY of GENERAL STORES

Name and Location	Date	Frequency of Visits	Proportion of Those Visiting a Median No. Times Who Purchased Distilled Spirits	Median Amount of Distilled Spirits Purchased
Thomas Store Day Bk. Morgan Co., Ga., GU	*Jun.* 1820	1/*week*	10/26	⅞ *pt.*
Rogers Store Day Bk. Hancock Co., Ga., G-Ar	1819	2/*year*	*NA*	⅓ *gal.*
Morton Store Acct. Bk. Clarke Co., Ga., G-Ar	*Feb.* 1822	*NA*	10/17	1¾ *qt.*

Location symbols: Georgia State Archives (G-Ar); University of Georgia (GU).

Table A1.5. GENERAL STORES' DISTILLED SPIRITS SALES as PERCENT of TOTAL SALES, in DOLLARS.

Name and Location	Date	Percent
Peirce Store Day Bks. and Ledgers	1798	.... 3.8%
Freetown, Mass., MH-BA	1803–1810	.... 21.2
Cox Store Acct. Bks.....................	1793–1800	.... 25.5
Salem, Mass., MSaE	1812–1815	.... 15.9
(1818–1820 includes wholesale business)	1818–1820	.... 6.5
	1824–1826	.... 6.4
Frost Store Day Bks.....................	1810–1812	.... 16.8
Durham, N.H., MH-BA	1813–1815	.... 2.7
	1816–1818	.... 19.9
	1819–1821	.... 26.7
	1822–1824	.... 26.6
	1825–1827	.... 15.9
	1828–1830	.... 14.2
	1831–1833	.... 8.5
Betts & Raymond Store Day Bks. and Ledgers	1801–1802	.... 17.6
Wilton, N.Y., MH-BA	1809–1812	.... 10.1
Hughes Store Cash Bk.	1817–1818	.... 43.8
Goshen, Ga., GU		
Stokes Store Ledgers	1818	.... 9.0
Petersburg, Ga., GU		
Rees & Co. Store Day Bks.	1826	.... 2.0
Eatonton, Ga., GU		
Thomas Store Day Bk....................	1835–1837	.... 5.0
Hamptonsville, Ga., GU		

Location symbols: Baker Business Library, Harvard University (MH-BA); Essex Institute, Salem, Mass. (MSaE); University of Georgia (GU).

APPENDIX TWO

Cross-National Comparisons of Consumption

THE FOLLOWING tables were constructed to show the annual per capita consumption of alcoholic beverages in various countries during past times. For the early nineteenth century, it was possible to obtain a large number of estimates of the consumption of distilled spirits. That data is presented in Table A2.1. Little information concerning beer, cider, and wine was available for the period before 1850; information for wine and beer is presented in Tables A2.2 and A2.3. Total consumption of alcohol from all alcoholic beverages appears in Table A2.4. Data for years prior to 1850 should be used with caution, for in many instances only a solitary estimate could be found, and its accuracy could not be verified.

Table A2.1. DISTILLED SPIRITS
consumption for selected countries, per capita of total population, in U.S. gallons [1]

Country	1800	1820–1823	1830–1836	1838–1840	1847–1853	1851–1860	1861–1870	1881–1890	1901–1905	1919–1922	1970–1974
U.S.A.	3.8	4.7	4.7	3.1	2.1	2.2	2.1	1.4	1.2	1.4	1.8
U.K.	1.2–2.4	-	1.3	1.3	1.1–1.2	1.4	1.3	1.4	1.4	.6	.6
England	-	-	1.3	1.1	3.1	-	-	-	-	-	-
Scotland	-	6.1	2.0–2.9	3.6	13.9	-	-	-	-	-	-
Ireland	-	1.9	1.5	2.0–2.8	4.4	-	-	-	-	-	-
Denmark	-	-	-	-	-	-	-	4.1	3.5	.3	.9
Norway	-	-	-	-	1.6	1.4	1.2	.9	.8	.2	1.0
Sweden	7.2	10.5	12.1–16.7	7.5–9.4	8.0	3.3	2.6	2.0	2.0	1.1	1.8
Holland	-	-	-	-	-	1.9	2.0	2.4	2.1	1.0	-
Germany	-	-	-	-	-	-	-	2.2	2.1	.7	-
Prussia	-	-	-	2.0–4.0	-	-	-	-	-	-	-
France	-	-	-	.4	3.7	1.1	1.3	2.1	1.9	1.2	1.6
Italy	-	-	-	-	-	-	-	.5	.4	.6	-

Table A2.2. WINE
consumption for selected countries, per capita of total population, in U.S. gallons [2]

Country	ca. 1839	1851–1860	1861–1870	1881–1890	1901–1905	1919–1922	1970–1974
U.S.A.	.3	.2	.3	.5	.4	-	1.3
Canada	-	-	-	.1	-	.2	1.4
U.K.	.3	.3	.5	.4	.4	.4	1.1
Denmark	-	-	-	.3	.4	.4	2.1
Finland	-	-	-	-	.1	<.05	1.5
Norway	-	-	-	.2	.4	1.0	.7
Sweden	-	.1	.1	.2	.2	.2	1.9
Holland	-	.5	.5	.6	.4	.4	2.0
Germany	-	1.2	1.6	1.5	1.7	.8	5.3
France	23.3	15.9	26.4	24.9	36.7	37.8	28.1
Italy	-	-	-	25.1	30.2	25.5	29.4

Table A2.3. BEER
consumption for selected countries, per capita of total population, in U.S. gallons [3]

Country	1830– 1839	1851– 1860	1861– 1870	1881– 1890	1901– 1905	1919– 1922	1970– 1974
U.S.A.	.6	2.7	4.2	10.5	16.4	-	18.4
Canada	-	-	-	3.5	-	4.7	21.7
U.K.	9.8–22	28.3	32.0	33.3	35.5	21.5	28.5
Denmark	-	-	-	15.1	9.7	18.4	27.7
Finland	-	-	-	-	2.8	-	12.8
Norway	-	-	3.2	4.3	5.5	-	10.0
Sweden	-	2.8	2.9	5.8	6.5	8.3	12.8
Holland	-	-	-	9.0	10.0	5.5	17.7
Germany	-	10.6	14.5	24.8	31.3	12.9	38.3
France	2.3	4.1	5.0	5.8	9.5	6.8	11.2
Italy	-	-	-	.2	.2	.8	3.4

Table A2.4. ABSOLUTE ALCOHOL IN ALL ALCOHOLIC BEVERAGES
consumption for selected countries, per capita of total population, in U.S. gallons [4]

Country	ca. 1839	1844– 1845	1861– 1870	1881– 1890	1901– 1905	1919– 1922	1937	1954	1965	1970– 1974
U.S.A.	1.8	1.0	1.3	1.3	1.5	.6	1.1	1.4	1.6	1.8
Canada	-	-	-	.8	-	.6	.6	1.1	1.4	2.0
U.K.	1.1	1.1	2.6	2.8	2.9	1.6	1.1	1.7	1.5	1.9
Denmark	-	-	-	2.7	2.2	.8	.6	.8	1.3	2.0
Finland	-	-	-	-	.5	.1	.4	.5	.6	1.4
Norway	-	-	-	.6	.7	.5	.6	.6	.7	1.0
Sweden	3.8	3.7	1.4	1.2	1.3	.8	.9	1.0	1.2	1.5
Holland	-	-	-	1.7	1.5	.8	.4	.5	1.2	1.8
Germany	-	-	-	2.3	2.6	.7	1.1	1.0	2.8	3.2
Prussia	1.1	1.1	-	-	-	-	-	-	-	-
France	4.5	3.9	3.8	4.3	5.7	4.7	5.7	5.3	5.2	4.5
Italy	-	-	-	3.5	4.1	3.6	2.6	3.4	3.4	3.6
Poland	-	2.5– 10.1	-	-	-	-	.3	.8	1.1	1.6

APPENDIX THREE

Cook Books

To DETERMINE if the use of alcohol declined after 1830, I consulted thirty-nine cook books published between 1796 and 1859. Each book's cake recipes, other than those for ginger bread, were examined in order to construct an index based on the percentage of recipes that used intoxicating beverages. While a few books had no recipes calling for liquor, most had some. The volumes were divided into low and high alcohol groups; a book was classed low when at least two-thirds of its cake recipes contained no alcohol. The groups were then plotted against time as a four-celled matrix:

	1796–1829	1830–1859
low alcohol	8	16
high alcohol	9	6

Visual inspection suggests that after 1829 a lower proportion of cake recipes used liquor. This conclusion can be supported mathematically, where phi $= -.26$; $Q = -.50$. A more elegant statistical test is also possible by correlating the percentage of cake recipes that used alcohol with each year in which a particular volume was published: $r = -.300$. I.e., as time passed, the percentage of cake recipes using alcohol tended to decline. I used books in collections at the American Antiquarian Society and at the Library of Congress. A list is in my dissertation, p. 271.

APPENDIX FOUR

Review of Drinking Motivation Literature

WHY DO people drink? In the nineteenth century it was widely accepted that people drank because they were undisciplined, ungodly, or degenerate. Temperance advocates claimed that drinkers had disordered appetites. Because reformers believed that either a corrupted soul or a lack of self-control motivated drinking to excess, they had little interest in examining the social, economic, or psychological correlates of drinking. With the rise of the social sciences the assumption that drinking was an immoral act was challenged. The development of survey research techniques and statistical methods for analyzing significant differences in collected data led investigators, at the end of the 1930s, to undertake the first scientific studies of drinking motivation. A pioneering account was Ruth Bunzel, "The Rôle of Alcoholism in Two Central American Cultures," *Psychiatry*, 3 (1940), 361–387. The *Quarterly Journal of Studies on Alcohol* began publication in 1940. An early, still uncompleted agenda is in Selden D. Bacon, "Sociology and the Problems of Alcohol," *QJSA*, 4 (1943), 402–445. (Also see Bacon's remarks in *Alcohol, Science and Society* [New Haven, 1945], 179–200.) Cross-cultural studies have been reviewed in Peter G. Bourne and Ruth Fox, ed., *Alcoholism, Progress in Research and Treatment* (N.Y., 1973), 171–194.

Donald Horton, in his path-breaking "The Functions of Alcohol in Primitive Societies," *QJSA*, 4 (1943), 199–320, related drinking behavior to social and psychological traits. Drawing his data from George P. Murdock's Human Relations Area Files, a collection of anthropological descriptions of primitive cultures, Horton was able to devise a cross-cultural method for correlating drinking with other characteristics. He concluded, "The primary function of alcoholic beverages in all societies is the reduction of anxiety." Horton made additional useful comments in *Alcohol, Science and Society*, 152–177. In 1951 Horton's theory was confirmed by John J. Conger in "The Effects of Alcohol on Conflict Behavior in the Albino Rat," *QJSA*, 12 (1951), 1–29. Animals who were made anxious by being subjected to stress were observed to increase their voluntary intake of alcohol. Two other important studies of rats have been done by Reginald G. Smart, "Effects of Alcohol on Conflict and Avoidance Behavior," *QJSA*, 26 (1965), 187–205, and U. G. Ahlfors, *Alcohol and Conflict, a Qualitative and Quantitative Study* . . . (Helsinki, 1969). There was, however, one significant difficulty with Horton's anxiety theory. Horton had been unable to define the theory in such a way that other researchers could easily build upon it. Some investigators did pursue Horton's ideas from a psychological perspective. See Morris E. Chafetz and Harold W. Demone, Jr., *Alcoholism and Society* (N.Y., 1962), 75; Francis T. Chambers, *The Drinker's Addiction* (Springfield, Ill., 1968), 3–16; Richard Lynn, *Personality and National Character* (Oxford, 1971).

In 1961 the 'anxiety hypothesis' was recast, when Peter B. Field used another cross-cultural study to suggest that Horton's measure of 'anxiety' was really a determination of a society's structural instability. See both his "Social and Psychological Correlates of Drunkenness in Primitive Tribes," Ph.D. thesis (Soc. Psych.), Harvard U., 1961, and "A New Cross-Cultural Study of Drunkenness" in *Society, Culture, and Drinking Patterns*, ed. David J. Pittman and Charles R. Snyder (N.Y., 1962), 48–74. Field noted that most of the high consumption groups which Horton had examined had suffered social disintegration after contact with western culture. Thus, while these primitive tribes may indeed have drunk to excess to reduce their anxiety, it was the crumbling of their native cultures that had produced the anxiety. Field's hypothesis was supported by Olav Irgens-Jensen, "The Use of Alcohol in an Isolated Area of Northern Norway," *British Journal of Addiction*, 65 (1970), 181–185. Irgens-Jensen showed, contra Horton,

that excessive drinking was more common in the socially dif-
fuse cities than in the more highly structured but also more
anxiety-prone fishing villages. This 'disintegration hypothesis,'
however, conflicted with several empirical studies of places
where investigators had located stable, well-integrated communities in which drinking to excess was the cultural norm. See,
e.g., Dwight B. Heath, "Drinking Patterns of the Bolivian
Camba," *QJSA*, 19 (1958), 491–508; Edwin M. Lemert, "Alcoholism and Sociocultural Situation," *QJSA*, 17 (1956),
306–317; William Madsen and Claudia Madsen, "The Cultural
Structure of Mexican Drinking Behavior," *QJSA*, 30 (1969),
701–718; Ozzie G. Simmons, "Ambivalence and the Learning
of Drinking Behavior in a Peruvian Community" in *Society,
Culture, and Drinking Patterns*, 37–47. These social scientists
explained inebriation, contra Field, as the consequence of the
integration of drunkenness into the social order. This 'normative hypothesis' has been most thoughtfully developed in an
important theoretical work, Craig MacAndrew and Robert B.
Edgerton, *Drunken Comportment* (Chicago, 1969). Their work
suggested the need for a new comprehensive view to explain
culturally derived variations in the use of alcohol.

Meanwhile, important work was being carried out on another front. One of the first in a series of intensive studies
reporting on drinking mores in particular cultures was Robert
F. Bales, "The 'Fixation Factor' in Alcohol Addiction: an Hypothesis Derived from a Comparative Study of Irish and Jewish Social Norms," Ph.D. thesis (Soc.), Harvard U., 1944.
(Much of his Irish material is in his essay in *Society, Culture,
and Drinking Patterns*, 157–187.) He compared and contrasted
the drinking of Irish and Jewish Americans. In a cultural interpretation, Bales suggested that frequent Irish-American intoxication reflected (1) ambivalent child-rearing in which Irish
parents produced anxiety by oscillating between overaffection
and withdrawal, (2) an Irish inability to succeed in terms of
Irish ideals, (3) a land tenure system in Ireland that denied
marriage to grown men, who responded by becoming drinking
'boys,' and (4) the insecurity of the Irish in America, where
their customs, especially Catholicism, subjected them to ridi-
cule. In contrast, he found that rare Jewish-American inebria-

tion reflected (1) child-rearing in which the drinking of alcohol was treated as a ceremonial rite, (2) a Jewish respect for liquor derived from its use in religious ceremonies, and (3) the insulation of Jews from anxieties concerning their minority status through the creation and maintenance of Jewish institutions. These two groups have also been studied by Andrew M. Greeley, *That Most Distressful Nation* (Chicago, 1972), 129–143, and Charles R. Snyder, *Alcohol and the Jews* (Glencoe, 1958).

In another study of a particular group Giorgio Lolli et al. compared drinking habits of Italians, Italo-Americans, and other Americans. The authors of *Alcohol in Italian Culture* (Glencoe, 1958) argued that the Italian pattern of high consumption of wine combined with rare inebriation reflected an Italian belief that wine was a food. Every meal in Italy had to have wine, but wine could only be drunk at a meal. Italians drank little hard liquor, because it was not recognized as a food. This Italian use of alcohol contrasted with consumption among the French, who drank both heartily and to intoxication. The French, according to Roland Sadoun et al., *Drinking in French Culture* (New Brunswick, 1965), took not only wine but also distilled spirits in the form of brandy. A more significant difference may have been that the French, unlike Italians, did not view wine as a food; indeed, they relaxed with mid-afternoon wine breaks. These authors suggested that French ambivalence about the proper role of alcoholic beverages led to drinking in order to achieve personal psychological escape. French culture, they concluded, encouraged escapism because it has promoted uniformity and has not tolerated eccentricity.

These studies of drinking in particular cultures made clear the inadequacy of the 'anxiety hypothesis.' The search began for a more satisfactory explanation for the motivation to drink. In a recent cross-cultural study entitled *The Drinking Man* (N.Y., 1972), David McClelland et al. presented what has become known as the power hypothesis. They contended that people drink in order to feel powerful. This theory of drinking motivation has encompassed the principal ideas contained in the earlier hypotheses. Powerlessness, as a concept, could be viewed as a refinement of what Horton called anxiety, it could be related easily to the idea of disintegration, and it was consonant with a normative interpretation. The 'power hypothesis' also was consistent with the intensive culture studies and explained apparent difficulties encountered by the earlier theories. High-anxiety, low-drinking societies were those in which fears did not produce a sense of powerlessness because those anxieties were successfully channeled through institutions. Or, as Field would have said, they were well integrated. On the other hand, low-anxiety, high-drinking societies could be stable, but they lacked the institutional mechanisms for the effective handling of the need to feel powerful.

Three aspects of the 'power hypothesis' made it particularly attractive. First, the theory explained all drinking without any reference to the degree or extent. Given the growing uneasiness with the concept of alcoholism among many theorists, any hypothesis that accounted for all kinds of drinking had an advantage over theories that primarily or exclusively considered 'deviant' behavior. Second, investigators have long noted that in all societies men have drunk as much or, most commonly, more than women. This difference could not be explained by the other theories, since neither anxiety nor the structural disintegration of a culture were sex-linked. But in most societies power has been a masculine concept. Women have been taught either that only men can achieve mastery of objects or others, including women, or that women's power is limited to the family. In the former case, women were culturally trained to accept powerlessness; in the latter case, the nature of family life made it unlikely for women to feel powerless. Finally, the power theory explained the often observed connection between religious conviction and abstinence: men who believed in the power of God no longer needed the power of alcohol. For critical comment see Henry S. G. Cutter et al., "Alcohol, Power and Inhibition," *QJSA*, 34 (1973), 381–389.

While the 'power hypotheses' has much utility, the most provocative recent theoretical work has focused on child-rearing. Margaret Bacon et al. in "A Cross-Cultural Study of Drinking: II. Relations to Other Features of Culture," *QJSA*, Supp. 3 (1965), 29–48, concluded that a culture's particular ways of using alcohol were related to its child-rearing practices. A high frequency of drunkenness was found in harsh cultures, where babies were given little nurturance, children were encouraged to assert themselves and strive for success without conformity, and adults were not competitive. Oddly, a high general consumption of alcohol was related to different characteristics, those of an autonomous culture, where babies were not indulged, children were pressured to be responsible for their acts, adults were expected to be independent, and folk tales were harsh, without rewards. In varying degrees, early nineteenth-century America partook of both stereotypes. Like other work on child-rearing, these conclusions are, given the present state of knowledge, tentative. This work appears to be pertinent to the experiences of many American Indian tribes. A recent study is Jerrold E. Levy and Stephen J. Kunitz, *Indian Drinking* (N.Y., 1974).

Social scientists thus far have suggested that drinking is a function of a culture's social organization. When social systems fail to meet individual needs, a high intake of alcohol and drinking to excess may occur. In particular, a high level of drunkenness is likely in cultures that are anxiety-ridden, structurally disintegrating, or incompetent in providing individuals with a sense of effectiveness. Such societies are most likely to be found under conditions of stress, when the social order has been wrenched either by contact with alien cultures or by internal dislocations caused by changes in ideology, institutions, structure, or economy. A high level of consumption of alcohol, however, need not be culturally abnormal, for drinking can be the means by which a society attempts to fulfill certain personal needs. Individual longings vary with the culture, partially because of different child-rearing practices. In any event, drinking mores can not be separated from and are functions of ideologies, customs, and social processes.

APPENDIX FIVE

Quantitative Measurements

MOST HISTORICAL sources are not quantitative, and this characteristic has led the historian, traditionally, to ignore the use of quantitative techniques. But it is possible to use such non-quantitative materials in a quantitative manner, provided that the historian is willing to use low-level techniques. The simplest involves the arrangement of data into hierarchical categories. A historian who has read a wide variety of sources will find that much of the data will fall naturally into clusters. If these clusters can be ranked according to some logical and useful scheme, then the data clusters can be used to produce a hierarchy: a quantitative model based on non-quantitative sources. This technique has been used to produce Tables A5.1 and A5.2 and Chart A5.1. Each is based on dozens of sources of the types used throughout this work; they are cited in the notes in my dissertation: Table A5.1, pp. 232–234; Table A5.2, pp. 237–239; Chart A5.1, pp. 250–251.

Table A5.1. DRINKING among WHITE MALES, by SOCIAL CHARACTERISTIC

Social Characteristic	Low Consumption	High Consumption
Region	New England	West
Locality Type	Rural	Urban
Roots	Low Mobility	High Mobility
Nativity	United States	Ireland
Age	45+	20–29
Social Class	Middle Class	Lower Class
Religion	Pietistic-Evangelical	Liturgical
Work Level	Employer	Employee
Skill Level	High Skilled	Unskilled

Table A5.2. DRINKING among ADULT WHITE MALES, by OCCUPATION

Lowest	Medium	High	Highest
Farm Owners (North)	Artisans	Fishermen	Canal Builders
Manufacturers	Planters (South)	Laborers (City and Farm)	River Boatmen
Merchants (except Spirits Merchants)	Professionals	Lumberjacks	Sailors
		Schoolmasters	Soldiers
		Stage Drivers	

Chart A5.1. RELATIVE INCIDENCE of DRINKING PATTERNS, 1790–1850

	1790–1820	1820–1830	1830–1840	1840–1850
Very Common		Communal Binges, rising	Solo Binges, peak	
Common	Daily Drams Communal Binges	Daily Drams, falling Solo Binges, rising	Communal Binges, falling Daily Drams, falling	Solo Binges
Rare	Solo Binges			Daily Drams Communal Binges

APPENDIX SIX

A Recipe

THE FOLLOWING recipe was published on the back cover of
Thomas Herttell's *An Expose of the Causes of Intemperate Drinking*
. . . (N.Y., 1820; orig. 1819), where it must have stimulated
liquor sales. It came with the advice that "Half a dozen tum-
blers of this legitimate liquor will put a gentleman in high
spirits, and make him 'ripe for sport of any sort.' "

ROYAL NECTAR, or the
PRINCE REGENT'S PUNCH

4 bottles Champagne
1 bottle Hock
1 bottle Curracoa (sic)
1 quart Brandy
1 quart Rum
2 bottles Madeira
2 bottles Seltzer Water
4 pounds Bloom Raisins
Some Seville Oranges, Lemons, Powdered Sugar
Add Green Tea, Highly Iced

BIBLIOGRAPHICAL NOTE

THIS WORK could not have been written without access to several major collections of temperance literature. Preeminent were the Congregational Society Library, Boston, and George C. Dempsey Collection (Soc 4300–4790), Widener Library, Harvard. Also helpful were the Presbyterian Historical Society, Philadelphia; Columbia Theological Seminary, Decatur, Georgia; Huntington Library, San Marino, California; Rare Books Division, Library of Congress; and Black Temperanceana Collection (VTZ), New York Public Library Annex. Temperance materials from the early nineteenth century were surprisingly judicious. In addition to the numerous exhortations of ministers, they included fact-filled annual reports of temperance societies. The reports of the American Temperance Society and its successor, the American Temperance Union, as well as those from the Maine and New York state societies, were outstanding. Other important sources were travel accounts and government documents, especially statistics concerning the production of alcohol in the New York and United States censuses and import records and surveys of Army and Navy drinking in the American State Papers. Occasional remarks appeared in letters, diaries, and, more frequently, in memoirs, particularly in those of Methodist ministers who took credit for starting the temperance movement. Also useful were novels on the South, *Niles' Register* and other periodicals, medical literature, reform society literature for the period preceding the organization of temperance societies, statistical compendia, distilling and brewing manuals, cook books, and nineteenth-century town and county histories. Excellent manuscripts were in the John H. Cocke Papers at the University of Virginia and the Benjamin Rush Papers at the Historical Society of Pennsylvania.

Secondary works were less helpful, because they have focused on temperance rather than drinking. Most valuable were two late nineteenth-century works, Daniel Dorchester, *The Liquor Problem in All Ages* (Cincin., 1884), and Henry A. Scomp, *King Alcohol in the Realm of King Cotton* (n.p., 1888). Also useful were Joseph Gusfield's highly interpretative sociological study, *Symbolic Crusade* (Urbana, 1963) and John Krout's classic *The Origins of Prohibition* (N.Y., 1925). Excellent bibliographies of early temperance literature are in the latter book and in J. C. Furnas, *The Life and Times of the Late Demon Rum* (N.Y., 1965). A list of all temperance publications issued before 1831 is in my dissertation: W. J. Rorabaugh, "The Alcoholic Republic, America 1790–1840," Ph.D. thesis (His.), U. Calif., Berkeley, 1976. Of the many recent studies of the temperance movement at the state level, the most thorough is C. C. Pearson and J. Edwin Hendricks, *Liquor and Anti-Liquor in Virginia, 1619–1919* (Durham, 1967). The investigations of social scientists concerning drinking were also important for this study, and that literature is discussed in Appendix 4. Here I will note that I was most influenced by David C. McClelland et al., *The Drinking Man* (N.Y., 1972), Craig MacAndrew and Robert B. Edgerton, *Drunken Comportment* (Chicago, 1969), and anthropological reports in the *Journal of Studies on Alcohol* (formerly, the *Quarterly Journal of Studies on Alcohol*).

GUIDE TO NOTES

INTELLECTUAL historians dissect sources; social historians devour them. Social historians are frustrated inevitably by the need to cite many items in a reasonable space. To save space, I have sometimes cited examples rather than all sources bearing upon a point. I have also used the following system. With rare exceptions, notes are keyed to an entire paragraph. Quotations are cited first and followed by a period. Other items are then cited in the order that they pertain to the paragraph. When necessary, topical heads are given in parentheses. Full citations are given only once, and subsequent citations use only an author's last name, unless an author's initials or an abbreviated title is necessary to avoid confusion. For printed works, citation from a note rather than from the text is indicated by an 'n' placed after the page number. For manuscript collections cited more than once, locations have been indicated by standard library symbols: American Antiquarian Society, Worcester, Mass. (MWA); Baker Business Library, Harvard University (MH-BA); Congregational Society Library, Boston (MBC); Duke University (NcD); Georgia State Archives (G-Ar); Graduate Theological Union, Berkeley, Calif. (CBGTU); Historical Society of Pennsylvania (PHi); Huntington Library, San Marino, Calif. (CSmH); Maine Historical Society (MeHi); Maryland Historical Society (MdHi); Massachusetts Historical Society (MHi); New York Historical Society (NHi); New York Public Library (NN); University of Virginia (ViU); Vassar College (NPV); and Yale University (CtY). Certain titles or parts of titles have been abbreviated according to the following key.

KEY TO ABBREVIATIONS

AR   Annual Report.

ASP   American State Papers, with Class, Volume, Page.

ATS   American Temperance Society. 1–9AR. 1828–1836.

ATU   American Temperance Union. 1–18AR. 1837–1854.

CtTS   Connecticut Temperance Society. 1, 3AR. 1830, 1832.

HR   U.S. House of Representatives.

MSSI   Massachusetts Society for the Suppression of Intemperance. 2, 14, 15AR. 1814, 1827, 1830.

MTS   Massachusetts Temperance Society. 21, 22, 24, 25AR. 1834–1837.

MeTS   Maine Temperance Society. 1–2AR. 1833–1834.

NHTS   New-Hampshire Temperance Society. 3, 5AR. 1831, 1833.

NYAD   New York Assembly Documents.

NYSD   New York Senate Documents.

NYATS New York Apprentices' Temperance Society. 1–2AR. 1830, 1832.

NYCTS New-York City Temperance Society. 1, 4, 6, 8AR. 1830, 1833, 1835, 1837.

NYSTS New-York State Temperance Society (also called: New-York Society for the Promotion of Temperance). 1–4AR. 1830–1833.

Niles   Niles' Weekly Register.

PSDUAS   Pennsylvania Society for Discouraging the Use of Ardent Spirits.

PaTS   Pennsylvania State Temperance Society.

QJSA   Quarterly Journal of Studies on Alcohol.

RITS   Rhode-Island State Temperance Society. 2, 3, 7AR. 1832, 1833, 1837.

SPPCNY   Society for the Prevention of Pauperism in the City of New-York. 1, 2, 4–6AR. 1818, 1820, 1821, 1823.

TS   Temperance Society.

VaTS   Virginia Society for the Promotion of Temperance. 3, 4AR. 1829, 1831.

NOTES

Chapter One

(Quote) Greene and Delaware Moral Soc. "Address" *Columbia Mag.* 1 (1815) 216. I found 'a nation of drunkards' in 13 other temperance publications.

1. *Columbia Mag.* 1 (1814) 45; (1815) 216; John Winslow *An Address, Delivered June 17th, 1816, before the Association, for the Suppression of Intemperance* . . . (Boston, 1816) 4; Mason L. Weems? *A Calm Dissuasive against Intemperance* (Phila., 1816) 6; Seth Williston *A Sermon upon Intemperance* (Otsego, N.Y., 1808) 2; Nathaniel S. Prime *The Pernicious Effects of Intemperance* . . . (Brooklyn, 1812) 40; Alex. Gunn *A Sermon, on the Prevailing Vice of Intemperate Drinking* . . . (N.Y., 1813) 3; Thos. Sewall *An Address Delivered before the Washington City TS* . . . (Wash., 1830) 5; Emerson Paine *A Discourse, Preached at Plympton* . . . (Boston, 1821) 15 (2 quo.); Albert Barnes *The Immorality of the Traffic in Ardent Spirits* . . . (Phila., 1834) 30.

2. Wash. to Thos. Green, Mar. 31, 1789, Washington *Writings* ed. W. C. Ford (N.Y., 1891) 11:377; Adams to Wm. Willis, Feb. 21, 1819, Adams *Works* ed. C. F. Adams (Boston, 1865) 10:365; Jeff. to Saml. Smith, May 3, 1823, Jefferson *Writings* ed. A. A. Lipscomb (Wash., 1903–1904) 15:431; Ticknor to Jeff., Dec. 8, 1821, Jefferson "Papers" Mass. His. Soc. *Coll.* 7 Ser. 1 (1900) 310.

3. C. D. Arfwedson *The United States and Canada* . . . (London, 1834) 1:145; Basil Hall *Travels in North America* . . . (Edinburgh, 1829) 2:90; Wm. Cobbett *A Year's Residence in the United States of America* (Carbondale, 1964; 1818) 197. Isaac Holmes *An Account of the United States of America* . . . (London, 1823) 352.

4. Peter Neilson *Recollections of a Six Years' Residence* . . . (Glasgow, 1830) 67; Isaac Candler *A Summary View of America* . . . (London, 1824) 452. Wm. Dalton *Travels in the United States of America* . . . (Appleby, Eng., 1821) 36.

5. Estwick Evans *A Pedestrious Tour* . . . ed. R. G. Thwaites (Cleveland, 1904; 1819) 261; Chas. Giles *Pioneer* (N.Y., 1844) 237; Tim. Dwight *Travels in New England and New York* (Cambridge, 1969; 1821–1822) 4:250; Anne N. Royall *Letters from Alabama* . . . (University, Ala., 1969; 1830) 93.

6. See Appendix 1.

7. See Appendix 2.

8. ATS 4AR 77.

9. *Boston Wkly. Mag.* 3 (1805) 118. (statistics) Cobbett 198; Jeremiah B. Jeter *The Recollections* . . . (Richmond, 1891) 14–15; *Niles* 7 (1814) 273; Nathaniel Cross *An Address, Delivered before the Young Men's TS* . . . (Morristown, 1832) 5; Geo. Osgood *An Address, Delivered in the Brick Meeting House* . . . (Salem, 1820) 10; Burleigh Smart *An Address, before the Kennebunk TS* . . . (n.p., 1830) 21; John I. Wells *Reflections on Intemperance* (Hartford, 1818) 14; ATS 4AR 77; 5AR 86; ATU 17AR 43; MSSI *Circular Addressed to the Members* (Boston, 1814) 4; NYCTS *Am. Temp. Almanac* (1833) 24. (comment) Adolphe de Bacourt *Souvenirs d'un Diplomate* (Paris, 1891) 104; Geo. Combe *Notes on the United States of North America* . . . (Phila., 1841) 2:138; F. Cuming *Sketches of a Tour* . . . ed. R. G. Thwaites (Cleveland, 1904; 1810) 319; B. Hall 2:77–78; Mrs. Basil Hall *The Aristocratic Journey* ed. Una Pope-Hennessy (N.Y., 1931) 100; Thos. Nuttall *A Journal of Travels* . . . ed. R. G. Thwaites (Cleveland, 1905; 1821) 49; Anne N. Royall *Sketches of History, Life, and Manners* . . . (New Haven, 1826) 49; Fred. J. Gustorf *The Uncorrupted Heart* ed. Fred Gustorf (Columbia, Mo., 1969) 35; Wm. Hill *Autobiographical Sketches* . . . (Richmond, 1968) 67; Hezekiah Prince, Jr. *Journals* (N.Y., 1965) 12, 18; Christiana H. Tillson *A Woman's Story of Pioneer Illinois* ed. M. M. Quaife (Chicago, 1919) 42; Harriet and Maria Trumbull *A Season in New York, 1801* ed. H. M. Morgan (Pittsburgh, 1969) 94; *Am. Museum* 4 (1788) 232; ATU 4AR 39; Robt. J. Breckinridge *An Address Delivered before the TS* . . . (Lexington, Ky., 1832) 2; Jos. I. Foot *Two Sermons on Intemperance* (Brookfield, Mass., 1828) 10; Gunn 16; Heman Humphrey *Intemperance* (Ballston Spa, 1814) 6; Saml. B. Woodward *Essays on Asylums for Inebriates* (n.p., 1838) 9; Lincoln and Kennebec Tract Soc. *Tract 7* (n.p., n.d.) 3; A. B. Longstreet *Georgia Scenes* (Gloucester, Mass., 1970; 1835) 139; O. A. Pendleton, Jr. "Temp. and the Evangelical Churches" *J. Presbyterian His. Soc.* 25 (1947) 15. Women dominated the temperance societies, as membership rosters attest. Two valuable pamphlets are *An Address to Females* (N.Y., 1831) and Oren Tracy *An Address, Delivered before the Female TS* . . . (Concord, N.H., 1834).

10. Wm. Sweetser *A Dissertation on Intemperance* . . . (Boston, 1829) 72 (2 quo.); Nuttall 49; Frances A. Kemble *Journal of a Residence in America* (Paris, 1835) 204; Delavan to J. H. Cocke, Nov. 1834, in C. C. Pearson and J. Edwin Hendricks *Liquor and Anti-Liquor in Virginia* . . . (Durham, 1967) 89. See also Arfwedson 2:11–12, 180; Duke Bernhard of Saxe-Weimar Eisenach *Travels through North America* . . . (Phila., 1828) 1:126; John M. Duncan *Travels through Part of the United States* . . . (Glasgow, 1823) 2:279–280; Mrs. Hall 24; John Woods *Two Years' Residence* . . . ed. R. G. Thwaites (Cleveland, 1904; 1822) 300; Wm. C. Howells *Recollections* . . . (Cincin., 1895) 125; Joshua N. Danforth *An Alarm to the Citizens of Washington* (Wash., 1830) 10; NYSTS 4AR 51; W. M. Whitehill "Perez Morton's Daughter Revisits Boston in 1825" *Mass. His. Soc. Proc.* 82 (1970) 21–47.

11. Michael Collins to a Warrenton, N.C., newspaper, ca. 1830, Collins Pap., NcD. Ephraim Beanland to J. K. Polk, Dec. 22, 1833, S. M. Caldwell to Polk, Feb. 7, 1836, John S. Bassett, ed. *The Southern Plantation Overseer as Revealed in His Letters* (Northampton, 1925) 54, 96; Fletcher to Jesse Fletcher, Jul. 4, 1812, Elijah Fletcher *Letters* ed. Martha von Briesen (Charlottesville,

1965) 57; Fred. Douglass *Narrative of the Life* (N.Y., 1968; 1845) 84; David
Ramsay *Memoirs of the Life of Martha Laurens Ramsay* (Phila., 1811) 150; Julia L.
Sherwood *Memoir of Adiel Sherwood, D.D.* (Phila., 1884) 114; Arfwedson 1:334;
B. Hall 3:125, 224; Henry C. Knight *Letters from the South and West* (Boston,
1824) 111; *Literary Mag. and Am. Reg.* 2 (1804) 67; *Niles* 7 (1814) 273; MSSI
Circ. 4; "PaTS 6AR" *Reg. Pa.* 11 (1833) 377–378; TS of Columbia, S.C. *Proc.*
(Columbia, 1829) 27; S. Henry Dickson *Address before the S.C. Soc. for the
Promotion of Temp.* . . . (Charleston, 1830) 33; Geo. Tucker *The Valley of Shen-
andoah* (N.Y., 1824) 1:65,170; Earl W. Cory "Temp. and Proh. in Ante-Bellum
Ga." M.A. thesis (His.), U. Ga., 1961, p. 24; Pearson and Hendricks 39, 63n;
H. A. Scomp *King Alcohol in the Realm of King Cotton* (n.p., 1888) 184–191, 257,
303; Jas. B. Sellers *The Prohibition Movement in Alabama* . . . (Chapel Hill,
1943) 11, 12, 29; Daniel J. Whitener *Prohibition in North Carolina* . . . (Chapel
Hill, 1946) 7, 35n, 39; Edmund Berkeley, Jr. "Prophet without Honor" *Va.
Mag. His. Biog.* 77 (1969) 182; Mason Crum *Gullah* (Durham, 1940) 258–259;
Eugene D. Genovese *Roll, Jordan, Roll* (N.Y., 1974) esp. 641–646; Lewis C.
Gray *History of Agriculture in the Southern United States to 1860* (Gloucester,
Mass., 1958; 1932) 490, 563; D. Clayton James *Antebellum Natchez* (Baton
Rouge, 1968) 172, 261; Guion G. Johnson *Ante-Bellum North Carolina* (Chapel
Hill, 1937) 533, 553, 558; Wendell H. Stephenson *Isaac Franklin* (University,
La., 1938) 112.

12. Thos. O. Larkin "A Yankee in N.C." ed. R. J. Parker *N.C. His. Rev.* 14
(1937) 333; Saml. Morewood *A Philosophical and Statistical History of* . . . *Inebriating Liquors* (Dublin, 1838) 338. See also Daniel Drake *Pioneer Life in Kentucky* ed. C. D. Drake (Cincin., 1870) 32–33, 54–56; Howells 130; Jeter *Recoll.*
33; Cobbett 197–198; Cuming 352; Holmes 352; Chas. W. Janson *The Stranger
in America* . . . (N.Y., 1935; 1807) 86; Johann D. Schoepf *Travels in the Confederation* . . . ed. A. J. Morrison (Phila., 1911; 1788) 1:362–363; Saml. B. H.
Judah *Gotham and the Gothamites* (N.Y., 1823) 18; *Boston Med. Surg. J.* 2 (1829)
729; *N. Eng. Farmer* 6 (1828) 398; *Niles* 7 (1814) 273; *Poughkeepsie Casket* 3 (1839)
126; Jesse Torrey *The National Flambeau* (Wash., 1816) 63; Benj. Waterhouse
Cautions to Young Persons . . . (5 ed., Cambridge, 1822) 29n; Jacob Carter
Twenty Years in the Life of a Drunkard . . . (N.Y., 1847) 3, 12–13; John Elliott
John Elliott, the Reformed (Boston, 1841) 11; Jas. Gale *A Long Voyage in a Leaky
Ship* . . . (Cambridgeport, Mass., 1842) 15; A. V. Green *The Life and Experi-
ences* . . . (Wooster, Oh., 1848) 5; John B. Lecraw *A Sketch of the Life* . . .
(Pawtucket, R.I., 1844) 7; Chas. T. Woodman *Narrative* . . . (Boston, 1843)
18; *My Native Village* (Phila., 1844) 20; ATS 1AR 60; Hingham TS *Address*
(Hingham, Mass., 1832) 31–32; MSSI 15AR 16; NYSTS 3AR 57; TS of
Columbia, S.C. *Proc.* 34; John S. Abbot *An Address Delivered before the TSs of
Waterford and Farmington* . . . (Augusta, Me., 1831) 14; Barnes 28; Daniel
Drake *A Discourse on Intemperance* (Cincin., 1828) 12, 25; Stephen Emery *An
Address, Delivered before the Temperate Society of Buckfield* . . . (Norway, Me.,
1828) 4; Gunn 21; Thos. Herttell *An Expose of the Causes of Intemperate Drinking*
. . . (N.Y., 1820; 1819) 10; H. Humphrey *Intemp.* 17; John B. O'Neall "The
Drunkard's Looking Glass" in *The Permanent Temperance Documents, Published by
Direction of the State TS* . . . (Columbia, S.C., 1846) 236; John G. Palfrey *Dis-
courses on Intemperance* . . . (Boston, 1827) 73n; Andrew Rankin *A Discourse, on
the Intemperate Use of Spirituous Liquor* . . . (Concord, N.H., 1827) 5; Lucius
M. Sargent *An Address Delivered before the TS of Harvard University* . . . (Cam-
bridge, 1834) 9; Caleb J. Tenney *The Intemperate Use of Ardent Spirits* (Newport,
R.I., 1815) 9.

13. (West) John J. Audobon *Delineations of American Scenery and Character* (N.Y., 1926; 1831–1839) 81–82; John Bradbury *Travels in the Interior of America* ed. R. G. Thwaites (Cleveland, 1904; 1819) 303; W. Faux *Memorable Days in America* ed. R. G. Thwaites (Cleveland, 1905; 1823) 11:192; Daniel H. Brush *Growing Up with Southern Illinois* . . . ed. M. M. Quaife (Chicago, 1944) 58; Howells 125; Royall *Sketches* 56; (East) Lyman Beecher *Autobiography* ed. B. M. Cross (Cambridge, 1961; 1864) 1:13; J. B. Bordley *Essays and Notes on Husbandry and Rural Affairs* (Phila., 1801) 324; "Rep. of the Select Comm." NYSD Doc. 73, vol. 3 (1840) 5; (South) Michel Chevalier *Society, Manners, and Politics in the United States* (Garden City, N.Y., 1961; 1839) 103; Geo. R. Gilmer *Sketches of Some of the First Settlers of Upper Georgia* . . . (Balt., 1965; 1855) 101, 129, 140; J. P. Kennedy *Swallow Barn* (N.Y., 1853; 1832) 89; (city) Duncan 2:322–323; Royall *Sketches* 158–159; Sandford C. Cox *Recollections of the Early Settlement of the Wabash Valley* (Lafayette, Ind., 1860) 145, 150; ASP 5:4:83; *N. Eng. Farmer* 3 (1825) 405; *Niles* 43 (1832) 25; 45 (1833) 169; 46 (1834) 85; Gale 104; (Army) ASP 5:4:83–86, 6:119–120. A good summary is in Francis P. Prucha *Broadax and Bayonet* (Madison, 1953) 45–51. (Navy) ASP 6:3:468–478, 4:85, 563; *Niles* 46 (1834) 320; Christopher McKee *Edward Preble* (Annapolis, 1972) 217–218; (middle class) S. A. Cartwright "Hygenics of Temp." *Boston Med. Surg. J.* 48 (1853) 376, 496–498; Mary P. Sturges *Reminiscences* . . . (N.Y., 1894) 31; A. V. Green 17–18; *A History of Temperance in Saratoga County, N.Y.* (Saratoga Springs, 1855) 26; Emery 6; A. L. Peirson *Address on Temperance* (Boston, 1830) 9; Sweetser 75; Woodward 9; (clergy) Thos. Robbins *Diary* ed. I. N. Tarbox (Boston, 1886) 1:443; *Telescope* 2 (1825) 49; A. V. Green 10; Joel Jewell *Temperance Jubilee* (Grand Haven, Mich., 1868) 6; ATU 7AR 9; Silas Adams *The History of the Town of Bowdoinham* . . . (Fairfield Me., 1912) 169; Daniel Dorchester *The Liquor Problem in All Ages* (Cincin., 1884) 213.

14. Bernhard 1:65–66; Duncan 2:247–248; Thos. Hamilton *Men and Manners in America* (Edinburgh, 1833) 1:43–44; Jacques G. Milbert *Picturesque Itinerary of the Hudson River* . . . ed. C. D. Sherman (Ridgewood, N.J., 1968; 1828–1829) 40; Hugo Playfair *Brother Jonathan* (London, 1844) 1:16; Beardsley "Reminiscences" in *Growing Up in the Cooper Country* ed. L. C. Jones (Syracuse, 1965) 83; Brush 57; John M. Peck *Forty Years of Pioneer Life* ed. Rufus Babcock (Carbondale, 1965; 1864) xlvi. See Table A1.3, Appendix 1. (genl.) J. Winston Coleman, Jr. *Stage-Coach Days in the Bluegrass* (Louisville, 1936); Willard R. Jillson *Kentucky Tavern* (Frankfort, 1943); Paton Yoder *Taverns and Travelers* (Bloomington, 1969).

15. Audobon 81–82; Faux 11:192; Gilmer 140; NYSD Doc. 73, vol. 3 (1840) 5; Saml. Nott, Jr. *An Appeal to the Temperate* . . . (Hartford, 1828) 62; Everett Dick *The Dixie Frontier* (N.Y., 1948) 188. Sales from Frost Genl. Store Day Books, Frost Coll., MH-BA. See Table A1.5, Appendix 1.

16. Quo. in Jas. T. Austin *An Address Delivered before the MSSI* . . . (Boston, 1830) 6. See also Arfwedson 1:144; B. Hall 3:71; Sidney G. Fisher *A Philadelphia Perspective* ed. N. B. Wainwright (Phila., 1967) 147.

17. Jas. Boardman *America and the Americans* (London, 1833) 101–102. See also Arfwedson 1:143–144; Bernhard 2:128; E. T. Coke *A Subaltern's Furlough* . . . (London, 1833) 69–71; B. Hall 2:382; T. Hamilton 1:76; Chas. F. Heartman, ed. *An Immigrant of a Hundred Years Ago* (Hattiesburg, 1941) 47; John A. Clark *Gleanings by the Way* (Phila., 1842) 49–50, 84; John Pintard to Eliza P. Davidson, Mar. 16, 1830, Pintard "Letters" N.Y. His. Soc. *Coll.* 72 (1941) 132; D. Drake *Discourse* 3.

18. Lecraw 9. Cobbett 197; Duncan 2:247–248; Jas. Flint *Letters from America* . . . ed. R. G. Thwaites (Cleveland, 1904; 1822) 60, 77; Holmes 352; Janson 306; Royall *Letters* 87, 180; Schoepf 2:220; Kennedy 89; Justin Edwards "The Well-Conducted Farm" in Am. Tract Soc. *The Temperance Volume* (N.Y., ca. 1835) 4; John H. Brown *Early American Beverages* (Rutland, 1966) esp. 23; Dorchester 139; Marie Kimball "Some Genial Old Drinking Customs" *Wm. and Mary Q.* 3 Ser. 2 (1945) 351; Thos. D. Clark *The Rampaging Frontier* (Indianapolis, 1939) 187.

19. Faux 11:106. See also Arfwedson 2:180; Bernhard 2:71; Bradbury 280n; Duncan 1:298; Faux 11:205–206; Fred. Marryat *A Diary in America* (London, 1839) 1:239; Nuttall 49; J. Woods *Two Years* 300, 347; Mrs. Hall 100; Howells 125; *Niles* 15 (1818) 151;21 (1821) 112; NYSD Doc. 73, vol. 3 (1840) 5; Saml. Mordecai *Virginia, Especially Richmond, in By-Gone Days* (Richmond, 1860; 1856) 250; Geo. H. Morgan *Annals, Comprising Memoirs, Incidents and Statistics of Harrisburg* (Harrisburg, 1858) 369; A. V. Green 6; Emery 5; Nott 57–58; Beverley W. Bond, Jr. *The Civilization of the Old Northwest* (N.Y., 1934) 461–462; Richard H. Collins *History of Kentucky* (Louisville, 1877) 30.

20. Henry P. Warren "Historical Address" in *The History of Waterford, Oxford County, Maine* (Portland, 1879) 189; Gen. Wilkinson quo. in Humphrey Marshall *The History of Kentucky* (Frankfort, 1812) 287. See also Cuming 199, 202, 231; Faux 11:106; Gustorf 58–59; S. B. Cloudman "Recollections of the Old Time Militia and the Annual General Muster" Me. His. Soc. *Coll.* 3 Ser. 2 (1906) 334, 340; Gilmer 163–164; *Niles* 46 (1834) 116; *Poughkeepsie Casket* 3 (1839) 126; Torrey *Natl. Flambeau* 37.

21. Royall *Letters* 180.

Chapter Two

(Quote) Increase Mather *Wo to Drunkards* (Cambridge, 1673) 4.

1. (genl.) Alice M. Earle *Home Life in Colonial Days* (N.Y., 1910; 1898) 146–148, 161–165; Dorchester 108–128; Pearson and Hendricks 3–22; Scomp 47–117, esp. 107; Whitener 1–11.

2. *The Indictment and Tryal of Sr Richard Rum* (3 ed., Boston, 1724) 24. Wm. Byrd *The Secret Diary* . . . *1709–1712* ed. L. B. Wright (Richmond, 1941) Jun. 25, Jul. 5, Aug. 27, 1709; May 3, Aug. 15, Sep. 21, Sep. 22, Dec. 11, 1710; Feb. 7, Apr. 4, 1711, pp. 53, 56, 75, 173, 218, 233, 234, 270, 298, 324; Wm. Byrd "History of the Dividing Line betwixt Virginia and North Carolina Run in the Year . . . 1728" in *The Prose Works of William Byrd of Westover* ed. L. B. Wright (Cambridge, 1966) 205; Cadwallader Colden "The Second Part of the Interest of the Country in Laying Duties . . ." (1726), Colden "Letters and Papers" N.Y. His. Soc. *Coll.* 68 (1937) 274–275, 278; Sarah Knight *Journal* (N.Y., 1935; 1825) 19; John Lawson *A New Voyage to Carolina* ed. H. T. Lefler (Chapel Hill, 1967; 1709) 70, 115; Wm. Penn "A Further Account of the Province of Pa." (1685), Albert C. Myers, ed. *Narratives of Early Pennsylvania* . . . (N.Y., 1912) 267; Saml. Sewall *Diary* ed. M. H. Thomas (N.Y., 1973) Feb. 24, 1681; Nov. 29, 1686; Dec. 20, 1687; Feb. 9, 1695; Mar. 24, 1705; Feb. 6, 1708; Sep. 18, 1711; Apr. 24, 1717, pp. 48, 126, 155, 327, 521, 588, 669, 853; John Urmston to [?], Jul. 7, 1711, Wm. L. Saunders, ed. *The Colonial and State Records of North Carolina* (Var. places, 1886–1914) 1:765.

3. Byrd *Diary* (Mar. 4, 1709) 12. Ibid. (Mar. 2, Oct. 12, Dec. 14, 1709) 11, 93, 118; John Archdale "A New Description of that Fertile and Pleasant Province of Carolina" (1707), Alex. S. Salley, Jr., ed. *Narratives of Early Carolina* . . . (N.Y., 1911) 290; Robt. Beverley *The History and Present State of Virginia* ed. L. B. Wright (Chapel Hill, 1947; 1705) 293, 306–307; Thos. Chalkley *A Journal or Historical Account of the Life* . . . (3 ed., London, 1751) 25–27; Hugh Jones *The Present State of Virginia* ed. R. L. Morton (Chapel Hill, 1956) 84; Lawson 93; W. K. Kay "Drewry's Bluff or Fort Darling?" *Va. Mag. His. Biog.* 77 (1969) 196n; John Watson *Observations on the Customary Use of Distilled Spirituous Liquors* (Balt., 1810) 8. (Potts) John Fiske *Old Virginia and Her Neighbours* (Boston, 1900) 1:239. In Byrd's time hard drinking prevailed at the meetings of the Governor's Council. Byrd *Diary* (Nov. 10, 1710; Apr. 23, Nov. 23, 1711; Mar. 12, 1712) 256, 334, 442, 500. At least one N.Y. governor has been accused of being "an habitual drunkard." Henry Sloughter reputedly signed Jacob Leisler's death warrant while intoxicated. Benson J. Lossing *The Empire State* (N.Y., 1887) 112. This legend has been rejected by Jerome R. Reich *Leisler's Rebellion* (Chicago, 1953) 121, note 98. See also Wm. Smith, Jr. *The History of the Province of New-York* ed. Michael Kammen (Cambridge, 1972; 1757) 1:83, 88–89; contra, Cadwallader Colden to Alex. Colden, Jul. 5, 1759, ibid. 295.

4. Byrd *Diary* (Jun. 25, 1709; Nov. 10, 26, 1710) 53, 256, 263; Byrd to Lord Egremont, Jul. 12, 1736, "Letters of the Byrd Family" *Va. Mag. His. Biog.* 36 (1928) 221. On the benign drinking style see John Bartram *Observations on the Inhabitants, Climate, Soil* . . . (London, 1751) 15–16. This style also prevailed in the British West Indies. Richard Ligon *A True & Exact History of the Island of Barbadoes* (London, 1673; 1657) 33.

5. E.g., Richard L. Bushman *From Puritan to Yankee* (Cambridge, 1967); Philip J. Greven, Jr. *Four Generations* (Ithaca, 1970); Kenneth A. Lockridge *A New England Town* (N.Y., 1970); Chas. S. Sydnor *American Revolutionaries in the Making* (N.Y., 1965; 1952); and esp. Jas. A. Henretta *The Evolution of American Society* (Lexington, Mass., 1973).

6. Edw. Field *The Colonial Tavern* (Providence, 1897) esp. 5, 7, 13, 144; Elise Lathrop *Early American Inns and Taverns* (N.Y., 1937); C. R. Barker "Colonial Taverns of Lower Merion" *Pa. Mag. His. Biog.* 52 (1928) 205–228; Saml. A. Drake *Old Boston Taverns and Tavern Clubs* (Rev. ed., Boston, 1917) esp. 30; E. P. McParland "Colonial Taverns and Tavern Keepers of British New York City" *N.Y. Gen. Biog. Rec.* 103 (1972) 193–202 and thereafter; H. S. Tapley "Old Tavern Days in Danvers" Danvers His. Soc. *His. Coll.* 8 (1920) 1–32; J. H. Brown 27, 29, 129–130; Hewson L. Peeke *Americana Ebrietatis* (N.Y., 1917) 145; Blackwell P. Robinson *William R. Davie* (Chapel Hill, 1957) 147–148; John A. Krout *The Origins of Prohibition* (N.Y., 1925) 41.

7. Gallus Thomann *American Beer* (N.Y., 1909) 8; Pearson and Hendricks 17; Barker 211, 217; Tapley 7, 27, 30; McParland. See also Bushman 111n.

8. S. Sewall (Feb. 6, 1714) 742. S. A. Drake 30. See also Chalkley *Jour.* 204.

9. On increased consumption see Appendix 1. (prices) Wm. B. Weeden *Economic and Social History of New England* (Boston, 1891) 2:502; Arthur H. Cole *Wholesale Commodity Prices in the United States* (Cambridge, 1938); (Ga.) Francis Moore *A Voyage to Georgia* (London, 1744) 17–18, 25; Patrick Tailfer et al. *A True and Historical Narrative of the Colony of Georgia* . . . (Charleston, 1741) v,

28–29; (industry) John J. McCusker, Jr. "The Rum Trade and the Balance of Payments of the Thirteen Continental Colonies, 1650–1775" Ph.D. thesis (Econ.), U. Pitt., 1970, pp. 435–439; Weeden 2:501–502; J. H. Brown 17; Geo. Duffield, Jr. *Samson Shorn* (Phila., 1855) 14; W. T. Baxter *The House of Hancock* (Cambridge, 1945) 51–52, 65; Lawrence H. Gipson *Jared Ingersoll* (New Haven, 1920) 15; Jas. B. Hedges *The Browns of Providence Plantations, the Colonial Years* (Cambridge, 1952) 41–42.

10. *Pa. Gaz.*, Jul. 22–Aug. 2, 1736. See also ibid., Jan. 13, 1736/7; Benj. Franklin *Papers* ed. L. W. Labaree et al. (New Haven, 1959–   ) 2:173; Alex. Hamilton *Gentleman's Progress, the Itinerarium* . . . ed. Carl Bridenbaugh (Chapel Hill, 1948) Jun. 15, 1744, p. 43; John Brickell *The Natural History of North-Carolina* (Dublin, 1737) 33–34.

11. I. Mather *Wo.* 3–4. Chalkley *Jour.* 25–27, 48–49, 81, 86, 140, 147, 199, 203–204, 229, 296, 301; Thos. Chalkley *A Letter to a Friend* (Phila., 1723); Saml. Danforth *The Woful Effects of Drunkenness* (Boston, 1710); Thos. Foxcroft *A Serious Address to Those Who Unnecessarily Frequent the Tavern* (Boston, 1726); Israel Loring *The Duty of an Apostatizing People* . . . (Boston, 1737) 50; Increase Mather *Diary* ed. Saml. Green (Cambridge, 1900) 43–44; Increase Mather *Testimony against Prophane Customs* (Charlottesville, 1953; 1687) 20–28; Benj. Wadsworth *An Essay to Do Good* (Boston, 1710); Geo. Whitefield *The Heinous Sin of Drunkenness* (Phila., 1740).

12. Cotton Mather *Sober Considerations* (Boston, 1708) 5, 3, 15, 18. See also Cotton Mather "Diary" (Jan. 14, 1696/7; Mar. 22, 1710/1; Apr. 22, 1711; Apr. 5, 1713; Aug. 9, 1724) Mass. His. Soc. *Coll.* 7 Ser. 7 (1911) 214–215; 8 (1912) 51, 65, 197–198, 747; Thos. Prince *A Chronological History of New-England* . . . (Boston, 1736) dedication, p. 3; Chalkley *Jour.* 204.

13. A. Hamilton *Itin.* (Jul. 9, 1744) 88. Ibid. (Aug. 28, Sep. 19, 1744) 165, 193.

14. Ibid. (intro., May 31, Jun. 15, Jul. 9, 1744) xvii, 6–7, 43, 88; Fred. P. Bowes *The Culture of Early Charleston* (Chapel Hill, 1942) 120–121.

15. Foxcroft 23. I. Loring 13, 50–51; Josiah Smith *Solomon's Caution against the Cup* (Boston, 1730) 10–11; Wm. Stephens Jour., Jan. 3, Apr. 9, 10, 1738; Feb. 27, Aug. 13, 1739, Allen D. Candler, ed. *The Colonial Records of the State of Georgia* (Atlanta, 1904–1916) 4:62, 121, 122, 291, 389; Thos. Jones to Harman Verelst, Feb. 17, 1738, ibid. 22 (pt. 2):84; Wadsworth 20–21; Carl Bridenbaugh *Cities in the Wilderness* (N.Y., 1955; 1938) 143n, 303n; McParland 103:193; H. B. Parkes "Morals and Law Enforcement in Colonial New England" *N. Eng. Q* 5 (1932) 440; Clinton Rossiter *The First American Revolution* (N.Y., 1956) 163.

16. J. Adams *Works* (Diary, May 29, 1760; Adams to Benj. Rush, Aug. 28, 1811) 2:84–85, 9:637.

17. Wm. Halsted *Speech Delivered at a Special Meeting of the TS* . . . (Trenton, 1835) 5; Pearson and Hendricks 19; Scomp 127, 131, 137, 139; Thomann *Am. Beer* 41; Whitener 3n, 7.

18. J. Adams *Works* (Diary, May 29, 1760) 2:85. Ibid. 2:111–112; Cadwallader Colden quo. in Alex. C. Flick, ed. *History of the State of New York* (N.Y., 1933–1937) 2:272; Stephens Jour., Apr. 14, 1741, A. D. Candler 4 Supp. 123. Ga. juries frequently refused to convict unlicensed retailers. Stephens Jour., Feb. 23, 1738, ibid. 4:91; Wm. Stephens *Journal* . . . *1741–1745*

ed. E. M. Coulter (Athens, 1958–1959) Jan. 30, 1742, v. 1:37; Lord Egmont *Jour.*, Jan. 6, 1742, Stephens to Trustees, Feb. 27, 1738, Oglethorpe to Trustees, Jul. 4, 1739, A. D. Candler vol. 5:583; vol. 22 (pt. 1):96; vol. 22 (pt. 2):165. See also Horatio Sharpe to Lord Calvert, Jan. 12, 1755, *Archives of Maryland* (Balt., 1883–   ) 6:164; unidentified Va. minister's remarks, Pearson and Hendricks 19n; Halsted 6.

19. *Niles* 13 (1817) 18; Halsted 6; J. H. Brown 138–139; E. Field 235–257; S. A. Drake 40, 45–46, 50, 83; Pearson and Hendricks 22, 27; Thomann *Am. Beer* 11; Whitener 4; Christopher Collier *Roger Sherman's Connecticut* (Middletown, 1971) 86; Gipson 32; Geo. C. Rogers, Jr. *Evolution of a Federalist* (Columbia, S.C., 1962) 36.

20. See, e.g., Henry F. May *The Enlightenment in America* (N.Y., 1976).

21. See, e.g., the merchant records cited in ch. 3, note 4.

22. Anthony Benezet *The Potent Enemies of America Laid Open* (Phila., 1774); Anthony Benezet *Remarks on the Nature and Bad Effects of Spirituous Liquors* (Phila., 1775); Roberts Vaux *Memoirs of the Life of Anthony Benezet* (Phila., 1817).

23. Soc. of Friends. Pa. Yearly Meeting *Rules of Discipline* . . . (Phila., 1797) 86–88. Similar to Soc. of Friends. N. Eng. Yearly Meeting *The Book of Discipline* (Providence, 1785) 117–118. See also John Hunt to Jas. Pemberton, Aug. 17, 1788, Pemberton Pap., PHi; Geo. Miller to Benj. Rush, Sep. 27, 1784, Rush Pap., PHi; Joshua Evans "Journal" ed. T. H. Fawcett, Friends' His. Assn. *Bull.* 28 (1939) 33; Fred. B. Tolles *George Logan* . . . (N.Y., 1953) 73–74. (funerals) Chalkley *Jour.* 81, 140; J. Wm. Frost *The Quaker Family in Colonial America* (N.Y., 1973) 44. Philadelphia zeal was not shared in all Meetings. Twelve Friends in Burlington, N.J., were distillers in 1795. Amelia M. Gummere "Friends in Burlington" *Pa. Mag. His. Biog.* 8 (1884) 169.

24. (Methodists) Henry Wheeler *Methodism and the Temperance Reformation* (Cincin., 1882) 46, 51–52, 59; Leroy M. Lee *The Life and Times of the Rev. Jesse Lee* (Nashville, 1860; 1848) 113–114; Rush to Jeremy Belknap, May 6, 1788, Benj. Rush *Letters* ed. L. H. Butterfield (Princeton, 1951) 460; Pendleton 20–21; Pearson and Hendricks 117–118; Scomp 94, 212–217; (Presbyterians) Pres. Ch., U.S.A. *The Presbyterian Church and Temperance* (n.p., n.d.); Scomp 222. I have located no eighteenth-century Baptist temperance activity.

25. (early) Geo. Cheyne *An Essay of Health and Long Life* (3 ed., London, 1725) 42–76; contra, Albert H. de Sallengre *Ebrietatis Encomium or the Praise of Drunkenness* (N.Y., 1910; 1723). (Ga.) Oglethorpe to Trustees, Feb. 12, 1742, A. D. Candler 23:486–487; Stephen Hales *A Friendly Admonition to the Drinkers of Gin, Brandy, and Other Spirituous Liquors* (London, 1734); Stephen Hales *Distilled Spirituous Liquors the Bane of the Nation* (London, 1736); Scomp 63, 69; (gripes) Thos. Cadwalader *An Essay on the West-India Dry-Gripes* (Phila., 1745); Stephens *Jour.* 2:175–176.

26. Benj. Rush *Autobiography* ed. G. W. Corner (Princeton, 1948) 42–52; Nathan G. Goodman *Benjamin Rush* (Phila., 1934) 14–15. Other Edinburgh medical students later active in the antiliquor movement were Americans Saml. Bard and Benj. Waterhouse and Englishman Erasmus Darwin. Martin Kaufman *American Medical Education* (Westport, 1976) 22, 25; Erasmus Darwin *Zoonomia* (London, 1794–1796) vol. 1, sec. 21.

27. Benj. Rush *Sermons to Gentlemen upon Temperance and Exercise* (Phila.,

1772) 5. Frank. to Rush, Aug. 22, 1772, Frank. *Pap.* 19:280–280n. A similar early view is in Jas. Iredell to Francis Iredell, Jr., Jun. 15, 1771, Jas. Iredell *Papers* ed. Don Higginbotham (Raleigh, 1976–   ) 1:68.

28. Rush *Let.* 143. Ibid. 270–272.

29. Ramsay to Rush, Aug. 16, 1784, Rush Pap., PHi. Publication date in Rush *Let.* 272n. There have been at least 20 reprintings (ibid. 273n), the first dated one being Boston, 1790 (Goodman 386). (circulation) John Marsh *A Half Century Tribute to the Cause of Temperance* (N.Y., 1851) 27. See Brackenridge to Rush, Aug. 23, 1785, Geo. Miller to Rush, Sep. 27, 1784, Rush Pap. Rush tried to have an English edition published. Rush to Granville Sharp, Jun. 5, 1785; reply, Oct. 10, 1785, J. A. Woods, ed. "The Correspondence of Benjamin Rush and Granville Sharp 1773–1809" *J. Am. Stud.* 1 (1967) 25–26.

30. Rush to John Lettsom, Aug. 16, 1788, Rush *Let.* 479.

31. "German Inhabitants," Benj. Rush *Essays, Literary, Moral and Philosophical* (Phila., 1806) 226–248. Written in 1789 according to Goodman 383. Rush noted Irish distilling and German abstinence from distilled spirits in an earlier travel diary. Benj. Rush "Dr. Benjamin Rush's Journal of a Trip to Carlisle in 1784" ed. L. H. Butterfield *Pa. Mag. His. Biog.* 74 (1950) 456. "Progress" (1786), Rush *Let.* 400–406. I would not argue that Rush invented the two-step analysis, but that he was one of the earliest practitioners.

32. Belknap to Rush, Aug. 16, 1788, Rush Pap., PHi; Rush to Belknap, Aug. 19, 1788, Rush *Let.* 482. Also important to this paragraph and the one following are Belknap to Rush, Mar. 1, 1789, Aug. 4, 1790, Rush Pap.; replies, May 6, 1788, Jan. 31, Jul. 13, 1789, Rush *Let.* 460, 500–501, 520; Oct. 7, 1788, Jeremy Belknap "Papers" Mass. His. Soc. *Coll.* 6 Ser. 4 (1891) 419–420.

33. The thermometer was first published in *Columbian Mag.* 3 (1789) 31. Repub. Boston, Feb. 28, 1789; *Gentleman's Mag.* 59 (1789) 399; *Poor Richard Improved* (Phila., 1790) 33; Benj. Rush *An Inquiry into the Effects of Spirituous Liquors* . . . (Boston, 1790) 12. An unidentified, undated letter from Rush is in Belknap's working papers on N.H. consumption. See Belknap "Estimate of the Annual Expense and Loss Sustained by the Unnecessary Consumption of Spirituous Liquors in the State of New Hampshire" (ca. 1790), Belknap Pap., MHi. On two occasions Belknap failed to obtain consumption estimates. Jeremiah Libbey to Belknap, Dec. 17, 1789, Bulkley Olcott to Belknap, Dec. 26, 1791, Belknap "Pap." 456, 508. See also Jeremy Belknap *The History of New-Hampshire* . . . (Dover, N.H., 1812) 3:199–200, 249–250.

34. "To American Farmers" (1789), Rush *Let.* 504–505; Rush to [Elias Boudinot?], Jul. 9, 1788, ibid. 476. "To the Ministers" (1788), ibid. 462; "An Oration on the Effects of Spirituous Liquors upon the Human Body" *Am. Museum* 4 (1788) 325–327. On Rush's promotion of beer see "Advantages of the Culture of the Sugar Maple-Tree" *Am. Museum* 4 (1788) 349–350; Belknap to Rush, Sep. 30, 1788, Rush Pap., PHi; Rush to Belknap, Nov. 5, 1788, to Thos. Jefferson, Jul. 10, 1791, Rush *Let.* 496, 593.

35. Filippo Mazzei in Chas. H. Sherrill, ed. *French Memories of Eighteenth-Century America* (N.Y., 1915) 78; J. P. Brissot de Warville *New Travels in the United States* . . . (Cambridge, 1964; 1791) 90, 348. See also Jeff. to M. de Warville, Aug. 15, 1786, Jeff. *Writ.* 5:403–404; Elizabeth Scott to Eliza Maynodier, Nov. 6, 1784, Key Coll., MdHi; Peeke 19.

36. Speed to Rush, Oct. 6, 1803, Rush Pap., PHi. Ramsay *M. L. Ramsay* 150; Ray W. Irwin *Daniel D. Tompkins* (N.Y., 1968) 19–21; Jedidiah Morse *The American Geography* (Elizabethtown, N.J., 1789) 89; Jedidiah Morse *Geography Made Easy* (Boston, 1790) 58–59; I. M. Sargent to Shattuck, Aug. 6, 1833, Shattuck Pap., MHi; Hopkins Pap., MdHi; John Vaughan "John Vaughan's Wilmington Medical Register for 1803" ed. D. B. Ivey *Del. His.* 14 (1971) 189.

37. *New Haven Gaz.* 1 (1786) 336; Belknap to Rush, Jul. 29, 1789, Belknap "Pap." 440. "Assn. of Litchfield for Discouraging the Use of Spiritous Liquors" (1864 copy of 1789 ms.), Litchfield Ct. His. Soc.; *History of Litchfield County, Connecticut* . . . (Phila., 1881) 142; *Am. Mag.* 1 (1788) 854–855; *Am. Museum* 4 (1788) 124; Wm. Bentley *Diary* (Salem, 1905–1914) Apr. 16, 1791, vol. 1:248; Schoepf 2:217; David Ramsay *The History of South-Carolina* . . . (Charleston, 1809) 2:393; Libbey to Belknap, Dec. 17, 1789, Belknap "Pap." 456.

38. Ramsay *S.C.* 2:395; *Mass. Mag.* 6 (1794) 341. Chalkley *Jour.* 229; J. Carroll to Rush, Jul. 18, 1789, Rush Pap., PHi.

39. Jos. Hadfield *An Englishman in America* ed. D. S. Robertson (Toronto, 1933) 8; Schoepf 2:218. See also Marquis de Chastellux *Travels in North America* . . . (Chapel Hill, 1963) 602; Comte de Ségur in Sherrill 78; "The St. George's Club" *S.C. His. Gen. Mag.* 8 (1907) 92–93; (N.Y.) Flick 4:347; (New England) Thos. Jones bill to Congregational Soc., Oct. 15, 1793, Liebmann Coll., NN. See also Robt. Rantoul "Mr. Rantoul's Establishment in Business . . ." Essex Inst. *His. Coll.* 5 (1863) 247; Harry B. Weiss *The History of Applejack* . . . (Trenton, 1954) 10.

40. Jenkins to Robison, Feb. 18, 1784, Robison Pap., MeHi. Morris to Messrs. Constable Rucker & Co., May 3, 1787, Livingston to John Taylor, Apr. 11, 1783, Liebmann Coll., NN; Hedges 311–312; Silas Deane "Papers" Ct. His. Soc. *Coll.* 23 (1930) 192, 215, 217; Wash. to Wm. A. Wash., Oct. 7, 1799, Liebmann Coll.; Ralph N. Hill *Yankee Kingdom* (N.Y., 1960) 133; Willard R. Jillson *Early Kentucky Distillers* . . . (Louisville, 1940) 56; Thos. E. V. Smith *The City of New York in the Year of Washington's Inauguration* (N.Y., 1889) 121.

41. *Am. Museum* 4 (1788) 234. (reform) ibid. 233; *New Haven Gaz.* 1 (1786) 336; Tench Coxe *Observations on the Agriculture, Manufactures and Commerce* . . . (N.Y., 1789) 46–47. This policy later appealed to others. Adams to Rush, Aug. 28, 1811, J. Adams *Works* 9:638; Jeff. to Saml. Smith, May 3, 1823, Jeff. *Writ.* 15:431. For an earlier colonial excise debate in which borrowed English rhetoric predominated see P. S. Boyer "Borrowed Rhetoric, the Mass. Excise Controversy of 1754" *Wm. and Mary Q.* 3 Ser. 21 (1964) 328–351. (Articles) Curtis P. Nettels *The Emergence of a National Economy* (N.Y., 1962) 33. See Mad. to Edmund Randolph, Mar. 11, 1783, Jas. Madison *Papers* ed. W. T. Hutchinson and W. M. E. Rachal (Chicago, 1962–   )6:326. While no excise was levied, imposts were imposed on wine and spirits. *Recommendations to the Several States, by the United States in Congress Assembled, April 18, 1783* (n.p., n.d.).

42. (Mass.) Thomann *Am. Beer* 13; (Va.) Mason to Wash., Nov. 6, 1787, Geo. Mason *Papers* ed. R. A. Rutland (Chapel Hill, 1970) 3:1011, 1012n; Mad. to Jeff., Dec. 9, 20, 1787, reply, Feb. 6, 1788, Thos. Jefferson *Papers* ed. J. P. Boyd (Princeton, 1950–   ) 12:411, 444, 570; W. F. Zornow "The Tariff

Policies of Va., 1755–1789" *Va. Mag. His. Biog.* 62 (1954) 308–313; (Pa.) Tolles *Logan* 73–74.

43. *New Haven Gaz.* 1 (1786) 336; petition quo. in *Universal Asylum* 6 (1791) 33. *Federalist #12*, Nov. 27, 1787 draft in Alex. Hamilton *Papers* ed. H. C. Syrett (N.Y., 1961–   ) 4:351; Speech, Jun. 28, 1788, ibid. 5:124; Coxe *Obs.* 46; Tench Coxe to Rush, Jan. 29, Feb. 2, 12, 1789, May 16, Jun. 4, 1790, Rush Pap., PHi; *Gaz. U.S.* 3 (1791) 130.

44. Sec. Treas. to HR "Report on . . . Distilled Spirits" (1792), Ham. *Pap.* 11:97. See also Fisher Ames to Ham., Jan 26, 1797, ibid. 20:484; Geo. That-cher to John Waite, May 26, 1789, Liebmann Coll., NN; Sec. Treas. to HR, Dec. 13, 1790, ASP 3:1:64–67; Coxe *Obs.* 88; Gallus Thomann *Liquor Laws of the United States* (N.Y., 1885) 4–21.

45. HR debate, Jun. 14–21, 1790, U.S. 1 Cong. *Annals* (Wash., 1834) 1694–1700; vote, Jun. 21, 1790, ibid. 1700. Tabulated with list of members in U.S. Cong. *Biographical Directory of the American Congress, 1774–1971* (Wash., 1971) 51–52. (excise) Ephraim Brown to Rep. Benj. Brown, Jan. 17, Feb. 3, 1791, Liebmann Coll., NN; W. D. Barber " 'Among the Most *Techy Articles of Civil Police*' . . ." *Wm. and Mary Q.* 3 Ser. 25 (1968) 58–84; Thomann *Liqr. Laws* 41–49; Robt. Ernst *Rufus King* (Chapel Hill, 1968) 173–174. (Williamson) Hugh Williamson "Letters of Sylvius" Trinity College His. Soc. *His. Pap.* 11 (1915) 5n, 29–30; J. W. Neal "Life and Public Services of Hugh Williamson" Trinity College His. Soc. *His. Pap.* 13 (1919) 62–111, esp. 105; Fleming Nevin "The Liquor Question in Colonial and Revolutionary War Periods" *W. Pa. His. Mag.* 13 (1930) 198–199.

46. HR debate, Jan. 5–6, 1791, U.S. 1 Cong. *Annals* 1890–1900; vote, Jan. 27, 1791, ibid. 1933–1934. Tabulated with U.S. Cong. *Biog. Dir.* 51–52. See also Mad. to Ham., Nov. 19, 1789, Ham. *Pap.* 5:525; Richard E. Welch, Jr. *Theodore Sedgwick* (Middletown, 1965) 100.

47. Quo. in Donald H. Stewart *The Opposition Press of the Federalist Period* (Albany, 1969) 83; Pres. Add., Oct. 25, 1791, ASP 1:1:16; Ham. to John Steele, Oct. 15, 1792, Rogers 225. Petitions in U.S. 2 Cong. *Annals* (Wash., 1855) 25, 30, 36, 176, 299; Pres. Add., Nov. 6, 1792, ASP 1:1:19; Sen. and HR replies, ibid. 1:1:20; Pres. Message, Nov. 22, 1792, ibid. 3:1:171–172; Sec. Treas. to HR, Dec. 13, 1790, Dec. 5, 1791, Jan. 23, Mar. 6, 1792, Feb. 21, 1798, ibid. 3:1:65, 67, 140, 145, 145n, 151–158, 557–575; Alex. Hamilton *Industrial and Commercial Correspondence* ed. A. H. Cole (Chicago, 1928) 107–108.

48. Albert Gallatin *Writings* ed. Henry Adams (Phila., 1879) 1:3; Sec. Treas. to HR, Mar. 6, 1792, ASP 3:1:156. Ibid. 157.

49. Tench Coxe to Ham., Aug. 5, 1794, Ham. *Pap.* 17:19. See also Ham. to Coxe, Dec. 18, 1793, Coxe to Ham., Aug. 8, 1794, ibid. 15:472, 17:77–78.

50. A good study of the rebellion is Leland D. Baldwin *Whiskey Rebels* (Rev. ed., Pittsburgh, 1968; 1939). Pres. Add., Nov. 19, 1794, ASP 1:1:24; New-port to Coxe, Nov. [?], 28, 1801, Coxe to Richard Peters, 1801, Tench Coxe Sec., Coxe Pap., PHi; Pres. Message, Dec. 8, 1801, ASP 1:1:58; Sec. Treas. to Sen., Dec. 21, 1801, ibid. 3:1:702.

51. Tench Coxe *An Address to an Assembly of the Friends of American Manufac-tures* (Phila., 1787) 26; Tench Coxe *A View of the United States . . .* (Phila., 1794) 493; Thomann *Liqr. Laws* 156.

52. Gallatin 1:3.

Chapter Three

(Quote) Cobbett 187.

1. McCusker 408–409; ASP 3:1:707, 2:712; Cole. This last work has been helpful throughout ch. 3.

2. E.g., *Indictment and Tryal* 9, 12; Gerard G. Beekman to Wm. Vanderspeigel, Nov. 23, 1747, to Wm. Beekman, Jun. 6, 1752, to Saml. Fowler, Mar. 29, 1753, to Thos. Cranston, Apr. 17, 1764, to John Peck, Apr. 30, 1765, Gerard G. Beekman et al. *The Beekman Mercantile Papers* ed. P. L. White (N.Y., 1956) 1:31, 143, 173, 465, 484.

3. Laurens to Thos. Mears, Feb. 15, 1763, Henry Laurens *Papers* ed. P. M. Hamer (Columbia, S.C., 1968–) 3:256.

4. Gerard G. Beekman to Vanderspeigel, Nov. 23, 1747, to Peleg Thurston, Aug. 23, 1748, to Saml. Fowler, Jul. 28, Dec. 15, 1752, Aug. 9, 1753, Jul. 10, 1755, to Southwick and Clark, Aug. 3, 1762, to Hugh Kirk, Jan. 20, 1769, Beekman 1:31, 58, 146, 160, 183, 258, 414, 520; Laurens to Foster Cunliffe, Jan. 20, 1748/9, to Mears, Feb. 15, 1763, to Meyler & Hall, Feb. 24, 1763, Laurens 1:202, 3:256, 270; Pringle to Humphrey Hill, Jul. 4, 1738, to Adam McDonald, Feb. 5, 1742/3, to John Dickinson, May 21, 1743, to John Erving, Jul. 29, 1740, Dec. 7, 1743, Robt. Pringle *Letterbook* ed. W. B. Edgar (Columbia, S.C., 1972) 1:18, 2:494–495, 556; 1:233, 2:616; Deane to Simeon Deane, Oct. 20, 1783, Silas Deane 192; Claude C. Robin *New Travels through North America* (Phila., 1783) 17; John Lord Sheffield *Observations on the Commerce of the American States* (London, 1784) 108–115; *Indictment and Tryal* 15,17. The triangular pattern was suggested by Weeden 2:501–502, 641. It has been shown to be true only for Rhode Island. G. M. Ostrander "The Making of the Triangular Trade Myth" *Wm. and Mary Q.* 3 Ser. 30 (1973) 635–644. See also Richard Pares *Yankees and Creoles* (Cambridge, 1956) 92–110, 121–122, 133; Jas. F. Shepherd and Gary M. Walton *Shipping, Maritime Trade, and the Economic Development of Colonial North America* (Cambridge, Eng., 1972) 49–53; McCusker 538; D. C. Klingaman "The Coastwise Trade of Colonial Massachusetts" Essex Inst. *Coll.* 108 (1972) 217–234; D. C. Klingaman "The Development of the Coastwise Trade of Virginia . . ." *Va. Mag. His. Biog.* 77 (1969) 26–45; Hedges 22–46.

5. Beekman to Thurston, Aug. 3, 1748, to John Channing, Jan. 22, 1749, Beekman 1:56, 75; Laurens to Gidney Clarke, Jul. 13, 1756, to Mears, Feb. 15, 1763, to Meyler & Hall, Feb. 24, 1763, Laurens 2:251, 3:256, 270; Pringle to Wm. Pringle, Aug. 21, 1739, to Erving, Feb. 11, 1742/3, to Thos. Goldthwait, Jan. 21, 1742/3, May 17, 1743, Pringle 1:123, 2:502, 485, 548; Edmund Pendleton to Col. Baylor, Feb. 4, 1772, "Baylor Letters" *Va. Mag. His. Biog.* 21 (1913) 94–95; Weeden 2:502; McCusker 478.

6. McCusker 434, 447–448. See also ibid. 408–409, 538; Tim. Pitkin *A Statistical View of the Commerce of the United States . . .* (N.Y., 1817) 21–23; Sheffield 108–116; Weeden 501–502.

7. Quo. in *Investigation into the Fifteen Gallon Law of Massachusetts . . .* (Boston, 1839) 65. See also Wm. Beekman to Jas. Beekman, Nov. 27, 1778, Gerard W. Beekman to Wm. Beekman, Jul. 9, 1778, to Abraham Beekman, Sep. 16, 1779, Beekman 3:1285, 1305, 1337; Wm. Pynchon *Diary* ed. F. E. Oliver (Boston, 1890) Sep. 1, 1777, p. 38; Francisco de Miranda *The New Democracy in*

America ed. J. S. Ezell (Norman, 1963) 118; Robin 82; Bordley 326; *Am. Museum* 4 (1788) 234; Watson *Obs.* 11; Geo. F. Willison *Patrick Henry and His World* (Garden City, N.Y., 1969) 35; Gipson 370. On the Army see Daniel O. Morton *'Wine is a Mocker, Strong Drink is Raging'* (Montpelier, 1828) 7; Robinson 120, 126; Rush *Let.* 142–143; David F. Hawke *Benjamin Rush* (Indianapolis, 1971) 207. There are numerous citations in the index to Geo. Washington *Writings* ed. J. C. Fitzpatrick (Wash., 1931–1944).

8. Brown & Benson to Hewes & Anthony, Mar. 9, 1789, Hedges 311; ibid. 312; White Acct. Bks., CtY; Hartford Co. TS 1AR (1831) 5; CtTS 1AR 7; 3AR 29; Robison Distillery Accts., Robison & Edgar to Saml. Brick, Jul. 12, 1784, Robison Pap., MeHi.

9. (markets) Deane to Deane, Oct. 20, 1783, Silas Deane 192; Adam Seybert *Statistical Annals* (Phila., 1818) 57–58; Coxe "Reflections on the Present Situation of the Distilleries of the United States . . ." (1791), Manufactures Box, Tench Coxe Sec., Coxe Pap., PHi; Belknap *N.H.* 3:250–251. (home consumption) McCusker 468; Wm. Constable to Gouverneur Morris, Dec. 6, 1788, Ham. *Corres.* 166–167. See also Sec. Treas. to HR "Report on . . . Distilled Spirits" (1792), Ham. *Pap.* 11:98–99.

10. Coxe *Obs.* 49. See also ibid. 23; Coxe *Add.* 26; Tench Coxe *Reflexions on the State of the Union* (Philla., 1792) 8, 15–16; Coxe *View* 106–110; *Am. Museum* 4 (1788) 234.

11. Geo. Thatcher to John Waite, May 26, 1789, Ephraim Brown to Benj. Brown, Jan. 17, Feb. 3, 1791, Liebmann Coll., NN; King to Gouverneur Morris, Sep. 1, 1792, Ernst 174; HR debate, Jan. 6, 1791, U.S. 1 Cong. *Annals* 1894–1900; Sec. Treas. to HR "Report on . . . Distilled Spirits" (1792), Ham. *Pap.* 11:98–99; Tench Coxe *A Brief Examination of Lord Sheffield's Observations* . . . (Phila., 1791) 9, 85; Morse *Am. Geog.* 89; Hedges 323–324; Thomann *Liqr. Laws* 16, 19; Benezet *Potent Enemies* 11n. The earliest reference to whiskey that I have located is for 1749 in W. J. Hinke and C. E. Kemper, ed. "Moravian Diaries . . ." *Va. Mag. His. Biog.* 11 (1903) 117. But this is a translation.

12. Cole; Stewart 83.

13. Molasses and rum imports as in Appendix 1, note 2. The War of 1812 reduced these imports. MSSI *Circ.* 6. In the 1820s distillers sought protectionist duties that would bar imported spirits. Ag. Com. to Sen. "Duty on Imported Spirits" (1826), ASP 3:5:368–371; Select Com. to HR "Duty on Imported and Excise on Domestic Spirit" (1826), ASP 3:5:506–521.

14. (immigrants) Saml. Morewood *An Essay on the Inventions and Customs . . . in the Use of Inebriating Liquors* (London, 1824) 187; Morewood *History* 335; Howells 100, 110; Laurens 3:469n; Jas. G. Leyburn *The Scotch-Irish* (Chapel Hill, 1962) 264–265; (stills) Harrison Hall *The Distiller* (2 ed., Phila., 1818) 44n–45n; Seybert 462; Morewood *Essay* 176; Rush *Let.* 400–403; *Reg. Pa.* 1 (1828) 170; Duffield 10–11; J. I. Wells 17–18; Jillson *Ky. Dis.;* Weiss 61; R. J. Forbes *Short History of the Art of Distillation* (Leiden, 1948) 233.

15. H. Hall *Dis.* 44n–45n; Seybert 462; Forbes 233.

16. An excellent fold out drawing is in H. Hall *Dis.* See also ibid. 34–35; Robt. Gillespie *A New Plan for Distilling* . . . (Balt., 1810); Saml. M'Harry *The Practical Distiller* . . . (Harrisburgh, 1809) 127–128; Hamlet Scrantom to

Abraham Scrantom, Jan. 24, 1815, Edwin Scrantom et al. "Letters" Rochester His. Soc. *Pub. Fund Ser.* 7 (1928) 190; Weiss 62–64, 67.

17. (patents) "All Patents Granted by the United States" HR Exec. Doc. 50, 21 Cong., 2 Sess., 2 (1831). On the difficulties still improvements caused excise agents see Sec. Treas. to HR "Duty on Stills" (1817), ASP 3:3:153–165. See also a tax case in Ways and Means Com. to HR "Duty on Stills" (1822), ASP 3:3:697–699; (technology) *Niles* 9 (1815) 35–36; 10 (1816) 347, 362; *Am. Farmer* 1 (1819) 45; *Plough Boy* 1 (1820) 411; *Reg. Pa.* 1 (1828) 170–171; Bordley 321–324; Gillespie; *The Grocer's Guide* . . . (N.Y., 1820) 124–168; H. Hall *Dis.* 34–35; M'Harry vii; (promoters) Coxe "Reflections on the Present Situation of the Distilleries," "An Account of a Cheap and Easy Method of Distilling Spirits . . ." (1790s?), Manufactures Box, Tench Coxe Sec., Coxe Pap., PHi; Coxe *Exam.* 74–75; Saml. L. Mitchill "Improvements in Distilling Spirits" *Niles* 3 (1812) 123–124. See also Mitchill in *Niles* 2 (1812) 227–228; Cooper in *Emporium of Arts and Sci.* n.s. 3 (1814) 498–499; Wash. to Jas. Anderson, Jan. 8, 1797, to John Fitzgerald, Jun. 12, 1797, to Wm. A. Wash., May 24, 1799, Wash. *Writ.* (Fitz.) 35:352, 465, 37:214; to same, Oct. 7, 1799, Liebmann Coll., NN; Peeke 72.

18. (grain) *Niles* 10 (1816) 336; Arfwedson 1:205; Cobbett 275–276; Cuming 247; Jas. Flint 293, 254; Janson 453; Jos. Pickering *Inquiries of an Emigrant* (London, 1831) 125; John S. Wright *Letters from the West* (Salem, N.Y., 1819) 54; (yield) *Reg. Pa.* 1 (1828) 170; H. Hall *Dis.* 13; M'Harry 55–56; Gillespie 4; *An Essay on the Importance and the Best Mode of Converting Grain into Spirit* (Lexington, Ky., 1823) 4, 17; Henry Wansey *The Journal of an Excursion to the United States* . . . (Salisbury, Eng., 1796) 176–177; (spirits prices) *Essay on Importance* 4, 5; M'Harry 74; J. S. Wright 55; Henry C. Wright "Human Life" *Growing Up in the Cooper Country* ed. Louis C. Jones (Syracuse, 1965) 153.

19. Symmes to Mr. and Mrs. Peyton Short, Mar. 17, 1800, John C. Symmes *The Intimate Letters* . . . ed. Beverley W. Bond, Jr. (Cincin., 1956) 61; H. Hall *Dis.* 27; Weiss 61; Neil A. McNall *An Agricultural History of the Genesee Valley* (Phila., 1952) 91.

20. H. Hall *Dis.* 27–32. See also Gillespie 14; M'Harry 125–128; John May "Journal" *Pa. Mag. His. Biog.* 45 (1921) May 15, 1789, pp. 110–111; Weiss 156–157.

21. Jas. Buchanan *Works* ed. J. B. Moore (Phila., 1908–1911) 1:358; Holmes 205, 284; Pickering 125; *Niles* 21 (1821) 225–227; 43 (1832) 176.

22. (production) "Digest of Manufactures" (1810), ASP 3:2:703; (transport) F. A. Michaux *Travels to the West* . . . ed. R. G. Thwaites (Cleveland, 1904;1805) 145; Coxe *Add.* 29; Coxe *View* 485; H. Hall *Dis.* 29; M'Harry 73.

23. Brissot de Warville 214–215. Faux 11:140, 236; Edwin James *Account of an Expedition* . . . ed. R. G. Thwaites (Cleveland, 1905;1823) 17:106; Janson 453; Harry Toulmin *A Description of Kentucky* ed. T. D. Clark (Lexington, Ky., 1945;1792) 7.

24. (fruit) Bradbury 281n; Howells 32, 76–77; Michaux 241–242; Johannes Schweizer "Journal" *The Old Land and the New* ed. R. H. Billigmeier and F. A. Picard (Minneapolis, 1965) 90–91; (prices) *Niles* 10 (1816) 269, 336; Cuming 183, 247; Holmes 284; Michaux 172; John Palmer *Journal of Travels in the United States* . . . (London, 1818) 83–84; Pickering 125; J. S. Wright 54–55;

(Europe) Seybert 60–61; *Niles* 10 (1816) 348; 13 (1817) 19–20; 23 (1822) 194–198; (carriage) *Niles* 6 (1814 Supp.) 249; Faux 11:161–162; (New Orleans) *Essay on Importance* 3; Faux 12:18; (pork) Frances Trollope *Domestic Manners of the Americans* ed. D. Smalley (N.Y., 1949;1832) 88–89; *Essay on Importance* 3–4. For a full discussion see Thos. S. Berry *Western Prices before 1861* (Cambridge, 1943) 215–246.

25. Symmes to Mr. and Mrs. Short, Mar. 17, 1800, Symmes 60; Arfwedson 1:205; Jas. Flint 293; J. S. Wright 54–55; *Essay on Importance* 4, 13–14; *Niles* 5 (1813) 41; 33 (1827) 153; *Reg. Pa.* 1 (1828) 170; Berry 103; Nettels 177.

26. Cole; Berry 104. The shortage of stills is noted by Baldwin *Whis. Reb.* 26.

27. (money) *Am. Museum* 4 (1788) 233; *Niles* 21 (1821) 225–227; Zerah Hawley *A Journal of a Tour* . . . (New Haven, 1822) 33; Brissot de Warville 215; Wm W. Sweet, ed. *Religion on the American Frontier: the Presbyterians* (N.Y., 1936) 65; Wm. T. Utter *Granville* (Granville, Oh., 1956) 87; (supply) ibid. 76; *Reg. Pa.* 14 (1834) 43; Elias P. Fordham *Personal Narrative of Travels* . . . ed. F. A. Ogg (Cleveland, 1906) 76; Howells 125; (Hope Distillery) Bernhard 2:132; Geo. W. Ogden *Letters from the West* ed. R. G. Thwaites (Cleveland, 1905;1823) 40; Collins 363.

28. *Essay on Importance* 4; *Niles* 10 (1816) 348.

29. (wages) *Niles* 33 (1827) 139; Holmes 284; Neilson 156; Benj. Smith, ed. *Twenty-four Letters from Labourers in America* . . . (2 ed., London, 1829) 36; (whiskey) Hawley 33; Holmes 266–268, 284; Pickering 27–28, 125; B. Smith 36, 45; R. Carlyle Buley *The Old Northwest* (Indianapolis, 1950) 1:527.

30. Compiled from sources in note 29 and *Niles* 21 (1821) 227; (1822) 381; Benj. H. Latrobe *Impressions Respecting New Orleans* (N.Y., 1951) 154; Neilson 157; Schweizer 96; J. Jakob Rütlinger "Journal" *The Old Land and the New* ed. R. H. Billigmeier and F. A. Picard (Minneapolis, 1965) 231–232; Horace Mann *Remarks upon the Comparative Profits of Grocers and Retailers* . . . (Boston, 1834) 8; ATS 6AR 51.

31. Wm. P. Dole "Wabash Valley Merchant and Flatboatman" ed. D. F. Carmony *Ind. Mag. His.* 67 (1971) 335–363; T. D. Clark 159; Leland D. Baldwin *The Keelboat Age on Western Waters* (Pittsburgh, 1941).

32. B. Hall 3:336; *Niles* 1 (1811) 10; 6 (1814 Supp.) 393; 12 (1817) 70; 24 (1823) 115; 27 (1824) 256. For a recent assessment see Eric F. Haites et al. *Western River Transportation* (Balt., 1975).

33. Farmer quo. in *Niles* 29 (1825) 180. On the long-range convergence of eastern and western prices see Berry.

34. Profits estimated in *Essay on Importance* 3–4. The classic study is Geo. R. Taylor *The Transportation Revolution* (N.Y., 1951).

35. (Dayton) *Niles* 42 (1832) 421; (New Orleans) Jas. Hall *Notes on the Western States* (Phila., 1838) 279; Berry 5; (Ohio) Board of Canal Cmrs., AR, Oh. Sen. J., 1834/5, p. 409; 1835/6, p. 380; *Hesperian* 3 (1839) 115–119; "Stat. of the Ag. and Man. and Dom. Trade, Currency, and Banks of the Sevl. States and Terr." Sen. Doc. 21, 28 Cong., 2 Sess. (1845) 330–376; Buley 1:535–539; (Erie) N.Y. statistics, 1821–1834, "Rep. of the Cmrs. of the Canal Fund," NYSD Doc. 58, vol. 2 (1835) Table D; NYSD Doc. 35, vol. 1 (1838) 58–74; *Niles* 48 (1835) 133; ATS 2AR 13; 6AR 76. Rochester's tag is from Blake

McKelvey *Rochester, the Flower City* (Cambridge, 1949) v. Its flour output doubled from 1826 to 1833. Blake McKelvey *Rochester, the Water Power City* (Cambridge, 1945) 171. See also Henry Hall *The History of Auburn* (Auburn, N.Y., 1869) 254–255; Jas. A. Frost *Life on the Upper Susquehanna* (N.Y., 1951) 82.

36. U.S. Cen., 1840 *Compendium of the Enumeration of the Inhabitants and Statistics of the United States* . . . (Wash., 1841) 363. (S.W. Pa.) *Reg. Pa.* 5 (1830) 79; 11 (1833) 380; *Niles* 48 (1835) 218; (Ohio) *Niles* 24 (1823) 32; Faux 12:18; (N.Y.) *Niles* 32 (1827) 388; NYSTS 3AR 37; (S.E. Pa.) *Am. Reg.* 5 (1809) 223; *Reg. Pa.* 2 (1828) 320; 16 (1835) 355; *Niles* 30 (1826) 21; 32 (1827) 113; 33 (1827) 154.

37. Coxe *Reflex.* 13; *Emporium of Arts and Sci.* n.s. 3 (1814) 499; *Reg. Pa.* 8 (1831) 236. See also Rush to John Adams, Jun. 27, 1812, Rush *Let.* 1145; Buchanan (July 4, 1815 oration) 1:5–6; PaTS *Anniversary Report of the Managers* . . . (Phila., 1834) 11. In Morristown, N.J., there were 19 distilleries in 1825, one in 1830. Mrs. E. P. Burton "Life and Labors of Rev. Albert Barnes . . ." (ca. 1870), Misc. Mss., Presbyterian His. Soc., Phila.

38. "Digest of Manufactures" (1810), ASP 3:2:703; U.S. Cen., 1840 *Comp.* 363; "PaTS 6AR" *Reg. Pa.* 11 (1833) 379; John S. Stone *An Address Delivered before the Young Men's TS* . . . (New Haven, 1831) 11. These figures should be considered estimates.

39. "Digest of Manufactures" (1810), ASP 3:2:703; U.S. Cen., 1840 *Comp.* 363. 1825 production estimated in Nott 13n. Other information from N.Y. Sec. State *Census* . . . *1855* (Albany, 1857) lix, lx; U.S. Cen., 1850 *A Digest of the Statistics of Manufactures* . . . (Wash., 1859) 47; U.S. Cen., 1860 *Preliminary Report on the Eighth Census* (Wash., 1862) 178. Much of the 1860 production was for industrial use. See U.S. Cen., 1860 *Manufactures of the United States in 1860* (Wash., 1865) 415. See also *New Yorker* 4 (1838) 810.

40. (England) T. G. Coffey "Beer Street: Gin Lane" *QJSA* 27 (1966) 669–692; Brian Harrison *Drink and the Victorians* (London, 1971); J. J. Tobias *Crime and Industrial Society in the 19th Century* (N.Y., 1967) 179–182; (Germany) Gallus Thomann *Real and Imaginary Effects of Intemperance* (N.Y., 1884) 21, 94; (Sweden) Walter Thompson *The Control of Liquor in Sweden* (N.Y., 1935) 9; (Russia) Wm. E. Johnson *The Liquor Problem in Russia* (Westerville, Oh., 1915) 126–131. See also ATU 4AR 60; 5AR 38; 12AR 17; 18AR 34.

41. On discretionary income see *Niles* 7 (1814) 273; 13 (1817) 19–20; 33 (1827) 138–144; Mann 8; David M'Kinney *Address of* . . . (Lewistown, Pa., 1835) 11–12.

42. Henry Ware, Jr. *The Criminality of Intemperance* (Boston, 1823) 19. (despair) MSSI *Report of the Board of Counsel* . . . (Boston, 1820) 7–8; John Ware *An Address Delivered before the MSSI* . . . (Boston, 1826) 3; (entrepreneur) Francis W. Halsey *The Pioneers of Unadilla Village* (Unadilla, N.Y., 1902) 137; Geo. B. Cheever *The True History of Deacon Giles' Distillery* (N.Y., 1844); (devil) Heman Humphrey "Debates of Conscience with a Distiller, a Wholesale Dealer, and a Retailer" Am. Tract Soc. *The Temperance Volume* (N.Y., ca. 1835); *The House Old Nick Built* (Albany, 1834).

43. H. Hall *Dis.* 17; Tardiveau to M. G. St. Jean de Crevecoeur, Aug. 25, 1789, Barthélemi Tardiveau *Barthélemi Tardiveau* ed. H. C. Rice (Balt., 1938) 33; Tilton "Real Independence" *Niles* 6 (1814) 192; John W. Townsend *O Rare Tom Johnson* (Lexington, Ky., 1949) 34 [one word corrected].

Chapter Four

(Quote)   Henry B. Fearon *Sketches of America* (London, 1818) 194.

1. Claude Lévi-Strauss *The Raw and the Cooked* (N.Y., 1969).

2. Audobon 334; Rebecca Burlend and Edw. Burlend *A True Picture of Emigration* (Chicago, 1936; 1848) 72; Sir Augustus J. Foster *Jeffersonian America* (San Marino, 1954) 21; Michaux 122; Chas. Sealsfield [born Karl Postl] *The Americans as They Are* (London, 1828; 1827) 83, 124; J. S. Wright 54; Richard C. Wade *The Urban Frontier* (Cambridge, 1959) 95.

3. Daniel Drake *Natural and Statistical View* (Cincin., 1815) 139. See also Daniel Drake "Notices Concerning Cincinnati" His. and Phil. Soc. of Oh. *Q. Pub.* 3 (1908) 30–31; Constance M. Green *Washington . . . 1800–1878* (Princeton, 1962) 41. Two exceptions were Pittsburgh and Philadelphia. [Beaufoy] *Tour through Parts of the United States . . .* (London, 1828) 28–29; Coke 44; Wade 95, 296–297.

4. Asa Greene *A Glance at New York . . .* (N.Y., 1837) 180; quo. in Morewood *History* 339. See also Theo. Dwight *Travels in America* (Glasgow, 1848) 83; Baron Axel Leonard Klinckowström *Baron Klinkowström's America 1818–1820* ed. F. D. Scott (Evanston, 1952; 1824) 68–69; (Croton) Philip Hone *Diary* ed. Allan Nevins (N.Y., 1936) Oct. 28, 1841, Oct. 12, 14, 1842, pp. 570, 624, 625; Ezekiel P. Belden *New York* (N.Y., 1850) 38–40; (July 4) Hone (Jul. 4, 1829, Jul. 4, 1844) 15, 708; Marryat *Diary* 1:102, 105–106, 111.

5. Quo. in Fred. Marryat *Second Series of a Diary in America* (Phila., 1840) 43; Fletcher to Jesse Fletcher, Oct. 31, 1810, Fletcher 21; John Randolph *Letters of John Randolph to a Young Relative* (Phila., 1834) 91. Frank. to Abbé Morellet, ca. 1776, Benj. Franklin *Works* ed. Jared Sparks (Boston, 1836–1840) 2:226–227; Pickering 23–24, 31; Jas. K. Paulding *Letters from the South* (N.Y., 1835) 1:21. See also Marryat *Diary* 2:154–155; *Pa. Gaz.* Jul. 12, 1764; *Niles* 14 (1818) 376.

6. (genl.) Burlend 59; Buley 1:216–217; (plentiful) Burlend 60, 71; Jas. Hall *Letters from the West* (London, 1828) 111; Nuttall 128; Royall *Sketches* 56; (scarce) Wm. Allen "Now and Then" Me. His. Soc. *Coll.* 1 Ser. 7 (1876) 272; Caroline M. Kirkland *A New Home . . .* ed. John Nerber (N.Y., 1953; 1839) 65–66; Faux 11:177; Adlard Welby *A Visit to North America . . .* ed. R. G. Thwaites (Cleveland, 1905; 1821) 249; (price) Richard Parkinson *A Tour in America* (London, 1805) 161; (milk sickness) Arfwedson 2:11; Harvey L. Ross *Lincoln's First Years in Illinois* ed. R. R. Wilson (Elmira, N.Y., 1946; 1899) 61; Buley 1:248–249; L. Furbee and W. D. Snively, Jr. "Milk Sickness, 1811–1966: a Bibliography" *J. His. Med. and Allied Sci.* 23 (1968) 276–285.

7. Neville B. Craig, ed. *The Olden Time* (Cincin., 1876; 1846–1847) 141. Bentley (May 25, 1805) 3:159; Buley 1:525; (New England) Playfair 1:34; (N.Y.) Fred F. DeRoos *Personal Narrative of Travels in the United States . . .* (London, 1827) 57; Duncan 2:280; (West) Edmund Flagg *The Far West* ed. R. G. Thwaites (Cleveland, 1906; 1838) 26:323; Buley 1:157; Dick 292; (prices) Holmes 266–268; Neilson 157; Godfrey T. Vigne *Six Months in America* (Phila., 1833) 194–195; Welby 177; Buley 1:527; Berry 120; (duties) Sec. Treas. to HR, HR Doc. 58, 15 Cong., 1 Sess., 7 (1818) 13; *Niles* 41 (1831) 327; (imports) (1790–1800) ASP 3:1:707; (1801–1826) 3:2:50, 110, 144, 149, 207, 249, 310, 376, 442, 498, 582, 654, 849, 3:36, 632, 685, 4:10, 378, 5:157, 258, 540, 652; (1827–1851) as in Appendix 1, note 2.

8. Quo. in *Niles* 44 (1833) 391. Ibid. 390; Royall *Sketches* 56; Burlend 71–72; Dick 292; (homemade) John Ball *Autobiography* ed. K. B. Powers et al. (Grand Rapids, 1925) 7; Hawley 32; Buley 1:157; (temp.) *N. Eng. Farmer* 8 (1830) 322; "Mem. of the Chamber of Commerce of the City of Phila." Sen. Doc. 124, 16 Cong., 1 Sess., 27 (1820) 8; anon. pam., ca. 1830, Dyer Coll., MeHi; (prices) *Niles* 44 (1833) 283; Cole; (duties and imports) as in note 7.

9. (prices) Kemble 85; Cole; (imports) as in Appendix 1, note 2; (Brande) ATS 5AR inside cover; PSDUAS *The Anniversary Report of the Managers* . . . (Phila., 1831) 12–13; PaTS *Anniversary Rep.* 12; S. H. Dickson in TS of Columbia, S.C. *Proc.* 52; John Adlum *A Memoir on the Cultivation of the Vine* . . . (Wash., 1823) 70–76. The publishing history of Brande's work is in *Address to the Young Men of Worcester County* (Worcester, 1835) 4.

10. Quo. in Josiah Quincy *Figures of the Past from the Leaves of Old Journals* (Boston, 1888) 189–190. Jeff. to Vine Utley, Mar. 21, 1819, Jeff. *Writ.* 15:187; Albert J. Beveridge *The Life of John Marshall* (Boston, 1916–1919) 3:9, 9n; Andrew Jackson *Correspondence* ed. J. S. Bassett (Wash., 1926–1935) 1:8, 3:408, 4:381n, 432, 5:169, 484; Marquis James *Andrew Jackson, the Border Captain* (N.Y.: Universal Lib., n.d.; 1933) 88, 110, 219; Harriette S. Arnow *Seedtime on the Cumberland* (N.Y., 1960) 424.

11. Robt. H. Gardiner *Early Recollections* . . . (Hallowell, Me., 1936) 83. Hone (May 14, 1836, Oct. 16, Dec. 15, 1841, Feb. 6, 1846, Feb. 3, 1847) 208, 568–569, 577, 755, 787–788; Edw. Pessen "Philip Hone's Set" N.Y. His. Soc. *Q.* 56 (1972) 285–308; Arfwedson 2:180; Bacourt 368; T. Hamilton 1:119, 121, 368; Playfair 1:96; Fisher (esp. Dec. 26, 1840) 108; Elbridge Gerry, Jr. *Diary* ed. C. G. Bowers (N.Y., 1927) 201; Robt. W. July *The Essential New Yorker* (Durham, 1951) 92–93, 276; Whitehill 21–47.

12. Bernhard 2:246; Mrs. Hall 89, 248; Kemble 203n; Michaux 207; Jeff. to M. de Neuville, Dec. 13, 1818, Jeff. *Writ.* 15:178; Fletcher to Jesse Fletcher, Jul. 2, 1814, Fletcher 82; Cal. to Col. G. Gibbs, Mar. 26, 1823, John C. Calhoun *Papers* ed. R. L. Meriwether and W. E. Hemphill (Columbia, S.C., 1959–   ) 7:543; Adlum; Alphonse Loubat *The American Vine Dresser's Guide* (N.Y., 1827); Wm. R. Prince and Wm. Prince *A Treatise on the Vine* (N.Y., 1830) esp. iii; *Am. Farmer* 1 (1819) 53; *Niles* 1 (1811) 139–140; 10 (1816) 99; 11 (1816) 141; 20 (1821) 304; 24 (1823) 283, 369; 28 (1825) 416; 29 (1825) 160; 31 (1826) 192; 32 (1827) 196, 289–290; 37 (1829) 76–77, (1830) 296; 38 (1830) 441–442.

13. J. Woods 240; Wm. N. Blane *An Excursion through the United States* . . . (London, 1824) 138; Nuttall 63. (Vevay) D. Drake *View* 142n; E. Evans 284; Cobbett 257–258; Michaux 207–208; Sealsfield 32; *Niles* 1 (1811) 139–140; 10 (1816) 347; 13 (1817) 224; 15 (1818) 111; 18 (1820) 399; (Longworth) Clara L. de Chambrun *The Making of Nicholas Longworth* (N.Y., 1933) 29–32; Longworth to Am. Inst. Trustees, Aug. 27, 1849, Am. Inst. "7AR," NYAD Doc. 199, vol. 9 (1850) 157; U.S. Cen., 1840 *Comp.* 359; U.S. Cen., 1850 *Statistical View of the United States* . . . (Wash., 1854) 174, 295.

14. L. B. Langworthy "The Grape," NYAD Doc. 131, vol. 6 (1842) 392; "Ann. State Fair Add.," Rochester, Sep. 19, 1851, N.Y. State Ag. Soc. *Trans.*, NYAD Doc. 126, vol. 6 (1852) 41. A Langworthy wine recipe is in *Niles* 38 (1830) 441–442; (Adlum) Adlum esp. 139–142; Theo. Dwight 29–30; *Niles* 24 (1823) 283; 34 (1828) 161, 192, 209.

15. E. S. Thomas *Reminiscences of the Last Sixty-Five Years* (Hartford, 1840) 2:117. (trade) Jeff. to de Neuville, Dec. 13, 1818, Jeff. *Writ.* 15:178; Geo. Ticknor to Jeff., Dec. 8, 1821, Jeff. "Pap." 310; Langworthy "Grape" 392–393; *Niles* 12 (1817) 416; 29 (1826) 316; 32 (1827) 307; 34 (1828) 251; "Mem. of the Chamber of Commerce of the City of Phila." Sen. Doc. 124, 16 Cong., 1 Sess., 27 (1820) 7–8; Sec. Treas. to HR, HR Doc. 58, 15 Cong., 1 Sess., 7 (1818) 13–14; Ways and Means Com. to HR (1818), ASP 3:3:296; (impurities) Boardman 361; Marryat *Sec. Ser.* 1:37; Rütlinger 218; Frost Genl. Store Daybks., Frost Coll., MH-BA; Moses Stuart *Essay on the Prize-Question* . . . (N.Y., 1830); Waterhouse 28n; ATU 3AR 41; John H. Cocke to Wm. Meade, Jun. 1846, Kane Coll., CSmH; (temp.) Humphrey *Intemp.* 31; Justin Edwards *Letter to the Friends of Temperance in Massachusetts* (Boston, 1836) 18; Stuart; MTS 25AR 22; (imports) as in Appendix 1, note 2.

16. John Spurrier *The Practical Farmer* (Wilmington, 1793) 246, 247. Rush *Inquiry* (1790) 7; Rush to Jeremy Belknap, Aug. 19, Nov. 5, 1788, Rush *Let.* 482, 496; Belknap to Rush, Jun. 22, Sep. 30, 1788, ca. 1789 [30 Rush Ms9], Rush Pap., PHi; Rush "Observations on the Federal Process in Phila." *Am. Museum* 4 (1788) 75–78; Rush on maple beer in ibid. 349–350; Jeremiah Libbey to Jeremy Belknap, Dec. 17, 1789, Belknap "Pap." 456; (guides) Bordley 325–326; Saml. Deane *The New-England Farmer* (Worcester, 1790) 21; Job Roberts *The Pennsylvania Farmer* (Phila., 1804) 61–62, 168; (associations) Saml. L. Mitchill "Address," Jan. 10, 1792, Soc. for the Promotion of Ag., Arts and Manufactures *Trans.* (Albany, 1801) 1:30; Tolles *Logan* 89.

17. Coxe *View* 493; Coxe *Add.* 14, 26; Tench Coxe *An Enquiry into the Principles on Which a Commercial System for the United States of America Should Be Founded* (Phila., 1787) 23; *The Complete Family Brewer* (Phila., 1805) iii–iv; Jos. Coppinger *The American Practical Brewer* . . . (N.Y., 1815) vii; *Am. Museum* 4 (1788) 234; "Rep. on Manufactures" (draft), Ham. *Pap.* 10:119; Wm. Barton to Ham., May 21, 1790, Nathaniel Hazard to Ham., Mar. 9, 1791, Ham. *Corres.* 116, 69; Stanley Baron *Brewed in America* (Boston, 1962) 118. Such views were expressed as late as the 1820s. John Pintard to Eliza P. Davidson, Dec. 16, 1828, Pintard 72:52.

18. Jas. Mease *The Picture of Philadelphia* . . . (Phila., 1811) 77; Bordley 326. *Complete Fam. Brewer;* Coppinger; Jeff. to Chas. Yancey, Jan. 6, 1816, Jeff. *Writ.* 14:380; Jeff. recipe for persimmon beer is in *Am. Farmer* 1 (1819) 22; Baron 140–142; (Phila.) Brissot de Warville 399; Coxe *View* 76, 487; Thos. Wilson *Picture of Philadelphia* (Phila., 1823) 8–9; *Niles* 27 (1824) 6; Edwin T. Freedley *Philadelphia and Its Manufactures* (Phila., 1859) 192; (Albany) Giles 46; *Niles* 29 (1825) 160; 31 (1826) 115; 33 (1827) 156; (Cincin.) D. Drake *View* 147; Bond 410; (Lexington) Cuming 186; (Pittsburgh) Saml. Jones *Pittsburgh in the Year Eighteen Hundred and Twenty-Six* . . . (Pittsburgh, 1826) 80–81; Anne N. Royall *Mrs. Royall's Pennsylvania* (Wash., 1829) 2:121; *Niles* 6 (1814) 208; (Richmond) Mordecai 244; (scarcity) Candler 45; David D. Field *A Statistical Account of the County of Middlesex in Connecticut* (Middletown, 1819) 17; Geo. F. Talbot "Temperance and the Drink Question in the Old Time" Me. His. Soc. *Coll.* 2 Ser. 6 (1895) 377; Coleman 62; (cost) Cobbett 186–187; Cuming 247; Faux 11:103; Gustorf 36; Pickering 27–28.

19. Faux 11:113, 118; Parkinson 1:60; Thos. C. Cochran *The Pabst Brewing Company* (N.Y., 1948) 19, 21; Morris Weeks, Jr. *Beer and Brewing in America* (N.Y., 1949) 20; (skill) Traugott Bromme *Reisen durch die Vereinigten Staaten und*

Ober-Canada (Balt., 1834–1835) 1:80, 85; Baron 127, 182; (climate) Coppinger 128; Robt. Sutcliff *Travels in Some Parts of North America* (Phila., 1812) 28; (other) Vassar to Henry Tucker, Apr. 15, 1816, Booth Coll., Vassar Pap., NPV; Thomann *Am. Beer* 54. Tavern and general store account books show only a few sales per day.

20. Holmes 204; Benj. Silliman *A Journal of Travels in England, Holland and Scotland* . . . (New Haven, 1820) 3:88; Freedley 195; Geo. Ade *The Old-Time Saloon* (N.Y., 1931) 137; Thomann *Am. Beer* 13, 55, 57, 65; Weeks 12–14, 21–22. The best account of lager is Baron 175–187. Coors is Dutch. The only thorough study of an American brewery is Cochran's. (Vassar) Baron 149–156; Matthew Vassar *Autobiography* . . . ed. E. H. Haight (N.Y., 1916); Vassar Pap., NPV.

21. Thomas Kelly *Thomas Kelly and Famaly's* [!] *Journal* ed. Margery West (Isle of Man? 1965) 38; Faux 11:172. Arfwedson 1:111; Bernhard 1:52, 2:176; Jas. Flint 254; B. Smith 43; D. Drake *View* 55; NYAD Doc. 150, vol. 5 (1847) 21; NYAD Doc. 125, vol. 4 (1848) 391, 412–414; NYAD Doc. 200, vol. 4 (1849) 461.

22. A good general discussion is in Weiss esp. 24, 36. Bernhard 2:176; Faux 11:172; (prices) Cuming 246–247; B. Smith 43; *Niles* 29 (1825) 288; (alcohol) estimate by David H. Fischer; Wm. Alcott "Cider Drinking" *Moral Reformer* 1 (1835) 121; ATS 5AR inside cover.

23. H. P. Warren 191; Tim. Dwight 1:27; *Niles* 6 (1814) 278. Bradbury 303; Dalton 210; Saml. G. Goodrich *Recollections of a Lifetime* (N.Y., 1856) 1:70; Neilson 129; Fletcher to Jesse Fletcher, Dec. 4, 1812, Fletcher 69; Wm. W. Snow to John B. Clopton, Oct. 13, 1826, Clopton Let., NcD; Rodolphus Dickinson *Geographical and Statistical View of Massachusetts Proper* (Greenfield, Mass., 1813) 12; D. D. Field 16; *Am. Farmer* 1 (1819) 72; *Moral Reformer* 1 (1835) 121; MTS *Temp. Almanac* (1841) 13; Myra Himelhoch "The Suicide of Sally Perry" *Vt. His.* 33 (1965) 285; Wm. Little *The History of Warren* (Manchester, N.H., 1870) 413; Gerald Carson *Rum and Reform in Old New England* (Sturbridge, Mass., 1966) 5; (champagne) Bacourt 207; Faux 11:70; T. Hamilton 2:173.

24. The early nineteenth-century American diet is a little studied subject. The starting point remains Arthur M. Schlesinger "A Dietary Interpretation of American History" *Mass. His. Soc. Proc.* 68 (1944–1947) 199–227. (This paper appears in an altered form without notes but with an updated bibliography in Schlesinger's *Paths to the Present* [Boston, 1964] 220–240.) See also Kathleen A. Smallzried *The Everlasting Pleasure* (N.Y., 1956). Harriette Arnow has noted that by 1800 American food tastes differed sharply from the English. Arnow esp. 389–390, 423. Bernhard 2:128; H. M. Brackenridge "The Southern States" *Travels in the Old South* ed. E. L. Schwaab (Lexington, Ky., 1973) 246; Jos. Doddridge *Notes, on the Settlement and Indian Wars, of the Western Parts of Virginia & Pennsylvania* (Wellsburgh, Va., 1824) 109; Jas. B. Finley *Autobiography* ed. W. P. Strickland (Cincin., 1853) 69; Goodrich 1:66–68; Chas. J. Latrobe *The Rambler in North America* (London, 1835) 2:13; Marryat *Sec. Ser.* 35–37; Pickering 27; Toulmin 7; J. S. Wright 39; *Niles* 33 (1827) 139.

25. Jeff. to Vine Utley, Mar. 21, 1819, Jeff. *Writ.* 15:187; Bernhard 2:128. Duncan 1:298; Tim. Dwight 4:249; Holmes 356; C. J. Latrobe 2:13; Michaux 247; Wm. H. Ely "Letters" ed. W. S. Hoole *Ala. Rev.* 3 (1950) 36–39; *Friend* 3

(1830) 90–91; Rush *Serm.;* Rush to Vine Utley, Jun. 25, 1812, Rush *Let.* 1142; "An Acct. of the Manners of the German Inhabitants of Pa.," Rush *Essays* esp. 230; Tucker 1:52; (slaves) Sealsfield 131–132; Gray 563–564; Albert V. House *Planter Management and Capitalism in Ante-Bellum Georgia* (N.Y., 1954) 47; John H. Moore *Agriculture in Ante-Bellum Mississippi* (N.Y., 1958) 61; (prisons) Francis Hall *Travels in Canada, and the United States* . . . (Boston, 1818) 187; Ignatz Hülswitt *Tagebuch einer Reise nach den Vereinigten Staaten* . . . (Münster, 1828) 173; Milbert 274; Neilson 59; Jos. Sturge *A Visit to the United States* . . . (London, 1842) 133.

26. Allen 272. H. C. Knight 71–73; Michaux 241–242; D. Drake *Pioneer* 44, 46–47; Finley 69; Gilmer 138–139; *Niles* 16 (1819 Supp.) 188; 29 (1826) 291; Kennedy 326; Tucker 1:76.

27. Prince Maximilian of Wied *Travels in the Interior of North America* ed. R. G. Thwaites (Cleveland, 1906; 1843) 24:123; quo. in Chas. McKnight *Our Western Border* . . . (Phila., 1876) 188; Bernhard 2:128. Arfwedson 2:11–12; Cuming 39, 209; Duncan 2:20; Tim. Dwight 4:41; Faux 11:211; A. J. Foster 21; C. J. Latrobe 2:13; Nuttall 69; Schoepf 1:173–174, 233; Welby 249; J. S. Wright 39, 57; Doddridge 109; Finley 69; Kirkland 65–66; Elizabeth A. Roe *Aunt Leanna* (Chicago, 1855) 15; *Am. Farmer* 9 (1827) 94; *Am. Museum* 4 (1788) 233; *Niles* 43 (1832) 25; Gunn 21.

28. Howells 77; Smallzried 131–134.

29. Tillson 123; Amelia Simmons *American Cookery* . . . (Hartford, 1796) 31. Kirkland 59; Smallzried 96.

30. Mrs. Hall 37; T. Hamilton 2:5. Boardman 30; Fordham 155; Wm. T. Harris *Remarks Made during a Tour through the United States* . . . (London, 1821) 86; Hülswitt 222; Marryat *Sec. Ser.* 35–36; Palmer 13; Welby 249; J. S. Wright 39; Ely 66; Tillson 84.

31. Faux 11:177. J. S. Wright 39.

32. Schweizer 88. Combe 2:82–83; DeRoos 106; Duncan 2:319; B. Hall 1:138; Edw. de Montulé *Travels in America* ed. E. D. Seeber (Bloomington, 1951; 1821) 124, 129; Palmer 151; Philippe Suchard *Mein Besuch Amerika's im Sommer 1824* (Boudry, Switz., 1947) 37.

33. Quo. in Yoder 130.

34. Combe 2:82–83. Mrs. Hall 285.

35. Sarah J. Hale *The Good Housekeeper* (Boston, 1839) 7. Benj. Rush *An Inquiry into the Effects of Spirituous Liquors on the Human Body* (Rev. ed., New Brunswick, N.J., 1805) 32; Rush *Serm.;* John Watson *An Alarming Portraiture of the Pernicious Effects* . . . (Phila., 1813) 40–41; Horace Greeley *Recollections* . . . (N.Y., 1873) 104–105; Edw. C. Delavan to John H. Cocke, Nov. 1834, Cocke Dep., Cocke Pap., ViU; Geo. C. Shattuck, Jr., to Lucy B. Shattuck, Oct. 26, 1834, Shattuck Pap., MHi; Mrs. John H. Kinzie *Wau-Bun* (Chicago, 1932) 134; Sarah J. Hale *Mrs. Hale's New Cook Book* (Phila., 1857) 401–419; Elisha Bartlett *The 'Laws of Sobriety,' and 'The Temperance Reform'* (Lowell, 1835) 10, 16; Thos. J. O'Flaherty *A Medical Essay on Drinking* (Hartford, 1828) 29; Osgood 5; ATS 9AR 8–10; Louis B. Wright *Culture on the Moving Frontier* (N.Y., 1961) 109. See Appendix 3.

36. Greeley 103–105; Sturge 107; Geo. C. Shattuck, Jr., to E. F. Prentiss, Apr. 14, 1832, Shattuck Pap., MHi; Wm. A. Alcott *The Young House-Keeper*

. . . (Boston, 1838) 89; Chas. C. Colton *Protestant Jesuitism* (N.Y., 1836) 73; D. Drake *Discourse* 22–23; O'Flaherty 24; Osgood 4–6; Palfrey 68–69; R. H. Shryock "Sylvester Graham . . ." *Miss. Valley His. Rev.* 18 (1931) 172–183.

37. Colton 71; ATS 7AR 87; Geo. C. Channing *Early Recollections of Newport* . . . (Newport, R.I., 1868) 167. Savannah *Georgian*, Jul. 29, 1830; Goodrich 1:63.

Chapter Five

(Quote) Edw. E. Bourne *The History of Wells and Kennebunk* . . . (Portland, Me., 1875) 413.

1. A perceptive comment is in Chas. M. de Talleyrand "Talleyrand in America as a Financial Promoter" ed. Hans Huth and W. J. Pugh, Am. His. Assn. *Ann. Rep.* 2 (1941) 155. See also Alexis de Tocqueville *Journey to America* ed. J. P. Mayer (Garden City, N.Y., 1971) 399; Vigne 42–43; Austin 26.

2. Arfwedson 2:99; Faux 11:213, 299; J. Hall *Let.* 114–115, 243–244; Heartman 50; H. C. Knight 94; Michaux 247; Jas. K. Paulding *Westward Ho!* (N.Y., 1832) 1:112; Amos Stoddard *Sketches, Historical and Descriptive, of Louisiana* (Phila., 1812) 306; J. Woods 317; *Panoplist* 14 (1818) 212–213.

3. Talleyrand 155; *N.Y. Farmer* 3 (1830) 118–119.

4. Harris 17. Cobbett 178, 180; Kemble 316–317; B. Smith 45; John Lowell *An Address Delivered before the Mass. Ag. Soc.* (Boston, 1818) 6; "Mem. of Sundry Citizens of Charleston, S.C. against the Tariff," HR Doc. 17, 16 Cong., 2 Sess. (1820) 5; J. P. Beekman "Address," NYSD Doc. 85, vol. 3 (1845) 36; Josiah Quincy "Address," NYSD Doc. 105, vol. 4 (1846) 15; J. Edwards "Farm" 4. Owners were alarmed at the increasing use of spirits among their hands. Bradbury 303; Saml. Bard "Address" Soc. of Dutchess Co. for the Promotion of Ag. *Trans.* 1 (1807) 10; Weiss 126; *N. Eng. Farmer* 3 (1824) 65; ATS 4AR 7; MSSI *Circ.* 8; Parker Cleveland *An Address, Delivered at Brunswick* . . . (Boston, 1814) 11; Tolles *Logan* 89. Part of the farmers' concern was self-interest. Beecher *Auto.* 1:13; D. Drake *Pioneer* 66; Rush *Let.* 270–272; *N. Eng. Farmer* 3 (1825) 405; Nott 64–66.

5. U. S. Cen., 1790 *Return of the Whole Number of Persons* . . . (Phila., 1791); U.S. Cen., 1830 *Fifth Census* (Wash., 1832). See also Coke 130; B. Hall 1:158. (genl.) Sam B. Warner, Jr. *The Private City* (Phila., 1968) 3–45; (eighteenth century) Carl Bridenbaugh *Cities in Revolt* (N.Y., 1955); Fred. B. Tolles *Meeting House and Counting House* (Chapel Hill, 1948); (nineteenth century) Roger Lane *Policing the City* (Cambridge, 1967); Raymond A. Mohl *Poverty in New York* (N.Y., 1971); Jas. F. Richardson *The New York Police* (N.Y., 1970); Stephan Thernstrom and Richard Sennett, ed. *Nineteenth-Century Cities* (New Haven, 1969); Wade. (drink) E.g., Duncan 2:322–323; Jas. Flint 312; Royall *Pa.* 2:89; Royall *Sketches* 158–159; Edw. Everett to [?], Dec. 14, 1833, Norcross Pap., MHi.

6. U.S. Cen., 1810 *A Statement of the Arts and Manufactures* . . . (Phila., 1814) Table 37; U.S. Cen., 1840 *Comp.* 360–364; Arfwedson 1:120–121; Chevalier 140; Sturge cxviii–cxx; D. D. Field 42; *Niles* 41 (1831) 250; *Reg. Pa.* 8 (1831) 236; RITS 2AR 8, 13, 17; (genl.) G. R. Taylor *Trans.;* Wm. A. Sullivan "The Industrial Revolution and the Factory Operative in Pa." *Pa. Mag. His.*

Biog. 78 (1954) 479; (drink) Gunn 4; Lecraw 9–10; Wm. Sullivan *A Discourse Delivered before the MSSI* (Boston, 1832) 17–18; Woodward 9.

7. (factories) Fearon 37–38; Wm. E. Channing "Rep. of the Comm. Appointed to Consider the State of Morals among the Young Men of the City . . ." (1825), Channing Pap., Andover Harvard Theological Library, Harvard U. (print shop) Greeley 136, 138, 140; Thurlow Weed *Life* . . . (Boston, 1883–1884) 1:45–46, 361; Jas. L. Crouthamel *James Watson Webb* (Middletown, Ct., 1969) 67–81; Eugene Exman *The Brothers Harper* (N.Y., 1965) 4; (genl.) David Montgomery "The Working Classes of the Pre-Industrial American City" *Labor His.* 9 (1968) 3–22.

8. Wm. E. Channing *An Address on Temperance* (Boston, 1837) 29; NYCTS 1AR 22; NYATS 1AR 4. (disappointed) Combe 1:310; Holmes 376; D. Drake *Discourse* 38; (occasions) Watson *Obs.* 13; Geo. Haydock *Incidents in the Life* . . . (Hudson, N.Y., 1845) 3; H. C. Wright 166; Woodman 37, 42; ATS 5AR 77–78; MeTS 2AR 129; MTS 22AR 8; NYATS 1AR 3; NYCTS 1AR 22; (apprentices) Jacob Carter 14–16; Gale 12; Jefferson J. Polk *Autobiography* (Louisville, 1867) 20–21; Woodman 35; ATS 9AR 21–22; ATU 5AR 43; Sweetser 78; (payday) Fearon 407; Haydock 4; Woodman 39.

9. Paper Makers Assn. quo. in Watson *Obs.* 14; Woodman 36. Royall *Sketches* 158–159; Bentley (Apr. 16, 1791; Feb. 10, 1818) 1:248, 4:501; Jacob Carter 14–16; A. V. Green 7; Woodman 36, 37, 41; Watson *Obs.* 14–16; ATS 5AR 78; NYATS 1AR 3; NYCTS 1AR 9–10.

10. E.g., Wilbur J. Cash *The Mind of the South* (N.Y., 1941) 14–17; contra, Ramsay *S.C.* 2:414.

11. Ely 67–68; Jas. Flint 142; Randolph 26; Benj. Drake *Tales and Sketches, from the Queen City* (Cincin., 1838) 27; Kennedy; Paulding *West.*; Tucker.

12. Achille Murat *The United States of North America* (London, 1833) 22; Wm. C. Preston *Reminiscences* ed. M. C. Yarborough (Chapel Hill, 1933) 10. Combe 2:13–14; Benj. H. Latrobe *Journal* (N.Y., 1905) 46; Schoepf 2:218; J. B. Dunlop " 'The Grand Fabric of Republicanism' . . ." ed. R. A. Mohl *S.C. His. Mag.* 71 (1970) 183; Fletcher 13; Gardiner 88; Henry Hitchcock "From the Green Mountains to the Tombigbee . . ." ed. D. E. Bigham *Ala. Rev.* 26 (1973) 217; Baron de Montlezun "A Frenchman Visits Charleston, 1817" ed. L. G. Moffatt and J. M. Carrière *S.C. His. Gen. Mag.* 49 (1948) 149; Saml. H. Perkins "A Yankee Tutor in the Old South" ed. R. C. McLean *N.C. His. Rev.* 47 (1970) 66; Ramsay *S.C.* 2:342; Paulding *West.* 2:39; Tucker 1:70; Thos. Adams *A Sermon on Intemperance* (Hallowell, Me., 1827) 9.

13. Combe 1:105; Jas. F. Cooper *Notions of the Americans* (London, 1828) 1:369; Tim. Dwight 2:345; Kemble 137; Suchard 81–82; Tocqueville 272–275; *Gaz. U.S.* 3 (1791) 130.

14. (M.D.s) M. S. Pernick "Politics, Parties, and Pestilence . . ." *Wm. and Mary Q.* 3 Ser. 29 (1972) 559–586; Jas. H. Young *The Toadstool Millionaires* (Princeton, 1961) 44–57; Alex. Berman "The Thomsonian Movement . . ." *Bull. His. Med.* 25 (1951) 405–428, 519–538; W. G. Smillie "An Early Prepayment Plan for Medical Care" *J. His. Med. and Allied Sci.* 6 (1951) 253–257; Kaufman esp. 57–70; (law) Maxwell Bloomfield *American Lawyers in a Changing Society* (Cambridge, 1976); Perry Miller *The Life of the Mind in America* (N.Y., 1965) esp. 171–182.

15. Lyman Beecher *A Reformation of Morals Practicable and Indispensable* (Andover, Mass., 1814) 22–23; Elizur Wright to Elizur Wright, Sr., Mar. 15,

1827, Wright Pap., Library of Congress. See also ibid., Nov. 16, 1826; to Susan Clark, Feb. 20, 1829; Beecher *Auto.* 1:128, 130, 140–142, 190; Lee 371; Peck 87; Playfair 2:210; Ebenezer Porter *A Sermon, Delivered in Boston . . .* (Andover, Mass., 1821) 16; Saml. Worcester *A Sermon, Preached in Boston . . .* (Andover, Mass., 1816) 22–23; Chas. I. Foster *An Errand of Mercy* (Chapel Hill, 1960) 128, 143; David M. Ludlum *Social Ferment in Vermont* (N.Y., 1939) 45–47.

16. D. Drake *Pioneer* 233; Jos. Speed to Benj. Rush, Oct. 6, 1803, Rush Pap., PHi; Northeastern Ct. Reg. Plan. Agency *History of the Northeast Region* (Brooklyn, Ct., 1972) 9. Beecher *Auto.* 1:179–180; A. V. Green 10, 17–18; Sturges 31; Sweet *Presb.* 66; John Bell *An Address to the Medical Students' TS . . .* (n.p., 1833) 6; David Hosack *Address Delivered at the First Anniversary . . .* (N.Y., 1830) 12; Jeremiah B. Jeter *The Life of Rev. Daniel Witt* (Richmond, 1875) 60; Silas Adams 170; Jewell 6; Benj. F. Riley *History of the Baptists of Alabama . . .* (Birmingham, 1895) 69.

17. Beecher *Auto.* 1:27; Irwin 18–21; Porter *Serm.* 16, 27; Worcester 23. Parental advice is in Martha L. Ramsay to David Ramsay, Jul. 18, Sep. 11, 1810, Ramsay *M.L. Ramsay* 286, 293–294; John Randolph to Theo. Randolph, Jan. 8, 1807, Randolph 25–26. See also Bertram Wyatt-Brown *Lewis Tappan . . .* (Cleveland, 1969) 13. (genl.) D. F. Allmendinger, Jr. "The Dangers of Ante-Bellum Student Life" *J. Soc. His.* 7 (1973) 75–85; Steven J. Novak *The Rights of Youth* (Cambridge, 1977) esp. 116, 136.

18. Joshua Darling quo. in ATS 9AR 25; Isaac A. Coles to J. H. Cocke, Aug. 30, 1825, Shields Sec., Cocke Pap., ViU. (genl.) Beecher *Auto.* 1:33; Bentley 2:52–53; Peirson 11n; John Pierce "Memoirs" Mass. His. Soc. *Proc.* 39 (1905) 364; John Pierce "Some Notes on the Anniversary Meetings of the Phi Beta Kappa Society, Alpha of Massachusetts" Mass. His. Soc. *Proc.* 29 (1894) 131, 136, 141–142; C. P. Curtis "Learning and Liquor at Harvard College" Mass. His. Soc. *Proc.* 70 (1957) 56–64; (eighteenth century) Beveridge 1:156; Peeke 41–42; (rules) Codman Hislop *Eliphalet Nott* (Middletown, Ct., 1971) 407; Peeke 40; Saul Sack "Student Life in the Nineteenth Century" *Pa. Mag. His. Biog.* 85 (1961) 258. Turmoil plagued many colleges. (Yale) Beecher *Auto.* 1:27; (Harvard) Jacob R. Motte *Charleston Goes to Harvard* ed. A. H. Cole (Cambridge, 1940) Jul. 18, 1831, p. 66; J. Edwards *Letter* 16; (Princeton) Novak 80–82; (Bowdoin) Parker Cleaveland to John Derby, Sep. 19, 1809, Derby Pap., Essex Inst., Salem, Mass.; (Dartmouth) John Wheelock to Jesse Appleton, Jun. 24, 1809, Appleton Pap., Bowdoin College; (U. Va.) Faculty Minutes (1826–1830), typescript pp. 231–232, 238–241, 383–384, 550–551, 553, ViU; Anne N. Royall *Mrs. Royall's Southern Tour* (Wash., 1830–1831) 1:92.

19. On isolation as a source of anxiety see Rollo May *The Meaning of Anxiety* (N.Y., 1950) 183. Frieda Fromm-Reichmann has suggested that undischarged tension, which produces anxiety, cannot be discharged when people live in a state of "not-being" or "nothingness." See her article in Maurice R. Stein et al., ed. *Identity and Anxiety* (Glencoe, 1960) 129–144, esp. 135.

20. Royall *Sketches* 100. Bernhard 2:18; Cobbett 55–56; Jas. Hemphill "A Visit to Md., 1802" *Del. His.* 3 (1948) 76–77; Royall *Pa.* 1:99; Royall *S. Tour* 2:103; *Niles* 47 (1834) 114.

21. Calvin Stowe quo. in Dorchester 213; John Bristed *America and Her Resources* (London, 1818) 383. Talleyrand 80; Elliott 17; MeTS 2AR 52, 95, 101; NYSTS 2AR 58; 4AR 64.

22. For a sympathetic, romantic account see Jas. Hall *Sketches of History, Life, and Manners in the West* . . . (Cincin., 1834) 136–137; contra, R. E. Oglesby "The Western Boatman . . ." *Travelers on the Western Frontier* ed. J. F. McDermott (Urbana, 1970) 258, 265. See also Audobon 25; Cuming 116; E. Evans 260; Faux 12:15; Fordham 196.

23. Quo. in Dick 320; J. Hall *Let.* 92. Ibid. 91–94; Blane 136; Cuming 303; B. H. Latrobe *Impress.* 129; J. Woods 244–245, 251; Thos. Smyth *Autobiographical Notes* ed. L. C. Stoney (Charleston, 1914) 37; Wm. Jenks *A Sermon, Delivered before the MSSI* (Boston, 1821) 33.

24. *New Mirror* 1 (1843) 88. Beaufoy 127; Boardman 262; Chevalier 97; Tim. Dwight 3:374–375; Fearon 369n; Isaac Fidler *Observations on Professions, Literature, Manners, and Emigration* . . . (N.Y., 1833) 91, 102; T. Hamilton 1:139; Kemble 181; Alfred Brunson *A Western Pioneer* (Cincin., 1872) 1:307–309; Saml. E. Edwards *The Ohio Hunter* (Battle Creek, 1866) 114–115; *Am. Reg.* 1 (1806–1807) 15; *Irish Shield* 1 (1829) 229; *Niles* 24 (1823) 71–72; 36 (1829) 317; 43 (1832) 25.

25. (brawls) Cox 145, 148, 150; Jas. B. Walker *Experiences of Pioneer Life* . . . (Chicago, 1881) 42–45; E. N. Kirk *A Sermon on the Traffic* . . . (n.p., ca. 1835) 13; *Niles* 36 (1829) 270–271, 409; 37 (1829) 216; 46 (1834) 85, 123; 48 (1835) 379, 393; (drink) Bernhard 1:180, 2:18; Bristed 437; J. A. Clark 172–177; Coke 139; Parkinson 1:179, 181; Pickering 17; Playfair 2:21–24; Royall *Let.* 239; Royall *Sketches* 16; Walker 147–148; Wied 22:137; D. Drake *Discourse* 34; Alex. M'Farlane *An Essay on the Use of Ardent Spirits* . . . (Carlisle, Pa., 1830) 37; NYSTS 2AR 17; (estimates) J. S. Buckingham *The Slave States of America* (London, ca. 1842) 1:169; Royall *Pa.* 1:126; Pintard 72:152; ATU 2AR 85; NYCTS 8AR 24; (Patch) Boardman 165–167; Coke 160–161; Kemble 320; Marryat *Diary* 1:97. (suicide) Boston *Am. Statesman and City Reg.*, Jan. 27, 1827; *Niles* 41 (1831) 102; 50 (1836) 129; Bacourt 215–217; Tardiveau 38; Saml. Breck *Recollections* . . . ed. H. E. Scudder (Phila., 1877) 296. In a journal recording public notices that came to his attention, Apr.–Oct. 1836, Dr. Benajah Ticknor listed 55 suicides, 60 homicides. Ticknor Pap., CtY. Nathaniel Bouton wrote Justin Edwards, Nov. 10, 1845, classifying 6 of 22 drunkards' deaths in Concord, N.H., over 20 years as suicides. Ms. note in Bouton's *History of the Temperance Reform in Concord* (Concord, N.H., 1843), MBC. See also Chas. Jewett *A Forty Years' Fight with the Drink Demon* . . . (N.Y., 1872) 17. For a theoretical link between alcohol consumption and suicide see Richard Lynn *Personality and National Character* (Oxford, Eng., 1971); Emile Durkheim *Suicide* (N.Y., 1951) esp. 77–81, 393. Durkheim's anomic theory is consistent with studies of drinking. In 1962 problem drinkers accounted for 20–30% of attempted suicides. Richard H. Blum and Lauraine Braunstein "Mind-Altering Drugs and Dangerous Behavior: Alcohol" *Task Force Report: Drunkenness* ed. President's Comm. on Law Enforcement and Admn. of Justice (Wash., 1967) 35.

26. (soldiers) Calhoun to Edmund P. Gaines, Oct. 24, 1818, J. C. Calhoun 3:231; ASP 5:4:83–86, 247–248, 275–276, 289, 291, 6:119–120; *Niles* 41 (1832) 340; (sailors) Bernhard 2:77; Blane 340–341; J. A. Clark 143–147; Gale 52–56; Heartman 7–9, 16; Elliott 25–26, 31; Lecraw 15–16; ASP 6:3:468–478; Danielle Hitz "Drunken Sailors and Others" *QJSA* 34 (1973) 496–505; (masters) D. Drake *Pioneer* 152–153; Gilmer 181–182; Jonathan Roberts "Memoirs . . ." *Pa. Mag. His. Biog.* 62 (1938) 69–72; H. C. Wright 116–118.

27. Bourne 413. For the development of the anxiety theory see Donald Hor-

ton "The Functions of Alcohol in Primitive Societies" *QJSA* 4 (1943) 199–320, esp. 223, and my Appendix 4.

Chapter Six

(Quote) Balt. TS *The Constitution and Address* . . . (Balt., 1830) 23.

1. (drams) G. C. Channing 248–249; D. Drake *Pioneer* 83; Gardiner 82; Weiss 125–126; Emery 4; Thos. G. Fessenden *Address Delivered before the Charlestown TS* . . . (Charlestown, Mass., 1831) 11; Chas. Sprague *An Address Delivered before the MSSI* . . . (Boston, 1827) 9. (tolerance) In one day a person can metabolize without intoxication up to .9 qt. of pure alcohol. Jan DeLint and Wolfgang Schmidt "Maximum Individual Alcohol Consumption" *QJSA* 26 (1965) 670–673.

2. (courts) Cuming 62–63, 136; F. Hall 208; D. Drake *Pioneer* 189–190; Rosser H. Taylor *Ante-Bellum South Carolina* (Chapel Hill, 1942) 169; (musters) Cloudman 334, 340; Cuming 231; H. P. Warren 189; (elections) B. Hall 2:78, 151; Hone (Sep. 28, 1843) 672; Morgan 369; (cvents) Howells 190; G. G. Johnson 678; (estimate) Jeremy Belknap "Estimate of the Annual Expense & Loss Sustained by the Unnecessary Consumption of Spirituous Liquors in the State of New-Hampshire" (ca. 1790), Belknap Pap., MHi.

3. On shifts see Chart A5.1, Appendix 5. (increasing communal drinking) Henry S. Foote *Casket of Reminiscences* (Wash., 1874) 264, 267; Gilmer 164, 182; Jas. Hall *Legends of the West* (Cincin., 1869) ix; E. Howitt *Selections from Letters Written during a Tour* . . . (Nottingham, Eng., 1820) xiii; Jeter *Recoll.* 14; Kirkland 23; Edw. Shippen "Reminiscences" *Pa. Mag. His. Biog.* 78 (1954) 223–224; G. G. Johnson 153.

4. Foote 264. Faux 11:178; Fidler 45; B. H. Latrobe *Jour.* 30; Gardiner 82–83; Wm. J. Grayson "Autobiography" ed. S. G. Stoney *S.C. His. Gen. Mag.* 49 (1948) 26; *Phila. Repertory* 2 (1812) 340; *The Substance of a Discourse Delivered before a Moral Society* (Cincin., 1824) 15; NYST *Temperance Tracts for the People. No. 9. Drinking Usages* (n.p., ca. 1830) 2.

5. Marryat *Diary* 1:111. J. A. Woodburn "Pioneer Presbyterianism" *Ind. Mag. His.* 22 (1926) 361. See also Count Francesco Arese *A Trip to the Prairies* (N.Y., 1934) 27; Audobon 243; I. Candler 490; Hone 15, 69, 162, 336, 548, 663, 708; Howells 126; Isaac Mickle *A Gentleman of Much Promise* ed. P. E. Mackey (Phila., 1977) 1:52–54; Pintard 71:59; R. H. Taylor 53; Foot 5; Bond 458–461.

6. Wash. to Jas. Wood, Jul. 1758, Wash. *Writ.* (Fitz.) 2:251; Foote 267; Vigne 72. Wash. *Writ.* (Fitz.) 1:130, 2:241n–242n; Peeke 66–68; Sydnor 44–59; Faux 11:106, 123; Flagg 26:322; H. C. Knight 94–95; Murat 67–69; Torrey *Natl. Flam.* 37; B. Drake 76–92; D. Drake *Discourse* 29; PSDUAS *Anniversary Rep.* 21; F. W. Halsey 163; Frank J. Heinl "Newspapers and Periodicals in the Lincoln-Douglas Country" Ill. State His. Soc. *J.* 23 (1930) 384.

7. Wm. Littell *Festoons of Fancy* (Lexington, Ky., 1940; 1814) 45; Gunn 19n. See also H. C. Knight 68. Many politicians were hearty drinkers. On Elihu Root see Henry van der Lyn Diary, Feb. 14, 1830, pp. 211–213, NHi. See also Polk 119–121.

8. Janson 87; Harriet Martineau *Society in America* (N.Y., 1837) 1:115–120;

Chilton Williamson *American Suffrage from Property to Democracy* (Princeton, 1960).

9. (genl.) Champlain Soc. and Hudson's Bay Record Soc. publications. In the latter series see esp. McLoughlin's "Letters" v. 4, 6, 7; Peter Ogden's "Journals" v. 23, 28. (liquor) "Peter Skene Ogden's Snake Country Journals, 1827–28 and 1828–29" ed. Glyndwr Williams, Hudson's Bay Record Soc. *Pub.* 28 (1971) 54, 54n; P. J. DeSmet, S.J. *Letters and Sketches* ed. R. G. Thwaites (Cleveland, 1906; 1843) 261–262; Henry Schoolcraft *Schoolcraft's Expedition to Lake Itasca* ed. P. P. Mason (E. Lansing, 1958; 1834) 19; Hiram M. Chittenden *The American Fur Trade of the Far West* (N.Y., 1902) 3:936–937; (Ore.) Thos. J. Farnham *Travels in the Great Western Prairies . . .* ed. R. G. Thwaites (Cleveland, 1906; 1843) 99–100.

10. Arese 60; Francis A. Chardon *Chardon's Journal at Fort Clark* ed. A. H. Abel (Pierre, 1932) 242n; Gurdon S. Hubbard *Autobiography* (Chicago, 1911; 1888) 16; Washington Irving *Adventures of Captain Bonneville* (London, 1837) 1:45, 3:151–153; Wied 24:99–100.

11. (genl.) Chittenden; LeRoy R. Hafen, ed. *The Mountain Men and the Fur Trade of the Far West* (Glendale, 1965–1972); Paul C. Phillips *The Fur Trade* (Norman, 1961). (liquor) A good summary is in ibid. 2:348–388. See also Robt. Campbell "Private Journal" ed. G. R. Brooks, Mo. His. Soc. *Bull.* 20 (1964) Nov. 29, 1833, p. 107; Robt. Campbell to Hugh Campbell, Nov. 16, 1833, Robt. Campbell *The Rocky Mountain Letters of Robert Campbell* (n.p., 1955) 15–16; Wm. Gordon to Wm. Clark, Oct. 27, 1831, K. McKenzie to Joshua Pilcher, Dec. 16, 1833, Chardon 350–352, 362–363; (effects) J. Archdale Hamilton to J. Halsey, Sep. 17, 1834, to Kenneth McKenzie, Sep. 17, 1834, Mar. 29, 1835, ibid. 286n, 287n–288n, 293n; Warren A. Ferris *Life in the Rocky Mountains* ed. H. S. Auerbach and J. C. Alter (Salt Lake City, 1940) 229; Hubbard 162–164; (exploitation) Robt. Campbell to Hugh Campbell, Dec. 8, 1833, Campbell *Let.* 19; [?] to H. Picott, Dec. 15, 1833, K. McKenzie to P. Chouteau, Jr., Dec. 16, 1833, to W. B. Astor, Dec. 16, 1833, Chardon 359–360, 364–367, 369; Zenas Leonard *Adventures . . .* ed. J. C. Ewers (Norman, 1959) x–xvii, 94; (Ashley) J. Cecil Alter *Jim Bridger* (Rev. ed., Norman, 1962; 1925) 98.

12. Statistical account in Hafen 10:9–14.

13. David L. Brown *Three Years in the Rocky Mountains* (n.p., 1950; 1845) 12–13, 20; Ferris 268; Irving 1:35–36. The early nineteenth-century longing for nature is apparent in Cooper's Leatherstocking novels. An important discussion is Henry N. Smith *Virgin Land* (Cambridge, 1950).

14. D. L. Brown 11, 15; John K. Townsend *Narrative of a Journey . . .* ed. R. G. Thwaites (Cleveland, 1905; 1839) 193, 230–231; Capt. Thing to Tucker & Williams, Jun. 29, 1834, Wm. M. Anderson *The Rocky Mountain Journals . . .* ed. D. L. Morgan and E. T. Harris (San Marino, 1967) 27; [McKenzie?] to Pratte Chouteau & Co., Dec. 10, 1835, Chardon 376–378; Alter 71–72, 88, 119, 137; Alpheus H. Favour *Old Bill Williams* ed. Wm. Brandon (Norman, 1962; 1936) 121–122; LeRoy R. Hafen and W. J. Ghent *Broken Hand* (Denver, 1931) 55, 101; Chittenden 3:943–944; Hafen 3:257.

15. Mary M. L. Hoyt "Life of Leonard Slater" *Mich. Pioneer Coll.* 35 (1907) 150; Arese 70; DeSmet 261; Edw. C. Delavan to J. H. Cocke, Dec. 3, 1834, Cocke Dep., Cocke Pap., ViU.

16. A similar pattern involving the breaking of sex taboos during intoxication has been noted by Ruth Bunzel "The Rôle of Alcoholism in Two Central American Cultures" *Psychiatry* 3 (1940) 366.

17. Favour 97–98, 128–129.

18. Anderson 209.

19. Gilmer 128–129; Pickering 27–28; J. W. Townsend 8, 15; Woodman 40; Elizabeth Scott to Eliza Maynodier, Nov. 6, 1784, Key Coll., MdHi; Catharine Harper to Robt. G. Harper, Feb. 27, 1814, Harper-Pennington Coll., MdHi; H. Humphrey *Intemp.* 28; Jonathan Kittredge *An Address Delivered before the TS of Bath, N.H.* . . . (Boston, 1829) 4; Daniel Remich *History of Kennebunk* . . . (n.p., 1911) 453.

20. (primitives) See Appendix 4; (Europe) Erik Allardt et al. *Drinking and Drinkers* (Helsinki, 1957) 15; Genevieve Knupfer "Female Drinking Patterns" N. Am. Assn. of Alcoholism Programs, 15th Ann. Meet. *Selected Papers* (n.p., ca. 1964) 141–142; Giorgio Lolli et al. *Alcohol in Italian Culture* (Glencoe, 1958) 96; Thos. F. A. Plaut *Alcohol Problems* (N.Y., 1967) 130–131.

21. J. B. Pinney to Leonard Bacon, Mar. 15, 1838. This unfortunate man's story can be gleaned from numerous letters, Boxes 1 and 2, Bacon Family Coll., CtY. Crucial is Leonard Bacon to David Bacon, Mar. 23, 1862. Important for understanding the family are a genealogy in the collection inventory; Wm. Hall to Leonard Bacon, Feb. 21, 1865; Theodore Bacon *Leonard Bacon* (New Haven, 1931). See drunkards' memoirs in ch. 1, note 12.

22. Quo. in Beecher *Auto.* 1:xiii. Leonard Bacon *A Discourse on the Traffic* . . . (New Haven, 1838); *One Hundred Years of Temperance* (N.Y., 1886) 124; Wyatt-Brown 13; Ernest Gordon *The American Way* . . . (Phila., ca. 1947) 24.

23. Jesse Torrey *The Moral Instructor* (2 ed., Albany, 1819) 43. A good example of the type is Mr. Rutherford in Kennedy 361. See also Murat 15; Nuttall 69; J. Woods 317; Nathan S. S. Beman *A Discourse Delivered in Stephentown* . . . (Troy, N.Y., 1829) 7; *Beman on Intemperance* (n.p., ca. 1830) 1; Foot 10; Ebenezer Porter *The Fatal Effects of Ardent Spirits* (Hartford, 1811) 22; Saml. Spring *The Only Safe Expedient* (Hartford, 1832) 7; *Temp. Recorder* 4 (1835) 29. On the idea of independence see Arfwedson 2:99; Boardman 12, 215–216; Tim. Dwight 1:123; Fearon 378; J. Hall *Let.* 114–115; J. Hall *Sketches* 150; Kemble 38; Murat 343; Royall *S. Tour* 3:178; Wm. Tudor *Letters on the Eastern States* (2 ed., Boston, 1821) 198; Ramsay *S.C.* 2:384.

24. On alcohol as a regressive means to escape responsibility see Francis T. Chambers *The Drinker's Addiction* (Springfield, 1968) 7. See also Blum and Braunstein 35.

25. B. Hall 2:78; quo. in O'Neall 129. On vitality see Cobbett 178, 180; Dalton 226; Mrs. Hall 27, 104–105; T. Hamilton 1:211; Kemble 92; Marryat *Sec. Ser.* 103; Playfair 2:9–10; B. Smith 45; J. Woods 317.

26. Thos. F. Marshall *Great Temperance Speeches* . . . (N.Y., 1842) 7. See *The Good Girl's Soliloquy* (N.Y., 1820); *Errors of Youth* (Phila., 1820s?).

27. E.g., Sweetser 82; "A Succinct His. of the Origins, Principles, Objects and Progress of TSs in the U.S.A." *Am. Q. Temp. Mag.* 1 (1833) 6. See Chart A5.1, Appendix 5.

28. (genl.) M. M. Gross et al. "Acute Alcohol Withdrawal Syndrome" *The Biology of Alcoholism: Clinical Pathology* ed. Benj. Kissin and Henri Begleiter

(N.Y., 1974) 3:191–263. Access to early materials was through *Index-Catalogue of the Library of the Surgeon-General's Office* (Wash., 1880–1895) 3:658–665. (early treatment) A good review is in B. H. Coates "Observations on DTs . . ." *N. Am. Med. Surg. J.* 4 (1827) 205–212. See also Stephen Brown "Observations on DTs . . ." *Am. Med. Recorder* 5 (1822) 193–215; Walter Channing "Cases of DTs . . ." *N. Eng. J. Med. Surg.* 8 (1819) 15–28; S. Henry Dickson *Essay on Mani a Potu* . . . (Charleston, 1836) 14–15, 20; Geo. Hayward "Some Remarks on Delirium Vigilans" *N. Eng. J. Med. Surg.* 11 (1822) 235–243.

29. (increasing) Neilson 309; Coates 32; Jesse Carter "Observations on Mania a Potu" *Am. J. Med. Sci.* 6 (1830) 321; Dickson *Essay* 4; J. C. Nancrede "On Mania a Potu" *Am. Med. Recorder* 1 (1818) 479; J. M. Staughton "Observations on Mania à Potu" *Phila. J. Med. Phys. Sci.* 3 (1821) 239; Chas. S. Tripler *Remarks on Delirium Tremens* (N.Y., 1827) 5–6; (Mexico) Bunzel 371–387; (Germany) Gross 3:200.

30. S. Brown 195. Jesse Carter 333, 335–336; Nancrede 480–481; Walter Channing 15–28; Coates 37–38; S. Brown 198–199.

31. Gale 131. (imagination) T. Hamilton 1:230; Kemble 123, 166–167; C. J. Latrobe 1:62. See also Chevalier 200, 262; Duncan 1:106–107; Fidler 94. (bankruptcy) Nancrede 480; Walter Channing 15–16.

32. See the suggestive account in Daniel Drake "Observations on Temulent Diseases" *Am. Med. Recorder* 2 (1819) 60–61.

33. Saml. K. Lothrop *An Address Delivered before the Massachusetts State TS* . . . (Boston, 1835) 23–24. Bordley 325–326; I. Candler 45; Holmes 135; Janson 31; Soc. for the Promotion of Ag., Arts and Man. 1:30; J. Woods 190; J. Leander Bishop *A History of American Manufactures* . . . (Phila., 1861–1864) 1:264.

34. See D. C. McClelland and S. C. Wilsnack "The Effects of Drinking on Thoughts about Power and Restraint" David C. McClelland et al. *The Drinking Man* (N.Y., 1972) 123–141, esp. 135–136. See also ibid., 173; Roland Sadoun et al. *Drinking in French Culture* (New Brunswick, 1965) 1–7. Because McClelland correlates alcohol consumption with power, see also D. C. McClelland and R. I. Watson, Jr. "Power Motivation and Risk-Taking Behavior" *Human Motivation* ed. D. C. McClelland and R. S. Steele (Morristown, N.J., 1973) 166–167.

35. T. Hamilton 2:378; Fearon 372. Ibid. 372–373; Arese 46; DeRoos 58; Gustorf 65; B. Hall 1:109; Mrs. Hall 126; Pickering 37; Sealsfield 24; Trollope ix–x, 303n, 404–409.

36. (genl.) David C. McClelland *The Achieving Society* (Princeton, 1961). See ch. 3, note 40 and Appendix 2.

37. (use) A. B. Snow *An Address, Delivered at the Formation of the Seamen's Bethel TS* . . . (Boston, 1833) 8; Robt. W. Scott *An Address, Delivered at the Request of the Franklin TS* (Frankfort, Ky., 1829) 15. In 1973 the Natl. Comm. on Marijuana and Drug Abuse estimated that 53% of adults used alcohol, 1.3% heroin. *U.S. News*, Oct. 29, 1973, p. 45. See also Geo. T. Strong *Diary* ed. Allan Nevins and M. H. Thomas (N.Y., 1952) May 16, 1843, v. 1:203; Henry Wolf *A Hasty Defence of the Farmers & Distillers* . . . (York, Pa., 1833) 6; D. Drake *Discourse* 23–24; Daniel H. Gregg *An Address Delivered before the Newton TS* (Boston, 1828) 9; Edw. Hitchcock *An Essay on Alcoholic & Narcotic Substances* . . . (Amherst, Mass., 1830) 9–10, 35; Palfrey 59–60; Spring 9–10;

MSSI 14AR 5–6; (Orient) Morewood *History* 102; (medicine) Gustorf 50–51; *Am. Museum* 4 (1788) 234; David Ramsay to Benj. Rush, Apr. 8, 1784, Rush Pap., PHi; Geo. C. Shattuck, Jr., to E. F. Prentiss, Apr. 14, 1832, Shattuck Pap., MHi; Rush *Inquiry* (1790) 9; Cory 110.

38. (treatment) Jas. Jackson "On a Peculiar Disease Resulting from the Use of Ardent Spirits" *N. Eng. J. Med. Surg.* 11 (1822) 351–353; Phila. Med. Soc. *Report of the Committee* (Phila., 1829) 10, 17; Stephen Davis *Notes of a Tour in America* (Edinburgh, 1833) 68; Sturges 105; (laudanum) Gerda Lerner *The Grimké Sisters from South Carolina* (N.Y., 1971) 43; Morewood *History* 130–133; Sturges 142; A. Bancroft to Nathaniel Cheever, Nov. 7, 1817, Cheever Pap., MWA; Dorchester 139; (patent medicine) J. H. Young 68–69.

39. (group control) Peter B. Field "Social and Psychological Correlates of Drunkenness in Primitive Tribes" Ph.D. thesis (Soc. Psych.), Harvard U., 1961, p. 245. (drive) E.g., Chas. Larpenteur *Forty Years a Fur Trader* . . . (N.Y., 1898) 1:77. See also Hosack 15; O'Flaherty 10–11. Opium was used frequently in suicide attempts. See Woodman 45; Nathaniel Bouton to Justin Edwards, Nov. 10, 1845, Bouton, MBC.

40. References are sparse. See Fisher (Nov. 3, 1863) 462; Strong (Sep. 1, 1856) 2:290–292; Warren Abbott *Address to the Danvers Auxiliary Society* . . . (Salem, 1822) 7. Fur traders occasionally mention Indian use. (India) G. M. Carstairs "Daru and Bhang" *QJSA* 15 (1954) 220–237. See also Joel Fort *Alcohol* (N.Y., 1973) 77, 92; John Rublowsky *The Stoned Age* (N.Y., 1974) 91–116.

41. (theory) John W. Atkinson and Norman T. Feather, ed. *A Theory of Achievement Motivation* (N.Y., 1966) 16–18, 174, 185–203, 327–329, 368–369; Margaret K. Bacon et al. "A Cross-Cultural Study of Drinking: II" *QJSA* Supp. 3 (1965) 46–47; McClelland *Ach. Soc.* esp. 150; (gambling) I. Candler 454; Chevalier 295; T. Hamilton 2:174, 190; Harris 18; Neilson 65–66; Pickering 15; Ephraim Abbot to Mary H. Pearson, Dec. 28, 1811, Abbot Pap., MWA; (economics) Geo. R. Taylor "American Economic Growth before 1840" *J. Econ. His.* 24 (1964) 427; Henretta 204.

42. Robt. McClorg to David McClorg, Sep. 1, 1821, Boling-Miller Coll., private. (theory) Atkinson and Feather 164–167; McClelland *Ach. Soc.* 342–344. See also M. K. Bacon 46–47; W. C. Becker "Consequences of Different Kinds of Parental Discipline" *Review of Child Development Research* ed. M. L. Hoffman and L. W. Hoffman (N.Y., 1964) 1:197–198; (early nineteenth century) Arthur W. Calhoun *A Social History of the American Family* (Cleveland, 1917–1919) entitled his chapter on the early nineteenth century "The Emancipation of Childhood," 2:51–77. See also ibid. 1:105–127, 285–298; Robt. H. Bremner, ed. *Children and Youth in America* (Cambridge, 1970) 1:131–132, 343–344. I have also profited from talking with Jacqueline Reinier of Berkeley, who has been investigating this neglected subject; (observers) Fidler 52; Janson 304; Martineau 2:271–272; I. Candler 453; NYCTS 4AR 29; (teachers) Fidler; Fearon 39, 230. On the popularity of the Lancastrian system, which depended upon highly motivated children see ibid. 38, 229.

43. (readers) McClelland *Ach. Soc.* 150; (attitudes) ibid. 47–48, 359–361; Atkinson and Feather 214. Based on Max Weber's work.

44. With few exceptions the reformers were gradualists (e.g., 'immediate emancipation gradually accomplished') who were as concerned with means as ends, an attitude that McClelland has linked to high achievement motivation. McClelland *Ach. Soc.* 103–104.

Chapter Seven

(Quote) Huntington Lyman *An Address Delivered before the TS of Franklin-ville* . . . (N.Y., 1830) 5.

1. One of the few early observations of pharmacology is Francis Wayland *An Address, Delivered before the Providence Association for the Promotion of Temperance* (3 ed., Boston, 1832) 4. On high intake see J. H. Mendelson and N. K. Mello "Ethanol and Whiskey Drinking Patterns in Rats . . ." *QJSA* 25 (1964) 1–25; De Lint and Schmidt "Max. Individual Alc. Cons." 670–673; Sadoun et al. 1–4.

2. I have been influenced by Ralf Dahrendorf *Essays in the Theory of Society* (Stanford, 1968); Clifford Geertz "Ideology as a Cultural System" *Ideology and Discontent* ed. D. E. Apter (N.Y., 1964) 47–76; Edw. Shils "The Concept and Function of Ideology" *Intl. Ency. Soc. Sci.* ed. D. L. Sills (N.Y., 1968) 7:66–76; Neil J. Smelser *Social Change in the Industrial Revolution* (Chicago, 1959).

3. Wm. A. Hallock *'Light and Love'* (N.Y., 1855) esp. 43; ATS 2AR 7; N. Eng. Tract Soc. *Tract No. 3* (Andover, Mass., 1814); Geo. F. Clark *History of the Temperance Reform in Massachusetts* (Boston, 1888) 7; Krout 89–91, 109.

4. Isaac N. Davis *An Address, Delivered before the Elberton TS* (Augusta, Ga., 1830) 10. (medical) Benezet *Remarks;* Rush *Inquiry* (1790); Rush *Let.;* Waterhouse xi; Neal 105; John W. Nevin *My Own Life* (Lancaster, Pa., 1964) 7; Tolles *Logan* 89; "Evil" *Am. Museum* 4 (1788) 233–234; Mem. to Cong. (1790), ASP 10:1:20–21; MSSI *Constitution* (Boston, 1813) 21–22; various TS reports, e.g., ATS 5AR 63; 7AR 60–64; NYCTS 8AR 29–30. A classic is Saml. Chipman *Report of an Examination of Poor-Houses, Jails, &c., in the State of New-York* . . . (Albany, 1834). See also Arfwedson 1:145–146. (moral) N. E. Johnson *An Address Delivered in Homer* (Homer, N.Y., 1832) 3; Lyman 5; Wm. Hines *An Address, Delivered at the Methodist Chapel* (Norwich [Ct.?], 1828) 6. Opponents responded in kind. E.g., David M. Reese *Humbugs of New-York* . . . (N.Y., 1838) 263. That anxieties could lead to abstinence as well as to drinking was suggested by Horton 230. See Selden D. Bacon "The Classic Temperance Movement . . ." *Br. J. Addiction* 62 (1967) 5–18.

5. ATS 4AR 6. An excellent record of an agent's activities is in NYSTS *Essays, &c* (n.p., ca. 1831) 1–12. See also Andrew Erwin to Geo. W. Erwin, Aug. 20, 1832, Erwin Pap., Filson Club, Louisville, Ky.; Emil C. Vigilante "The Temperance Reform in New York State, 1829–1851" Ph.D. thesis (His.), N.Y. U., 1964, p. 31. Many temperance societies kept minutes of their meetings. Newton TS and Lyceum *Constitution* (Newton, 1829); "Young Men's TS of New Gloucester" (Me., ca. 1826–1830), Stinchfield Pap., MeHi; Scituate [Mass.] Auxiliary Soc. for the Suppression of Intemperance Records, 1817–1836, MWA; Harwinton [Ct.] TS Acct. Bk., 1829–1836, Litchfield Ct. His. Soc.; Litchfield Co. TS Records, 1829–1840, LCHS; "The Book of Records for the TS of the Fork, 1829–1833" (Clinton, Mo.), Lewis Pap., NcD; (battle) MeTS 1AR 66; (anti-TS) C. J. Latrobe 2:60–62; *Niles* 44 (1833) 423; 45 (1833) 8; *Am. Q. Temp. Mag.* 2 (1834) 87–88; NYSTS 1AR 35.

6. Eliakim Phelps *Intemperance* (Geneva, N.Y., 1830) 20. Elisha Mitchell *Arguments for Temperance* (Raleigh, N.C., 1831) 29; Philadelphus *The Moral*

Plague of Civil Society (Phila., 1821) 10; "Natl. Circ." ATS 5AR 84–85; East-Hartford TS *Annual Report* (n.p., ca. 1833) 3; Scomp 371.

7. (inns) Coke 26; Combe 1:viii, 34; Theo. Dwight 215–216; ATU 4AR 40; NYSTS 2AR 96; PSDUAS *The PSDUAS to Innkeepers* (Phila., 1832); ATU *J.* 11 (1847) 48; *Natl. Era* 3 (1849) 198; Vigilante 57–62; (boats) J. A. Clark 84; Chas. F. Mayer *An Address Delivered by the Hon* . . . (Annapolis, 1833) 9; NYSTS 3AR 23; 4AR 21; Vigilante 34; (business) Lyman Beecher *Six Sermons on* . . . *Intemperance* (Boston, 1827) 91; ATU 1AR 19–20; NYATS 1AR 5–7; Lee Co. Va. Auxiliary TS Constitution, 1833, ViU; (insurance) Boardman 358; *Niles* 41 (1831) 326; ATS 6AR 37; 7AR 15; NYCTS 1AR 18; August F. Fehlandt *A Century of Drink Reform in the United States* (Cincin., 1904) 76; (politics) Josiah T. Hawes *An Address Delivered before the Falmouth TS* (Portland, 1831) 5; Balt. TS 35; Soc. for the Promotion of Temp. in Ware Village *Report of the Managers* (Belchertown, Mass., 1827) 4–5; Woburn TSs *AR* (Boston, 1834) 1–8.

8. Delavan to John H. Cocke, Sep. 14, Nov. 1834, Cocke Dep., Cocke Pap., ViU; Mad. to Jack., Oct. 11, 1835, Madison Pap., ViU; NYSTS "5AR" *Am. Q. Temp. Mag.* 2 (1834) 10; NYSTS *Temp. Almanac* (1837) back cover; Marsh 27; Vigilante 37–38; C. I. Foster 173. From 1801 through 1825 there were 98 temperance works published; from 1826 through 1830, 158. There were 62 issued in the peak year of 1830. Only 49 were published in 1831, but this latter figure may be a less complete inventory. Compiled from Ralph R. Shaw and Richard H. Shoemaker *American Bibliography, 1801–1830* (Var. places, 1958–1973); Scott Bruntjen and Carol Bruntjen *A Checklist of American Imprints for 1831* . . . (Metuchen, N.J., 1975).

9. *Boston Temp. Songster* (Boston, 1844) 57; Chas. R. Fisk *Poem* (n.p., 1834) 5; *Pa. and N.J. Temp. Almanac* (1835) 13; Hines 17; Josiah Moore *An Address Delivered at Pembroke* . . . (Plymouth, 1836) 19; Henry Ware *A Sermon Delivered at Dorchester* (Boston, 1820) 4; E. Hitchcock 36.

10. MeTS 2AR 70. N. Cross 16; M'Farlane 24.

11. Wm. Goodell *Reasons Why Distilled Spirits Should Be Banished* . . . (N.Y., 1830) 9.

12. N. S. S. Beman 7; Randolph to Theo. Randolph, Dec. 30, 1821, Randolph 232. See also Wm. Shedd *The Influence of Temperance upon Intellectual Discipline* . . . (Burlington, Vt., 1844) 22; Geo. W. Wells *The Cause of Temperance the Cause of Liberty* (Kennebunk, Me., 1835) 8; NYSTS *Temp. Almanac* (1836) 24.

13. (equality) Merritt Caldwell *An Address Delivered before the Readfield TS* . . . (Hallowell, Me., 1832) 6; W. M. Cornell *An Address Delivered before the Temperance Association of Quincy* . . . (Boston, 1836) 6–11; E. Phelps 20; Bellamy Storer *An Address Delivered before the Cincinnati TS* (Cincin., 1833) 3; (renunciation) J. Edwards *Letter* 18; Herttell 20–21; ATS 6AR 39; *Biblical Repertory and Theological Rev.* n.s. 3 (1831) 46–47.

14. E.g., Joshua B. Flint *An Address Delivered before the MSSI* . . . (Boston, 1828) 17; Goodell 3; Jos. Harvey *An Appeal to Christians* (Middletown, Ct., 1831) 6; (ATS) ATS 4AR 38; 7AR 14; (N.Y.) NYSTS *Temp. Almanac* (1839) 18.

15. Kemble 92; Kelly 46; Guillaume Merle d'Aubigné *La Vie Américaine* . . . ed. Gilbert Chinard (Paris, 1935) 97; T. Adams 9. (pace) Marryat *Diary*

1:18–19; Ramon de la Sagra *Cinq Mois aux Etats-Unis* . . . (Bruxelles, 1837) 120–121; Mrs. Hall 27, 104–105; Lydia M. Child *The American Frugal Housewife* . . . (30 ed., N.Y., 1844) 3–4; (idle) Chevalier 200; Kemble 123; (leisure) Arfwedson 1:121; Theo. Dwight 261; *Niles* 44 (1833) 257; (warning) C. P. Beman *An Address, Delivered before the TS* . . . (Mt. Zion, Ga., 1830) 7; Emery 7–8; Lyman 14–15.

16. Sealsfield 186; quo. in T. Hamilton 2:246. Chevalier 200–201; Marryat *Sec. Ser.* 103; Ely 68; Boston *Atheneum* 2 Ser. 3 (1825) 355; (deference) Douglas T. Miller *Jacksonian Aristocracy* (N.Y., 1967). One explanation for a money cult has been suggested by Margaret Mead "Culture Change and Character Structure" Stein et al. 95.

17. Arfwedson 1:120–121; Bentley (Feb. 10, 1818) 4:501; Rantoul 243; *Niles* 41 (1831) 250; J. B. Flint 41; ATS 9AR 16; W. A. Sullivan 479; (poor) SPPCNY *Documents Relative to Savings Banks, Intemperance, and Lotteries* (N.Y., 1819) 4; M'Kinney 11–12; Palfrey 98; (banks) SPPCNY *Docs.* 3, 6; Newton TS 1–12; Saml. Martin to Calhoun, Dec. 21, 1822, J. C. Calhoun 7:392; (capital) *African Repository* 5 (1830) 381; *Am. Museum* 4 (1788) 124; SPPCNY *Docs.* 16; Gardner B. Perry *An Address, Delivered before the Society for Promoting Temperance* (Haverhill [Mass.?], 1828) 10; NYSTS *Temp. Almanac* (1836) 5. One recent study shows deposits growing more rapidly 1820–1830 than 1830–1850. Alan L. Olmstead *New York City Mutual Savings Banks* (Chapel Hill, 1976) 182–183.

18. Mann esp. 4–6, 10, 12. See also *Niles* 49 (1835) 126; Mark Doolittle "Temp. a Source of Natl. Wealth" *Am. Q. Temp. Mag.* 2 (1834) 42; N. S. S. Beman 20; E. Hitchcock 36; Wm. S. Potts *Effects of Intemperance on National Wealth* (St. Louis, 1839) 3–4; MTS 25AR 5; NYCTS 1AR 15. The producer mentality is considered in Graham J. Barker-Benfield *The Horrors of the Half-Known Life* (N.Y., 1976). Many early temperance leaders were also early advocates of industrialization. John F. Kasson *Civilizing the Machine* (N.Y., 1976).

19. John McGee to Thos. L. Douglass quo. in John B. M'Ferrin *History of Methodism in Tennessee* (Nashville, 1869–1873) 1:297. Similar instances are in Henry Smith *Recollections* . . . (N.Y., 1854) 55; Chevalier 309. Good references are in C. A. Johnson "The Frontier Camp Meeting" *Miss. Valley His. Rev.* 37 (1950) 91–110. See in general Edw. P. Humphrey and Thos. H. Cleland *Memoirs of the Rev. Thomas Cleland, D.D.* (Cincin., 1859); John B. Boles *The Great Revival* (Lexington, Ky., 1972); Niels H. Sonne *Liberal Kentucky* (N.Y., 1939).

20. Jas. Flint 261; Brunson 1:30; D. Drake *Pioneer* 195; Finley 305–306; H. Smith 100–101, 106–107; Jos. Thomas *The Life of the Pilgrim* (Winchester, Va., 1817) 63–64; H. C. Wright 148–149; G. G. Johnson 407; (Cartwright) Wm. H. Milburn *The Pioneers, Preachers and People of the Mississippi Valley* (N.Y., 1860) 383–384; (Thomas) J. Thomas 100.

21. (Methodists) Wheeler esp. 46, 68, 70, 71, 79; Wm. W. Sweet *Methodism in American History* (N.Y., 1933) 171. See also D. Drake *Pioneer* 83; H. Smith 62; I. Candler 214; (Presbyterians) Pres. Ch., U.S.A. 1. See also *Centenary Memorial of the Planting and Growth of Presbyterianism* . . . (Pittsburgh, 1876) 238; Levi Parsons *History of Rochester Presbytery* . . . (Rochester, N.Y., 1889) 22–23; Pendleton 14–45.

22. Barton W. Stone *The Biography of Eld. Barton Warren Stone* ed. John Rogers (Cincin., 1847) 33. See also Barbara M. Cross' introduction in Beecher *Auto.*

23. See, e.g., Boles; Chas. R. Keller *The Second Great Awakening in Connecticut* (New Haven, 1942); Wm. Sweet's works; Bernard A. Weisberger *They Gathered at the River* (Boston, 1958).

24. Asahel Nettleton "Spirit of the Pilgrims" ATS 2AR 53; Foot 19; Tenney 19–20. See also Richard Dunning to John A. Murray, Apr. 5, 1838, Am. Home Missionary Soc. Pap., CBGTU film; John H. Cocke to Wm. Meade, Jun. 1846, Kane Coll., CSmH; Solomom [!] Adams *An Address, Delivered at North-Yarmouth* (2 ed., Portland, 1830) 14; Gamaliel Bradford *An Address Delivered before the MSSI* (Boston, 1826) 6; E. Nelson *The Use of Ardent Spirits . . .* (Boston, 1830) 6; Dudley Phelps *An Address, Delivered January 24, 1830 . . .* (Haverhill [Mass.?], 1830) 7; *Portland Mag.* 2 (1836) 123; *Southern Literary Messenger* 1 (1834) 36–39; *Telescope* 1 (1824) 110.

25. *Biblical Recorder*, Jul. 10, 1832, quo. in Pearson and Hendricks 69; Thos. Brown to A. Peters, Sep. 16, 1834, Sweet *Presbyterians* 682; quo. in Wm. H. Townsend *Lincoln and Liquor* (N.Y. 1934) 28. The best description of Hard Shells is Edw. Eggleston *The Hoosier Schoolmaster* (N.Y., 1928; 1872) 84–85, 91. See also Sweet *Presbyterians* 697; Wm. W. Sweet, ed. *Religion on the American Frontier: Congregationalists* (Chicago, 1939) 260–261; Wm. W. Sweet, ed. *Religion on the American Frontier: Baptists* (N.Y., 1931) 206; Riley 61, 69; Cory 50–52; Pearson and Hendricks 69.

26. (churches) Neilson 14; Humphrey and Cleland 105; Jas. H. Hotchkin *A History of the Purchase and Settlement of Western New York* (N.Y., 1848) 136, 151; Scomp 210; Ralph N. Hill *The Winooski* (N.Y., 1949) 154; (revival first) *A Narrative of the Late Revivals of Religion* (Geneva, N.Y., 1832) 16, 18, 25; Bloomer Kent to Absalom Peters, Apr. 14, 1836, Am. Home Missionary Soc. Pap., CBGTU film; Jewell 8; MeTS 1AR 17; Talbot 370, 373; (temp. first) Brunson 1:414; *Narrative of the Late Revivals* 6, 10, 18, 20, 25–26; ATS 4AR 82; 5AR 38; MeTS 1AR 15; NYSTS 3AR 24, 56; Scomp 226–227, 231; C. I. Foster 173, 210. A recent work that relates temperance and revivalism to industrialization in a perceptive way is Paul E. Johnson *A Shopkeeper's Millennium* (N.Y., 1978).

27. Young Men's Domestic Missionary Soc. *An Appeal to the Citizens of Philadelphia* (Phila., 1824) 15. See also Isidor Thorner "Ascetic Protestantism and Alcoholism" *Psychiatry* 16 (1953) 169–170 (based on Max Weber); S. D. Bacon 6; Goodell 9–10.

28. (workers) Arfwedson 1:120–121; Mrs. Hall 104–105; T. Hamilton 1:167; Kemble 123; Lydia M. Child *The Frugal Housewife* (2 ed., Boston, 1830) 5, 7–8; NYATS 1–2AR; NYCTS 1, 4, 6, 8AR; Jas. D. Knowles *Spirituous Liquors Pernicious and Useless* (Boston, 1829) 6; (businessmen) Arfwedson 2:189; Duncan 1:106; T. Hamilton 1:127, 230; J. B. Flint 41; (Tappan) Wyatt-Brown 226–247; (Harpers) Exman.

29. (Millerites) *Niles* 41 (1831) 102; Mary S. Bull "Woman's Rights and Other 'Reforms' in Seneca Falls" ed. R. E. Riegel *N.Y. His.* 46 (1965) 43; Boles 90, 103; I. V. Brown "Watchers for the Second Coming" *Miss. Valley His. Rev.* 39 (1952) 451; Whitney R. Cross *The Burned-Over District* (Ithaca, 1950); Alice F. Tyler *Freedom's Ferment* (Minneapolis, 1944) 47–195, esp. 76; (progress) Nelson Tift "Address to Young Men's Polemick Society" (1835), Tift Diary, G-Ar; Bourne 411; Leo Marx *The Machine in the Garden* (N.Y., 1967).

30. See, e.g., John R. Bodo *The Protestant Clergy and Public Issues* (Princeton, 1954); C. I. Foster; Clifford S. Griffin *Their Brothers' Keepers* (New Brunswick,

1960). The most vivid sources are the autobiographies of ministers. E.g., Beecher *Auto.;* Peck.

31. D. Phelps 7. (connections) Striking examples of the shared opposition include two southern-born planters who freed their slaves, Thomas P. Hunt (*One Hundred Years* 145) and James G. Birney (Betty Fladeland *James Gillespie Birney* [Ithaca, 1955] 33–34, 52); a Tennessee Methodist bishop, James Axley (M'Ferrin 2:45–48, 243); a Kentucky Methodist minister, Jefferson J. Polk (Polk); Georgian J. L. Lumpkin (Scomp 301); and abolitionists William Lloyd Garrison (W. M. Merrill "Prologue to Reform—Garrison's Early Career" Essex Inst. *His. Coll.* 92 [1956] 164–167), Gerrit Smith (Smith to Mathew Carey, Jul. 13, 1832, Carey Sec., Carey Pap., PHi; Sturge 117), and Theodore Weld (Theo. D. Weld et al. *Letters* ed. G. H. Barnes and D. L. Dumond [N.Y., 1934] 19, 43). See also Cory 34–35; Scomp 299, 303. (rum worse) Eliphalet Gillet *Evils of Intemperance* (Hallowell, Me., 1821) 13; Heman Humphrey *Parallel between Intemperance and the Slave Trade* (Amherst, Mass., 1828) esp. 6, 14, 20, 25–26; Enoch Mudge *A Temperance Address* (New Bedford, 1837) 10; Nott 116; W. Sullivan 42; G. W. Wells 6.

32. The trend is predicted in Colton 61, 71.

33. Marryat *Diary* 3:182. For the law and its background see M.L.V. *'Licensed Houses'* (Boston, 1833); *Proceedings of the Convention of the Young Men of Massachusetts* (Boston, 1834); *Investigation into the Fifteen Gallon Law;* Leonard Withington *A Review of the Late Temperance Movements in Massachusetts* (Boston, 1840).

34. Quo. in Martineau 2:361. See the penetrating observation in Combe 2:272. I am not the only one intrigued by the comment in Martineau's account. See Ann Douglas *The Feminization of American Culture* (N.Y., 1978 paperback; 1977) 48.

Appendix One

1. (ca. 1710)   Richard B. Sheridan *Sugar and Slavery* (Balt., 1974) 341–342. See also G. M. Ostrander "The Colonial Molasses Trade" *Ag. His.* 30 (1956) 82n, 83; *Calendar of State Papers. Colonial Series, America and West Indies* (London, 1893–   ) 29:267; McCusker 437; (1710–1770) *Arch. Md.* 14:90; Thos. C. Barrow *Trade and Empire* (Cambridge, 1967) 142–143; W. D. Houlette "Rum-Trading in the American Colonies before 1763" *J. Am. His.* 28 (1934) 147; David MacPherson *Annals of Commerce . . .* (Edinburgh, 1805) 3:176, 403n; "Jasper Mauduit, Agent in London . . ." Mass. His. Soc. *Coll.* 74 (1918) 173; Ostrander "Col. Mol." 78, 80n, 83; Richard Pares *War and Trade in the West Indies* (Oxford, 1936) 488n; Pringle 2:436, 684; Scomp 78, 142–143; Sheridan 353, 356; "State of the Trade, 1763" Col. Soc. Mass. *Trans.* 19 (1916–1917) 386–387; (ca. 1770) McCusker 468, 477, 584; Shepherd and Walton 228–230. See also an earlier estimate by Sheffield 109, 111, 115; Barrow 134, 142; MacPherson 3:573; A. E. Martin "The Temperance Movement in Pennsylvania Prior to the Civil War" *Pa. Mag. His. Biog.* 49 (1925) 196; Ostrander "Col. Mol." 83n; Scomp 142–143; Julia C. Spruill *Women's Life and Work in the Southern Colonies* (Chapel Hill, 1938) 66; (1785) Brissot de Warville 389–390; MacPherson 4:161; Morse *Am. Geog.* 89; [?] to Jeff., Jun.–Jul. 1784, Jeff. *Pap.* 7:335; Jeff. to Lafayette, Jul. 17, 1786, ibid. 10:148; Wm. Maclay

Journal . . . ed. E. S. Maclay (N.Y., 1890) Jun. 4, 1789, p. 66; Benezet *Potent Enemies* 11n.

2. (wine) Imports and exports (1790–1800) ASP 3:1:707; (1801–1826) 3:5:880–882; (1827–1862) Sec. Treas. "Commerce and Navigation" AR in U.S. Serials Set [vol.:doc.], 174:253, 182:86, 193:95, 204:76, 220:230, 234:109, 241:289, 269:149, 283:375, 299:225, 318:446, 342:306, 361:577, 379:238, 399:356, 416:247, 435:289, 456:125, 472:4, 494:7, 504:5, 541:42, 553:3, 604, 628, 662, 703, 750, 865, 886, 960, 989, 1034, 1087, 1140, 1170; (rum and molasses) as above except (1790–1826) ASP 3:5:890; (whiskey tax) ASP 3:1:64–67, 110–111, 140–141, 145, 151–161, 171–175, 191, 249–251, 280, 557–576, 593, 618–619, 683–684, 702, 706–708, 720–722; Ham. *Pap.* 10:103, 119, 11:95–99, 15:472, 17:19, 77–78, 20:484; White Acct. Bks., 1791–1801, CtY; Distillery Box, Tench Coxe Sec., Coxe Pap., PHi; Material Relative to Collecting Revenue from the Distilling and Retailing of Liquors in Pa., 1794–1803, Am. Philosophical Soc., Phila.; Distillers' Licenses, 1798–1801, MdHi; (Ky.) e.g., ASP 3:1:720; Jillson *Ky. Dis.*; (W. Pa.) Baldwin *Whis. Reb.*; (Phila.) "Est. by Jas. Newport of Phila. Distillers, with Amt. Distilled and Amt. on Which Tax Has Been Paid, Oct. 5, 1801–Nov. 11, 1801," Newport to Coxe, Nov. 28, 1801, Coxe to Richard Peters, 1801, Distillery Box, Tench Coxe Sec., Coxe Pap.; (1814) ASP 3:3:51, 183, 207, 216, 298, 634, 5:371, 511–512.

3. "Digest of Manufactures" (1810), ASP 3:2:666–812. (imperfect) *Niles* 6 (1814) 333; (estimates) *Niles* 2 (1812) 54; Joshua Bates *Two Sermons on Intemperance* . . . (2 ed., Dedham, Mass., 1814) 15; Gunn 20; (reaction) Gillet 6; H. Humphrey *Intemp.* 17; Jas. Mott *An Address to the Public* (N.Y., 1814) 8; Tenney 14–15; MSSI *Circ.* 4; N. Eng. Tract Soc. 4; (1820) ASP 3:4:28–223, 291–299; (criticism) *Niles* 23 (1823) 382; 24 (1823) 130; (1830s) "Docs. Relative to the Manufactures in the U.S." House Doc. 308, 22 Cong., 1 Sess. (1833).

4. Ms. note, Jul. 22, 1842, U.S. Cen., 1840 *Comp.* 1, U. Calif., Berkeley. U.S. Cen., 1850 *Report of the Superintendent of the Census* . . . (Wash., 1853) 75, 159; U.S. Cen., 1850 *Stat. View* 182; U.S. Cen., 1850 *Digest* 47, 138; U.S. Cen., 1860 *Prelim. Rep.* 65, 178; U.S. Cen., 1860 *Manufactures* 415, 738; U.S. *Statistical Abstract* (1921) 616. (industrial use) A Physician *Desultory Notes on the Origin, Uses and Effects of Ardent Spirit* (Phila., 1834) 30; MTS 22AR 28; Edgar W. Martin *The Standard of Living in 1860* (Chicago, 1942) 79; Thomann *Liqr. Laws* 197; *The Whisky Problem* (Wash., 1876) 6, 13. This use of spirits has not been considered in the standard estimates of alcohol consumption. Vera Efron et al. *Statistics on Consumption of Alcohol and Alcoholism* (New Brunswick, 1972) 4; E. M. Jellinek "Recent Trends in Alcoholism and in Alcohol Consumption" *QJSA* 8 (1947) 8.

5. (taverns) Jan DeLint and Wolfgang Schmidt "Consumption Averages and Alcoholism Prevalence" *Br. J. Addiction* 66 (1971) 100. Many New York City licenses are at NHi. G-Ar has records for several Georgia counties. (distillers) Robison Distillery Accts., Robison Pap., MeHi; Hurd Pap., CtY. The haphazard nature of most distilleries is suggested by the records of excise collector Dyer White. White Acct. Bks., CtY. (brewers) Rhinelander Brewery Day Bk., 1794–1795, Frederick & Philip Rhinelander Brewery Ledger, 1793–1801, Rhinelander Pap., NHi. The Vassar Pap., NPV, are the only extensive papers of an early nineteenth-century brewer.

6. Ham. *Pap.*, 11:98; (1814–1817) ASP 3:2:854–855, 3:635, 5:371; *Niles* 10 (1816) 348; 12 (1817) 273; Bristed 61–62; (1818–1822) *Niles* 20 (1821) 211; 21

(1821) 225–227; *Am. Farmer* 2 (1820) 176; *Plough Boy* 1 (1820) 411; H. Hall *Dis.*
15; Utter 77; (1823–1827) *Niles* 32 (1827) 217; 33 (1827) 139; *Friend* 2 (1828) 13;
N. Eng. Farmer 2 (1823) 134; *Reg. Pa.* 11 (1833) 379; B. Hall 2:82; Holmes 205;
Utter 134; (1828–1832) *Ariel* 5 (1831) 112; *Literary Reg.* 1 (1828) 61; *Reg. Pa.* 5
(1830) 389; 8 (1831) 236; 11 (1833) 379; Utter 135; (1833–1836) ibid. 135.

7. (1814–1817) *An Address to the Inhabitants of the State of Vermont* (Montpe-
lier, 1817) 5; Hallock 47; H. Humphrey *Intemp.* 18; (1818–1822) SPPCNY
Docs. 18–19; MeTS 1AR 9, 54; *Beman on Intemp.* 3; Gillet 8; Henry Warren *An
Address Delivered at Roxbury* (Boston,1821) 8; Wm. Willis *An Address. Delivered be-
fore the New-Bedford Auxiliary Society* . . . (New Bedford, 1819) 13; (1823–1827)
ATS *Constitution* (Boston? 1826) 6; 1AR 66; 2AR 12, 15; 4AR 1, 45; 5AR 46;
ATU 3AR 52; 5AR 27; Bucks Co. Soc. for the Promotion of Temp. *1AR* 4;
CtTS 1AR 5, 7, 11; 3AR 23–24; MeTS 1AR; 2AR; MISSI *A Letter to the Mechanics
of Boston* (Boston, 1831) 9–10; MTS 22AR 12; NHTS 3AR 4; NYSTS 1AR 23,
25, 28; 2AR 49, 54; 3AR 56; VaTS 4AR 14; J. H. Agnew *Address on Intemperance*
. . . (Phila., 1829) 16; N. S. S. Beman 9; Bouton 4; Reuben Buck *An Address
Delivered before the York County TS* (Kennebunk, Me., 1831) 4; David Damon
Address Delivered at Amesbury (Boston, 1829) 9; Luther F. Dimmick *Intemperance*
(Newburyport, 1824) 16n; Daniel Dow *A Discourse, Delivered in Chepachet, R.I.*
(Providence, 1831) 8; A. D. Eddy *An Address to Young Men* (Canandaigua,
N.Y., 1830) 21; Elijah Foster *An Address Delivered before the Salisbury and Ames-
bury Society* . . . (Exeter, N.H., 1831) 7; Chas. Griswold *An Address, Delivered
at Hadlyme* (Middletown, Ct., 1828) 6; Elisha James, Jr. *An Address, Delivered
before the Scituate Auxiliary Society* . . . (Hingham, Mass., 1833) 17; Jonathan
Kittredge *An Address, Delivered before the TS of Plymouth, N.H.* (Boston, 1830) 7;
Reuben D. Mussey *An Address on Ardent Spirit* . . . (Boston, 1829) 13; Nott
13n; Palfrey 17; Addison Parker *An Address Delivered before the Southbridge TS*
. . . (Southbridge, Mass., 1830) 5, 14n; Rankin 7; Jonathan C. Southmayd *A
Discourse on the Duty of Christians* . . . (Montpelier, 1828) 16; Wm. B. Sprague
Intemperance (N.Y., 1827) 8; Thos. H. Stockton *Address Delivered in the Methodist
Episcopal Church in Easton* (Balt., 1833) 10; H. Ware, Jr. 13; (1828–1832) *Am. Q.
Temp. Mag.* 1 (1833) 282–283; ATS 2AR 12, 15, 48; 4AR 45, 76; 5AR 46, 47,
63, 77; ATU 6AR 44; 7AR 26; 8AR 44; CtTS 1AR 6, 7, 11; Hartford Co. TS
5; MeTS 1AR; 2AR; MSSI *Letter* 10; NHTS 3AR 5, 16; NYSTS 1–4AR;
PaTS *Anniversary Rep.* 8; Providence Assn. for the Promotion of Temp. *Total
Abstinence* (Providence, 1832) 5; VaTS 3AR 5–6; 4AR 14; Agnew 6, 11, 16;
Wm. J. Armstrong *The Evils of Intemperance* (Richmond, 1829) 5; E. H. Barton
A Discourse on Temperance . . . (New Orleans, 1837) 13; Bell 2; C. P. Beman 7;
Breckinridge 2; N. Cross 5; J. N. Danforth 13; Dow 8, 21; Elon Galusha *An
Address, Delivered before the Rome TS* (Utica, 1830) 6; Goodell 7; J. F. Halsey *An
Appeal to Patriots* . . . (Pittsburgh, 1830) 2; E. Hitchcock 35; Saml. B. How
An Address on Intemperance (Carlisle, Pa., 1830) 5; Alvan Hyde *An Example from
the Holy Scriptures* (Albany, 1829) 17; Edw. Jarvis *Financial Connection of the Use
of Spirits and Wine* . . . (Boston, 1883) 7; Kittredge *Plymouth Add.* 7; Knowles
9; Levi Loring *The Origin, Evils, and Remedy of Intemperance* (Portland, Me., 1828)
10; Humphrey Moore *A Discourse, to Encourage Abstinence* . . . (Amherst, Mass.,
1830) 3; Morton 8; Nott 13; A. Parker 14n; Joel Parker *An Address Delivered
before the Association in Keene* (Keene, N.H., 1830) 9; Benj. Patton, Jr.
Address, Delivered by . . . (Lewistown, Pa., 1832) 4; Arthur A. Ross *An Address,
Delivered before the Society* . . . (Providence, 1830) 7; Frederick A. Ross *A Sermon, on Intemperance* . . . (Rogersville, Tenn., 1830) 4; Scott 10; John A. Shaw

An Address Delivered before the Bridgewater Society . . . (Boston, 1828) 7, 9; J. S. Stone 15; W. Sullivan 31; Wayland 19; John C. Young *An Address on Temperance* (Lexington, Ky., 1834) 5; (1833–1836) *Am. Q. Temp. Mag.* 1 (1833) 143; ATS 8AR 4; Young Men's TS of the City of Albany *Proceedings* . . . (Albany, 1836) inside cover; MeTS 2AR 117; NYCTS 4AR 22; NYSTS *Temp. Almanac* (1836) 17; PaTS *Anniversary Rep.* 10; Pa. Young Men's Temp. Convention *Proceedings* (n.p., 1834) 5; *Pennsylvania and New-Jersey Temperance Almanac for 1835* (Phila., 1835) 29; (1838–1840) ATU 2AR 53; 3AR 52; 5AR 27; 6AR 44; A. T. Judson *Temperance Report* (Brooklyn, Ct., 1838) 18–20.

8. (Concord) Jarvis. See also Utter 125–136.

9. (beer) Bernhard 2:128; Burlend 71; I. Candler 45; Faux 11:113–114, 118; B. Hall 2:138; T. Val. Hecke *Reise durch die Vereinigten Staaten* . . . (Berlin, 1820) 1:95; Holmes 204; Janson 31; Parkinson 1:60; (cider) ms. tax assessments for Concord, Mass. courtesy of David H. Fischer and Robert Gross; *Moral Reformer* 1 (1835) 122; Bouton 5, 17; R. M. Hartley in ATU 4AR 60; MeTS 1AR 12. Horace Greeley claimed that a typical Vermont family used a barrel of cider each week. Greeley 98–99. (decline) Bouton 17; ATU 5AR 28; N.Y. State Ag. Soc. *Trans.*, NYAD Doc. 126, vol. 6 (1852) 486; Am. Inst. 7AR, NYAD Doc. 199, vol. 9 (1850) 156.

10. (congener effects) McClelland et al. *Drinking* 135–138; E. S. Katkin et al. "Effects of Alcoholic Beverages Differing in Congener Content . . ." *QJSA* Supp. 5 (1970) 101–114; contra, DeLint and Schmidt "Cons. Ave." 97–107. (statistics) Efron et al. 4; Wm. T. Brande *A Manual of Chemistry* (N.Y., 1821) 521–522.

11. (drinking pop.) Suggested by E. M. Jellinek "The Interpretation of Alcohol Consumption Rates . . ." *QJSA* 3 (1942) 267–280. Used by several recent studies. (drinking age pop.) Suggested by ibid. 267–280 and refined in E. M. Jellinek "Recent Trends" 1–42. (changing customs) Cobbett 197–198; D. Drake *Pioneer* 32–33; Holmes 352; Larkin 333; Neilson 67; Schoepf 1:363; Woodman 18; Geo. L. Maddox and Bevode C. McCall *Drinking among Teen-Agers* (New Brunswick, 1964).

12. Robt. V. Wells *The Population of the British Colonies in America before 1776* (Princeton, 1975) 72, 83, 92, 102, 116, 137, 152, 168; U.S. Cen., 1830 *Fifth Cen.* 26–27, 162–163; U.S. Cen., 1840 *Sixth Census or Enumeration of the Inhabitants of the United States* . . . (Wash., 1841) 476; U.S. Cen., 1870 *Ninth Census, Vol. II, the Vital Statistics* . . . (Wash., 1872) 560–577; U.S. Cen., 1970 *Characteristics of the Population, Vol. I. United States Summary. Part 1. Sec. 1.* (Wash., 1973) Ch. B, Table 51.

Appendix Two

1. (U.S.) Appendix 1; (early) *Am. Mag. Knowledge* 2 (1836) 192; *New Yorker* 4 (1838) 810; *Temp. Recorder* 2 (1833) 32; NYSTS *Temp. Almanac* (1838) 34; ATU 4AR 54, 60, 70, 72; 5AR 38; 12AR 34; 15AR 41; 18AR 34; (Scotland, 1822) Forbes 235; (U.K., 1800) Harrison 66; (Sweden, 1800) Thomann *Real* 94; (Sweden, 1820–1830) Thompson 9; (1851–1922) Rudolf Wlassak *Grundriss der Alkoholfrage* (2 ed., Leipzig, 1929) 154–155, except (Germany, 1851–1870) Walther G. Hoffmann *Das Wachstum der Deutschen Wirtshaft seit der Mitte des 19.Jahrhunderts* (Berlin, 1965) 172–173, 651 (both sources courtesy of James S.

Roberts); (1970–1974) U.K. *Annual Abstract of Statistics* (1976) 241; Denmark *Statistisk Årbog* (1976) 47, 244; Sweden *Yearbook of Nordic Statistics* (1976) 32, 232; *Annuaire Statistique de la France* (1976) 20, 207.

2. As in note 1, except (1839) ATU 4AR 60; (1970–1974) *Statistical Yearbook of Finland* (1975) 454–455.

3. As in note 2, plus (U.K., 1830) Coffey 679.

4. As in note 2, plus (1845) ATU 12AR 17; (Poland, 1844; 1937–1965) *Drinking and Drug Practices Surveyor* #5 (1972) 2.

INDEX

Abbot, Abiel, 192
abolition, 37, 214-215
abstinence, 189, 202, 209, 217; *see also* temperance
achievement motivation, 174-176, 178-182
Adams, John, 6, 34, 35, 111
Adams, John Quincy, 196
Adams, Solomom, 197
Adlum, John, 105
aggression, 178, 179
Alabama, 115, 214
Albany, N.Y., 107, 198
alcohol: electoral symbol, 154; in cider, 111; in cook books, 120; in different beverages, 229-230; in wine, 101-102; properties, 189; tolerance, 149; uses, 227
American Fur Company, 159
American Temperance Society, 197, 198, 202, 214
American Temperance Union, 198
American Tract Society, 196
Amherst, Mass., 197
Anderson, William M., 162-163
Andover Seminary, 15, 191
Annapolis, Md., 32
anomie, 140-144, 190
antimasonry, 173
antitemperance societies, 194
anxiety, 123, 125-146, 161, 166-167, 168, 169, 172-173, 174-175, 176, 180, 188, 189, 193, 212, 241-242, 245
Appalachian Mountains, 77-79, 126
Arfwedson, Carl D., 6

army, 15, 40; *see also* soldiers
artisans, 15, 131-133, 140
Ashley, William, 157
aspirations, 165, 174-176, 178, 180
Astor, John Jacob, 159, 160
attorneys, 15, 135
Axley, James, 290

Bacon, David, 164-166, 167
Bacon, Delia, 165
Bacon, Leonard, 164-165, 167
Bacon, Selden D., 241
Bales, Robert F., 243
Baptists, 209-210
Bard, Samuel, 263
Bath, N.H., Temperance Society, 197
Beecher, George, 166
Beecher, Henry Ward, 166, 218
Beecher, James, 166
Beecher, Lyman, 137, 166
beer, 9, 45, 65, 106-110, 173-176; consumption, 229; *see also* brewing industry
Belknap, Jeremy, 43, 45, 47
Benezet, Anthony, 36-37, 39, 225
beverage choice, 173-176; achievement motivation, anxiety, aspirations, 174-175
beverages: cordials, 12-13, 16; juleps, 19, 98; peach brandy, 53; syllabubs, 116; toddies, 19, 97-98; *see also* beer; cider; coffee; milk; rum; spirits, distilled; tea; water; whiskey; wine

binges, *see* communal binges; communal drinking; episodic drinking; solo drinking
Birney, James Gillespie, 214, 290
blacks, *see* slaves
boatmen, 142-143
Boston, 28-29, 32, 68, 197
Bourne, Edward, 123, 146
Bouton, Nathaniel, 280
Brackenridge, Hugh Henry, 41
Braintree, Mass., 34
Brande, William, 101
brewing industry, 108-110, 228; *see also* beer
British fur trade, 155
Brown, John, 217
Brown family, 49, 66
Buchanan, James, 76
Bunzel, Ruth, 241
Burr, Aaron, 102
Byrd, William, 26
Byrne, Frank, 187
Byron, Lord, 200

Cadwalader, Thomas, 39
Calhoun, John, 104
Calvinists, 191
camp meetings, 206-207
Canada, 238-239
canal laborers, 143-144
Candler, Isaac, 7
capital, 204, 211-212, 219
Cartwright, Peter, 206
change, 218-229; and drink, 125, 145; cultural, 190; economic, 129-130
Channing, William E., 132
character, American, *see* ideals
Charles Town, S.C., 32
children, 14, 168, 177, 180-182, 190, 198, 199, 230, 245-246
Chittenden, Thomas, 49
cider, 9-10, 45, 110-113, 116; consumption, 229
Cincinnati, 78, 96, 107, 108
cities, 96-97, 107, 128-129, 131-133; consumption, 248
class, *see* lower classes; middle classes; social class; upper classes
Clay, Henry, 104
Clinton, George, 32, 48

Cobbett, William, 6, 59, 108
coffee, 100, 101
colleges, 138-140; Amherst, 197; Andover Seminary, 15, 191; Dartmouth, 139; Harvard, 139; Harvard Divinity School, 138; Oberlin, 120; Philadelphia College of Medicine, 46; Princeton, 140; Union College, 139; University of Virginia, 139; William and Mary, 139; Yale, 165; *see also* students
colonial era, 25-40, 56-57, 61-69, 149-150, 152, 261; consumption, 225-226
Combe, George, 118-119
communal binges, 149-151, 159-160; *see also* elections, fur trappers
communal drinking, 150-152, 163, 169; consumption, 249
compartmentalization, 168
Concord, Mass., 228
Concord, N.H., 280
Congregationalists, 28, 48, 208
Congress, 51-53, 55, 67
Connecticut, 47
consumption, 7-11, 45, 89, 113, 128, 132-133, 139-140, 141, 187, 225-239; beer, 107, 229; cider, 111, 229; coffee, 100, 101; colonial, 29, 64-65, 225-226; cross-national, 237-239; drinking patterns, chart, 249; occupational chart, 248; regional chart, 248; rum, 64-66, 225; social class chart, 248; tea, 99, 101; U.S. statistics, 232-233; wine, 106, 229
Continental Army, 40, 65
cook books, 116, 120, 240
cookery, 116-118
Cooper, Thomas, 73
Coxe, Tench, 73, 226
crime, *see* social order
culture, 120, 168, 170-171, 178, 190, 212, 219-221, 242-244
Cumberland County, Me., Temperance Society, 197

D.T.'s, *see* delirium tremens
daily drams, 149, 169, 249
Dalton, William, 6

Danvers, Mass., 28
Darwin, Erasmus, 263
Dayton, Ohio, 85
Deane, Silas, 49
Delavan, Edward, 13, 196
delirium tremens, 169-173, 177, 189
Denmark, 238-239
Dickson, S. H., 102
diet, 78, 93, 95-122, 275
distillation process, 69-73
distilled spirits, *see* spirits, distilled
distilleries, number of, 86-87
distilling industry, 29, 48-49, 61, 65,
    66, 72-73, 75-77, 80-81, 85-87, 90,
    228; illicit, 55
distilling manuals, 73, 75-76
distilling technology, 73-74
doctors, *see* physicians
Dodge, Rev., 138
Dorchester, Daniel, 187
Douglas, Stephen A., 105
Drake, Daniel, 96
Drew, Daniel, 217
drinking clubs, 32
drinking motivation, 125, 146, 241-
    246
drinking occasions: auctions, 19, 26,
    37; barbecues, 19, 151; courts, 20,
    26; funerals, 37; militia musters,
    19-20, 26; ordinations, 48; *see also*
    camp meetings; elections; Inde-
    pendence Day; meals; rendezvous;
    social drinking; steamboats; treat-
    ing
drinking patterns, 149-183, 189, 249;
    see also communal binges; com-
    munal drinking; daily drams; de-
    lirium tremens; episodic drinking;
    intoxication; opium; solo drinking
drunkenness, *see* intoxication
Dun and Bradstreet, 212

East, 79, 84
economic growth, 88, 165, 172, 176,
    180-182, 204-205, 211-212
economics: banks and temperance,
    204; grain, 80, 84, 88; Hope Distil-
    lery, 81; insurance discounts, 196;
    money, 54, 203-204; purchasing
    power, 82; triangle trade, 63;

wealth, 203-204; *see also* Ap-
    palachian Mountains; brewing in-
    dustry; capital; change; distilling
    industry; economic growth; excise;
    factories; fur trappers; industrial-
    ization; merchants; population
    growth; price; tariff; trade
Edgerton, Robert B., 243
Edinburgh College of Medicine, 39
Edwards, Justin, 191, 280
eighteenth century, *see* colonial era
elections, 20, 26, 35, 152-155, 196
emotion, 121-122, 161, 168, 188,
    210-213, 219
England, 10-11, 89, 175-176, 238
Enlightenment, 39, 47
Episcopalians, 205
episodic drinking, 163-168
equality, 56, 104, 111, 135-136,
    138-139, 151, 154-155, 157-159,
    165, 180-183, 195, 201, 212
Europe, 5, 10-11, 89, 163, 175-176,
    237-239
Evarts, Jeremiah, 191
excise, 49, 51, 53-55, 68, 71, 107, 226

factories, 18, 131-132, 140, 176
Falmouth, Me., distillery, 66
family, *see* children; women; youths
farm guides, 107
farm laborers, *see* laborers, farm
farmers, 14, 47, 56, 65, 75, 83-85, 88,
    107, 110-111, 127, 128, 203, 248;
    southern, 133-135
Fearon, Henry, 93, 175
Federalists, 45, 50, 154
feelings, *see* emotion
Field, Peter B., 242
Finland, 163, 238-239
Fletcher, Elijah, 97
food, *see* diet
Foote, Henry, 151
Fourth of July, *see* Independence Day
France, 10-11, 163, 238-239
Franklin, Benjamin, 30, 34, 40, 97
Fraunces, Samuel, 49
freedom, *see* liberty
French Canadians, 156
Friends, *see* Quakers
frontier, 26, 47, 54-55, 69, 77, 96, 99,
    115, 126-127, 142-143, 206

fur trappers, 155-163
Furnas, J. C., 187

Gale, James, 172
Gallatin, Albert, 54, 56
gambling, 180
Gardiner, Robert, 103
Garrard, James, 49
Garrison, William Lloyd, 214, 290
general stores, 17-18, 231, 235-236
Genovese, Eugene, 14
Georgetown, D.C., 105
Georgia, 29, 38
Germany, 170-171, 175-176, 238-239
Goodell, William, 199-200
Gough, John B., 98
Graham, Sylvester, 121
Grimké, Sarah, 121
groceries, 204-205
guilt, 167, 172-173, 181
Gusfield, Joseph R., 188

Hale, Sarah J., 120
Hales, Stephen, 38
Hall, Basil, 6
Hall, Harrison, 75-76, 91
Hamilton, Alexander, 50-51, 53-54, 56, 226, 228
Hamilton, Dr. Alexander, 32
Hamilton, Thomas, 175
Hamilton County, Ohio, 105
Harper, James, 97
Harper brothers, 212
Hartford County, Conn., 66
Harvard Divinity School, 138
health, 39, 41-42; medicine, 38, 177; milk sickness, 99; West Indies Dry Gripes, 39; *see also* delirium tremens; diet; patent medicines; physicians; suicide; Thomsonians
Henry, Patrick, 65
Hitchcock, Edward, 197
Hodgenville, Ky., 96
Holland, 238-239
Holmes, Isaac, 6
Hone, Philip, 103-104
Hopkins, Richard, 46
Horton, Donald, 146, 174, 241-242
Hosack, David, 138
Hudson's Bay Company, 155-156

Humphrey, Heman, 215
Hunt, Thomas P., 290

ideals, *see* equality; independence; liberty; materialism; patriotism; progress; revolutionary ideals; romanticism
immigrants, 143-144, 188, 248
import duties, *see* tariff
independence, 142, 151-152, 154, 157-163, 168, 172, 177-178, 180-181, 194-195, 200-201
Independence Day, 45, 97, 152, 193-195
India, 178-179
Indians, 156, 159, 178, 246
industrialization, 88-90, 129-130, 167-168, 175-176, 182, 188, 211-212, 217
Inquiry into the Effects of Spirituous Liquors, 40-41
intoxication, 25-27, 30, 149, 151-152, 161, 168, 170, 206
Ireland, 10-11, 238
Irish immigrants, 69, 143-144, 243-244
Italy, 238-239

Jackson, Andrew, 102-103, 196
Jackson, James, 52
Jefferson, Thomas, 6, 102, 104, 114, 139
Jefferson City, Mo., 115
Jenkins, Robert, 49
Johnson, Tom, 91
Journal of Humanity, 198

Kemble, Frances, 13
Kentucky, 53, 77, 153-154
Kirby, Abner, 66
Kittredge, Jonathan, 197
Krout, John A., 188

laborers, 15, 26, 29, 47; farm, 14, 47, 65, 127-128; skilled, 131-133; unskilled, 140-144; *see also* occupations

lager beer, *see* beer; brewing industry
Lancaster County, Pa., 87
laudanum, 177
law, 13-14, 34, 49-50
lawyers, *see* attorneys
Leisler, Jacob, 261
Liberia, 164-165
liberty, 35, 37, 135-136, 138-139,
    151-152, 154-155, 157-159, 165,
    167, 181-183, 195, 200-201, 212
licensing, 28, 32-34, 227
Lincoln, Abraham, 96, 99
liquor, hard, *see* rum; spirits, distilled;
    whiskey
Litchfield, Conn., 47
Livermore, Samuel, 53
Livingston, Peter, 49
Logan, George, 50
Lolli, Giorgio, 244
Long Island, N.Y., 108
Longworth, Nicholas, 104-105
Louisville, Ky., 81, 83
Lowell, Mass., 88
lower classes, 34-35, 47, 135-136,
    199, 204, 248
lumberjacks, 141-142
Lumpkin, J. L., 290
Lyman, Huntington, 185

MacAndrew, Craig, 243
McClelland, David, 176, 244
McCusker, John J., Jr., 65, 225
Mackinaw, Mich., 159
Madeira wine, 32, 101, 103, 104, 106
Madison, Dolly, 13
Madison, James, 52, 196
Maine, 141, 199
Mann, Horace, 204-205
marijuana, 178-179
Marshall, John, 103
Marshall, Thomas, 169
Maryland, 77
Massachusetts, 28, 34, 43, 49, 217
Mass. Society for the Suppression of
    Intemperance, 191-192
materialism, 182-183, 202-205, 213,
    217, 219
Mather, Cotton, 30-31
Mather, Increase, 23, 30
meals, 13, 18-19, 48, 103-104, 118-
    119, 149

medicine, *see* health
merchants, 36, 62-63, 66; ledgers, 212
Methodists, 14, 38, 137, 152, 188,
    206-208, 212
Mexico, 170
middle classes, 188, 204, 248
milk, 98-99
Millerites, 213
Milwaukee, 108-110
ministers, 5, 15, 28, 30-31, 48, 81,
    136-139, 152, 191-193, 202, 220,
    228
Mississippi, 151-152
Mitchill, Samuel L., 73
molasses, 61-69
Mormons, 213
Morris, Robert, 49
Morse, Jedidiah, 46, 192
motivation to drink, 125, 146,
    241-246
mountain men, *see* fur trappers

Natchez, Miss., 96
Neilson, Peter, 14
New England, 32, 48, 66, 99,
    110-111, 226, 248
New England Tract Society, 191
New Hampshire, 45, 47
New Haven, Conn., 65-66, 165
New Orleans, La., 78, 83, 85
New York (city), 96-97, 99, 103-104,
    107, 138, 197, 203
New York (state), 32, 48, 76-77, 85,
    87, 107, 226
N.Y. State Temperance Society, 196
N.Y. Young Men's Society, 197
Newport, James, 55
Niles, Hezekiah, 104
Niles' Register, 228
North, 110-111
Norway, 238-239

Oberlin College, 120
occupations, 248; *see also* artisans; at-
    torneys; boatmen; canal laborers;
    farmers; fur trappers; laborers;
    lumberjacks; merchants; minis-
    ters; physicians; planters; sailors;
    schoolmasters; soldiers; stage driv-
    ers; students

Oglethorpe, James, 29, 38
Ohio, 77, 85, 104-105
opium, 170, 176-178

Paine, Tom, 139
Panoplist, 191
Patch, Sam, 144
patent medicines, 177
patriotism, 99, 104, 107
Pennsylvania, 50, 54-55, 69, 77, 85, 107, 154
Pennsylvania Gazette, 34
Peters, Richard, 50
Philadelphia, 32, 45, 55, 64, 80, 107, 226, 272
Philadelphia College of Medicine, 46
Philadelphia College of Physicians, 50
physicians, 15, 26, 38-39, 46, 50, 136-138, 164, 171-172, 177, 202; *see also* health
Pickering, Joseph, 97
Pittsburgh, 107, 272
planters, 14, 48, 133-135
Poland, 239
politics, *see* antimasonry; Congress; elections; excise; Federalists; law; licensing; Revolution; tariff; Whiskey Rebellion; Workingmen's Party
Polk, Jefferson J., 290
Pomfret, Conn., 138
population growth, 126-128
Porter, Ebenezer, 191
Portland, Me., 197
Potts, John, 26
Poughkeepsie, N.Y., 110
Presbyterians, 207-208
price, 26, 98-100, 106, 108, 111, 159, 173
Priestly, Joseph, 73
prisons, 114
progress, 212-213, 217, 220
prohibition, 217, 220-221; *see also* temperance
Providence, R.I., 66
Prussia, 10-11, 89, 238-239
psychology, *see* achievement motivation; aggression; anomie; anxiety; aspirations; compartmentalization; emotion; guilt; rapid eating; suicide, symbols; time
Putnam, Gen., 65-66
Pynchon, William, 65

Quakers, 36-38

Ramsay, David, 41, 47-48
Ramsay, Martha Laurens, 46
Randolph, John, 97-98, 201
rapid eating, 118-119, 203
recipe books, *see* cook books
Reeve, Tapping, 47
regions, 248; *see also* East; New England; North; South; West
religion, 120-121, 165-167, 181-183, 192-193, 205-211, 213, 216-217, 219, 248; *see also* Baptists; Calvinists; Congregationalists; Episcopalians; Methodists; Millerites; Mormons; Presbyterians; Quakers; Second Great Awakening; Unitarians
rendezvous, 159-160
retailers, 49
revivals, 205-206, 210
Revolution, 35, 37, 40, 65, 135 136, 194-195
revolutionary ideals, 56, 67, 104, 134-135, 137-139, 151-152, 157-163, 165, 181, 194-195, 200-201, 213-214
Rhode Island, 67
Robison, Thomas, 49, 66
Rochester, N.Y., 85, 144
romanticism, 199-200
Royall, Anne, 7
rum, 29-30, 38-39, 47, 61-69, 72-73; consumption, 225
Rush, Benjamin, 39-46, 48, 50, 107, 114, 120, 136, 187, 192
Russia, 89, 175-176

Sadoun, Roland, 244
sailors, 144
St. Louis, 95-96

schoolmasters, 145, 151, 164, 180-181
Scomp, Henry, 187
Scotland, 10-11, 238
Scots, 69
Second Great Awakening, 137, 181-183
Sedgwick, Theodore, 52
Sewall, Samuel, 28-29
Shattuck, George C., 46
Shipman, Elias, 66
Silliman, Benjamin, 109
skilled craftsmen, *see* artisans
slaves, 13-14, 25, 46, 63, 114; *see also* abolition
Sloughter, Henry, 261
Smith, Gerrit, 290
Smith, N.R., 147
social class, 135-136, 140, 248
social drinking, 13, 18, 19
social order, 30-31, 89-90, 121-122, 126-127, 144, 190-191, 211, 245
sociology, *see* change; children; cities; frontier; immigrants; Indians; Irish immigrants; lower classes; middle classes; prisons; slaves; social class; social order; students; upper classes; women; youths
soldiers, 144, 146
solo drinking, 163-169, 189, 249
South, 52-53, 115, 141, 151, 214, 248
South Carolina, 48, 153, 227
Speed, Joseph, 46, 138
spirits, distilled, 29, 45, 65, 74, 88-90, 170, 173-176, 179-180; consumption, 7-8, 225-228; *see also* rum; whiskey
stage drivers, 140-141
steamboats, 18, 83, 195-196
Steele, John, 52
still, *see* distillation process
Story, Justice, 103
Stowe, Harriet Beecher, 166
Stuart, Moses, 191
students, 138-140
suicide, 166, 280
Sweden, 10-11, 89, 175-176, 238-239
symbols, 154, 194-195

Tappan, Benjamin, 139
Tappan, Lewis, 212

Tappan, William, 139
Tappan family, 166
tariff, 51, 67, 99-100, 106
taverns, 16, 27-29, 32-35, 189, 195, 227, 231, 234; *see also* groceries
taxes on alcohol, *see* excise; tariff
tea, 99-101
temperance, 5, 90, 97-98, 106, 141, 152, 169, 176, 187-221, 227; and graham cracker, 121; hotels, 195; insurance discounts, 196; magazines, 198; pamphlets, 196-198, 201-202, 228; pies, 120; pledges, 193-194, 196, 216; poems, 198; societies, 189, 193-195, 198, 257; songs, 198; striped pig, 217, 218; *see also* abolition; abstinence; prohibition; vegetarianism
Temperance Almanac, 196
Temperance Recorder, 198
Tennessee, 138, 206
Thanksgiving, 114
theory of drinking, 146, 241-246
thermometer, 43-45
Thomas, Joseph, 206
Thomson, Samuel, 136
Thomsonians, 137
Ticknor, Benajah, 280
Ticknor, George, 6
Tillson, Christiana, 116
Tilton, James, 91
time, 18-19, 202-203
Tompkins, Daniel D., 46
trade, 62-63, 77-78, 80, 83-85, 88, 110, 129-130, 226
travellers, 6-7, 99-100, 112, 115, 118-119, 175, 228-229
treating, 152-154

Unitarians, 137
United Kingdom, 238-239
upper classes, 27, 31-32, 35-39, 46, 48, 57, 100-104, 106, 128, 135-136, 177, 199, 204, 248, 261
urban development, *see* cities

Vanderbilt, Cornelius, 218
Van Rensselaer, Stephen, 196

Vassar, Matthew, 110
Vaughan, John, 46
vegetarianism, 120-121, 189
Vevay, Ind., 104
vineyards, 104-106; *see also* wine
violence, *see* social order
Virginia, 27, 46, 48, 50, 97, 138, 152
Virginia Gazette, 35
Virginia Temperance Society, 196

Washington, George, 5, 49, 53, 55, 73, 152
Washington, D.C., 96
water, 95-98
Waterhouse, Benjamin, 263
Weld, Theodore, 121, 214, 290
Wesley, John, 38
West, 76-78, 80-85, 99, 103-105, 110-111, 115, 126-127, 142-143, 160-161, 248

West Indies, 63-64, 66-67, 225
whiskey, 61-92, 106, 108, 112-113, 117-119, 159-160, 226, 268
Whiskey Rebellion, 55, 226
whiskey tax, *see* excise
Whitefield, George, 30
Williams, Old Bill, 161-162
Williamson, Hugh, 52
wine, 100-106, 111-112, 173-175, 216-217; consumption, 10, 229; *see also* vineyards
women, 11-13, 19; in temperance societies, 257
Woods, Leonard, 191
Worcester, Samuel, 192
Workingmen's Party, 140

youths, 14, 138-140, 165, 197, 199, 230; *see also* students